The
Gorbachev
Strategy

The Gorbachev Strategy

Opening the Closed Society

Thomas H. Naylor

Duke University

Lexington Books

D.C. Heath and Company/Lexington, Massachusetts/Toronto

Library of Congress Cataloging-in-Publication Data

Naylor, Thomas H., 1936–   .
   The Gorbachev strategy.

Includes index.
1. Soviet Union—Politics and government—1953–   .
   2. Gorbachev, Mikhail Sergeevich 1931–
                    I. Title.
DK288.N38   1987   947.085′4   86-40219
         ISBN 0-669-13831-2 (alk. paper)

Published simultaneously in Canada
Printed in the United States of America
Casebound International Standard Book Number: 0-669-13831-2
Library of Congress Catalog Card Number: 86-40219

The paper used in this publication meets the minimum requirements of
American National Standard for Information Sciences—Permanence
of Paper for Printed Library Materials, ANSI Z39.48–1984.
                    ∞ ™

        ISBN 0-669-13831-2

     88 89 90 91 8 7 6 5 4 3 2

Contents

Preface and Acknowledgments

When Soviet leader Mikhail S. Gorbachev used the term "radical reform" in his February 25, 1986, speech to the Communist Party Congress in Moscow, few Soviet citizens realized that this was the beginning of an extremely well planned, direct assault on the legacy of Joseph V. Stalin—the centrally planned Soviet economy, the inflexible government bureaucracy, and the police state mentality. Few Americans realized they were witnessing the opening of *the closed society*—the Soviet Union.

Gorbachev meant exactly what he said. The name of the game is indeed radical reform—of Soviet culture, economy, political structure, and foreign policy. But Gorbachev's message has gone right over the heads of the Reagan administration, the Congress, the press, and most American Sovietologists.

My first contact with the Soviet economic reforms was in May 1982, six months before the death of Leonid I. Brezhnev, when I visited ten major Soviet research institutes in Moscow. I interacted with over 250 Soviet economists, management scientists, and computer scientists who were using state-of-the-art management science and computer modeling techniques to evaluate the effects on the Soviet economy of introducing decentralized planning and marketing, flexible prices and wages, profits and incentives, and credit and banking. Their objective was to convince Brezhnev's successors of the merits of emulating the Hungarian experience with decentralized, market-oriented planning. But it was not until May 1985 that I learned that Yuri V. Andropov and Mikhail S. Gorbachev had been the sponsors of this extremely interesting research.

Since 1982 I have made six trips to the Soviet Union, Hungary, and Poland, where I have had the opportunity to observe the economic reforms at very close range as a consultant to the general managers of numerous large state-owned enterprises. While introducing Soviet and Eastern European managers to market-oriented strategic planning, I have observed first hand the successes and frustrations of radical economic reforms. The planning methods that I use with the Soviets and Eastern Europeans are identical to the approaches I have used with my American corporate clients such as IBM, Shell Oil, Squibb, Northwest Industries, Burroughs Wellcome, SCANA, Florida Power, and the Federal Reserve Bank.

To analyze the dramatic changes that have taken place in the Soviet Union since Gorbachev was named General Secretary of the Communist Party on March 11, 1985, I shall employ an analytical approach known as *strategic analysis*. My approach to the Soviet Union is similar to that which a company like IBM might use to assess the relative strengths and weaknesses of a major competitor, to understand the competitor's long-term goals and objectives, and to evaluate the consequences of alternative strategies that might be employed by the competitor—in this case, the Soviet Union.

I show that Gorbachev is being driven toward radical economic, political, and foreign policy reforms by a combination of internal problems and a number of international forces. The domestic problems, many of which predate the 1917 Revolution, include a stagnant economy, inefficient agriculture, an inadequate supply of consumer goods and services, a substantial technological gap with the West, a rigid political and governmental structure, a police-state mentality, a high death rate, and an increasingly alienated population. On the international side, Hungary, China, Soviet bilateral trade needs, and the Reagan administration's foreign policy are not only pushing Gorbachev towards radical reform, but also enhancing the possibility that he will be successful in implementing radical reforms.

For nearly thirty years, the Hungarians have been quietly moving towards a less-centralized, market-oriented economic system. Unlike the situation in 1956 when the Soviets resorted to force to snuff out Hungarian initiatives, this time around the Soviets appear to be motivated by a desire to emulate some of Hungary's economic successes. They seem to be much more interested in learning from the Hungarians than in trying to control them.

The dramatic results of the Chinese economic reforms have not gone unnoticed in the Kremlin. China is too big and too important to be ignored. The fact that China has successfully replicated the Hungarian experiment with a population 100 times the size of Hungary in less than one third the time not only validates the Hungarian experience in the eyes of Soviet leaders, but also greatly enhances its credibility.

In no other area are Gorbachev's reforms more sweeping than in the field of international trade. His fundamental objective is to strengthen the Soviet economy and reduce international political tensions through a strategy of increased global interdependence based on bilateral trade between the Soviet Union and the rest of the world. To achieve his goal of integrating the Soviet economy into the global economy, Gorbachev has centralized Soviet foreign trade policy while simultaneously decentralizing foreign trade.

The relatively poor performance of the Soviet economy is obviously an important force motivating Gorbachev to pursue a strategy of international trade and tension reduction. The Soviets must increase their exports to the West to finance their much-needed imports of consumer goods, technology, and foodstuffs. Gorbachev also seems to have learned from Japan that the rules of international politics have changed and that the number of nuclear warheads in a nation's arsenal is not nearly as important a measure of political power as it once was. Economic clout has become a more important indicator of political influence than military might. International trade has replaced the arms race as the driving force of international politics.

When Ronald Reagan was elected President in 1980, he called for drastic reductions in government regulations, claiming that more often than not such regulations end up causing more harm than good. Yet he has spent his entire Presidency trying to regulate, manipulate, and control the Soviet Union, which is now stronger economically, politically, and militarily than at any time in its history. The Reagan administration's foreign policy has created precisely the kind of psychological environment in Moscow to make all of this possible. If Gorbachev had written Reagan's script, he would not have changed one word of it.

If the new CEO of a major American company such as General Motors wants to introduce fundamental policy changes, then he must come to grips with the company's culture—the attitudes, values, and customs of its managers and employees. The failure to address strongly ingrained cultural factors has led to the demise of many a new CEO in the United States.

This is precisely the situation in which Soviet leader Gorbachev finds himself as he attempts to de-Stalinize the Soviet Union and open the closed society. He has embarked on a systematic strategy to change the centrally planned economy, the Communist party, the vast government bureaucracy, the military establishment, and the KGB. For over thirty years various Soviet leaders, including Khrushchev, Kosygin, and Brezhnev, have unsuccessfully attempted to "change the economic mechanism" in the Soviet Union—that is, introduce decentralized, market-oriented planning. In each case, these efforts got bogged down in a sea of bureaucratic resistance and inertia. Each of these Soviet leaders learned the hard way that it is impossible to change the economic system of a country such as the Soviet Union without first coming to grips with the uniqueness of its culture.

If Gorbachev is to succeed, he must confront the culture of the largest risk-free society in the world—a society characterized by full employment, inexpensive housing, free education and medical care, low-cost transportation, the absence of bankruptcy, and cradle-to-grave socialism. But that is exactly what he is doing, and he is doing it very effectively. The alcohol reforms, the clampdown on corruption, increased openness, the release of political dissidents, and the call for secret balloting and a choice of candidates in elections are all examples of significant changes taking place in the Soviet culture under Gorbachev.

The United States has missed countless opportunities to play a constructive role in shaping Gorbachev's radical economic, political, cultural, and foreign policy reforms. Our failure to appreciate the international significance of the sweeping changes introduced by Gorbachev has stymied our ability to respond in a creative and imaginative fashion. Gorbachev's foreign policy initiatives deserve a more positive response from Washington. It is not business as usual in Moscow, and it is no longer in our self-interest to continue pretending otherwise.

Acknowledgments

Funding for this book was obtained from the Rockefeller Foundation, the International Research and Exchanges Board (IREX), the Soros Foundation, The Dow Chemical Company, and Abbott Laboratories. I also wish to acknowledge with appreciation the assistance provided by Dr. Wesley A. Fisher and Dr. Margit Serenyi, IREX; Margaret Chapman, American Committee on U.S.-Soviet Relations; Nancy A. Graham, Institute for Soviet-American Relations; and countless Soviets and Eastern Europeans who provided me with an enormous amount of information and data.

Some of the material in this book previously appeared in op-ed pieces by the author in *The New York Times, Los Angeles Times, The Journal of Commerce, The Miami Herald,* and *The Raleigh News & Observer.*

Multiple drafts of the constantly changing subject matter of this manuscript were typed and edited by Forrest Smith and Stacy Miller. Yvonne M. Lamvik also contributed editorial assistance. My wife Dr. Magdalena Raczkowska Naylor was my most severe critic and closest friend throughout this project. Her experiences in Warsaw have not only helped me keep my feet on the ground, but have given me a number of useful insights into life in Eastern Europe and the Soviet Union.

Part I
A Strategic Approach

———

1
The USSR:
The Closed Society

It was not by chance alone that General Secretary Mikhail S. Gorbachev chose 25 February 1986 as the opening date of the twenty-seventh Congress of the Communist Party of the Soviet Union. Thirty years earlier on that date, the full extent of Stalin's reign of terror was disclosed by Nikita S. Khrushchev to officials at the twentieth party congress. Gorbachev's five-and-a-half-hour speech was a clear signal that the second attempt to de-Stalinize the Soviet Union had begun in earnest. Only this time around it was not being orchestrated by a village peasant, but rather by a well-educated, sophisticated statesman who in less than six-and-a-half years had made a leap from party secretary of the Stavropol territory to general secretary of the Soviet Union. This was the beginning of an extremely well-planned, direct assault on the legacy of Joseph V. Stalin—the centrally planned Soviet economy, the self-serving Communist party, the inflexible government bureaucracy, and the police-state mentality. Few Soviet citizens realized that what they were witnessing was the opening of *the closed society*—the Soviet Union.

Gorbachev repeatedly used the term "radical reform" in his speech. However, because he neither denounced Marxist-Leninist ideology nor embraced capitalism, we were told by our government and by the press that nothing had changed in the Soviet Union and that it was business-as-usual in Moscow. I believe that Gorbachev meant exactly what he said. The name of the game is indeed radical reform—radical reform of the Soviet culture, economy, political structure, and foreign policy. Unfortunately, Gorbachev's message to the Soviet people seems to have gone right over the heads of the U.S. press, U.S. Sovietologists, the Reagan administration, and Congress.

Over forty years have gone by since Winston Churchill, Franklin D. Roosevelt, and Joseph V. Stalin met at Yalta to carve up Europe. That meeting gave birth to a system of international relations between the Soviet Union and the United States based on competition, fear, and mistrust. Within a matter of months after the end of World War II, the Soviet Union and the United States, who had been allies since 1941, would embark on a cold war characterized by a never-ending series of hostile acts on both sides and a military buildup of almost unbelievable proportions. Since 1945 the cold war has been fueled by U.S. and Soviet politicians, journalists, and so-called "experts"—many of whom have based their entire careers on anti-Soviet or anti-U.S. rhetoric, as the case may be.

Although Stalin died in 1953, and the Soviet Union has changed a great deal since then, most of the assumptions underlying U.S. foreign policy today are the same as they were in the 1950s. Isn't it high time we reexamined the USSR—its culture, its new leaders, their aspirations, and their strategies? Might it *not* be business-as-usual in the Kremlin? In what kind of business will the Soviet Union be in 1990? What are the implications of Gorbachev's reforms on the arms race, U.S. foreign policy, and the U.S. balance of payments problem? Do we need to rethink our political, military, and foreign-trade policies towards the Soviet Union and Eastern Europe? What if Gorbachev does succeed in opening the door to the closed society?

To analyze the dramatic changes that have taken place in the Soviet Union since Gorbachev was named general secretary of the Communist party on 11 March 1985, I will use an analytical approach known as *strategic analysis,* a technique used by many U.S. companies to analyze the behavior of their competitors. This approach is similar to that which a company like IBM might use to analyze a significant change in the strategic direction of one of its foreign competitors, such as Hitachi or Siemens. Strategic analysis is a technique for assessing the relative strengths and weaknesses of a major competitor, understanding its long-term objectives, and evaluating the consequences of alternative strategies that might be employed by the competitor.

Because most people in the United States view the Soviet Union as their foremost adversary, I propose to formulate a comprehensive strategic analysis of the objectives and strategies of the USSR to the year 2000. I begin with an assessment of the strengths and weaknesses of Soviet agriculture, industry, commerce, trade, politics, foreign policy, military, and culture. I will also evaluate the impact that several important international forces—Hungary, China, and the United States—may have in shaping the long-term strategic direction of the Soviet Union. My primary aim is to improve our understanding of the Soviet Union and to evaluate the implications of alternative Soviet objectives and strategies on the United States and the rest of the world.

The Soviet Union suffers from a plethora of well-known problems associated with a tightly controlled military state and a rigid, highly centralized economic system. These problems include economic stagnation, low productivity, shortages of food products and consumer goods, poor morale on the part of managers and workers, and a serious gap with the West in terms of the development of computers and other sophisticated technologies. There are serious shortages of raw materials and energy that give rise to production imbalances, unfulfilled production quotas, the need for imports from the West, rising costs, and foreign currency shortages. The sharp drop in the price of crude oil, the Soviet Union's principal source of foreign currency, is yet another source of pressure on the tightly squeezed Soviet economy. The huge Soviet military buildup during the 1970s and early 1980s pushed the country's scarce resources to the limit.

During the 1950s and 1960s the rate of economic growth, as measured by GNP, averaged over 5 percent per year; industrial production increased by 7 percent per year; and agricultural output grew by 3 percent per year. The Soviets were able to maintain a high rate of investment in plant and equipment, raise the standard of living, and achieve a large military buildup. However, in the mid 1970s, economic stagnation began to set in. Since 1975, growth in GNP has averaged only a little more than 2 percent a year. During the eleventh five-year plan (1981–85), annual growth in GNP averaged 2.2 percent; industrial growth, 2.3 percent; and agricultural growth, 2.2 percent. This represents the worst performance of the Soviet economy during any five-year plan since the end of World War II. Shrinking farm output held the growth in GNP in 1985 to about 1.5 percent for the second year in a row. However, industrial output in 1985 increased by nearly 3 percent—about equal to the rate of growth for 1983 and 1984.[1] The sharp drop in economic growth after 1975 was associated with a decline in labor force growth rate, reduced growth of investment in plant and equipment, and an absolute decline in the productivity of labor and capital. These economic problems alone go a long way towards explaining why Gorbachev has little choice other than to make radical changes in the economic mechanism of the Soviet Union.

The Soviet economic system as we know it today is essentially the same system that was put in place by Stalin in the 1930s. It is characterized by highly centralized state ownership, management, and control of the industrial, agricultural, and military resources of the country. It is managed by a complex hierarchy of government and Communist party organizations, including the Central Committee of the Communist Party, the Politburo, the State Planning Commission (Gosplan), fifty economic ministries, and dozens of regional ministries. Until recently, managers of most state-owned enterprises had little or no discretion over such matters as product prices, product mix, production volume, marketing, production inputs, international trade, financing, and joint ventures. All of these decisions were top-down decisions passed on to managers of enterprises through layers of government ministries and subministries.

The Soviet Union is also plagued with a number of persistent social problems often associated with a closed society. These include corruption of government officials; an extensive yet illegal black market for consumer goods and services; social alienation of many of its people; high death rates and infant mortality rates; widespread alcoholism; and more recently a significant drug abuse problem. Thus, internal economic and social pressures are strong enough to push Gorbachev towards radical reform, even if there were no outside forces such as Hungary, China, and the United States driving him in the same direction.

Agriculture

Six poor grain harvests in a row and the demands of a rapidly urbanizing population with increasing personal income have made it more and more difficult for Soviet agriculture to keep pace with demand. Because of these poor harvests, the Soviet Union found it necessary to import an average of 30 million metric tons of grain per year between 1981 and 1984, much of it from the United States and other Western countries. Between 1976 and 1980 Soviet grain production averaged 205 million metric tons per year. Since 1980, the U.S. Department of Agriculture estimates that Soviet grain harvests have averaged only 175 million metric tons per year. In spite of the fact that the winter of 1984–85 was the coldest winter in the Soviet Union in twenty years, grain production in 1985 was estimated to be 190 million metric tons—the best harvest since the record 237 million tons in 1978, and 20 million tons above the 1984 results. But this achievement, together with increased production of sunflower seeds, fruits, and cotton, was offset by lower output of potatoes, sugar beets, vegetables, and more importantly, livestock. The total value of agricultural output actually declined by one-half percent in 1984 and 1985.

The Soviets' agricultural problems stem from two primary sources—excessive centralization of agriculture and an extremely harsh climate. Inefficiency, waste, fertilizer shortages, transportation bottlenecks, and a lack of incentives are all characteristics of a rigid, unwieldy system that gives all too little attention to the feelings and attitudes of individual managers and workers. When these problems are confounded by short growing seasons and erratic rainfall, frequent production shortfalls are the rule.

That agricultural reform should rank highly on Gorbachev's list of priorities is fully understandable when one considers the importance of agriculture in his personal and political background. Mikhail Sergeevich Gorbachev was born on 2 March 1931 in the small village of Privolnoye located in the Caucasus region between the Black and Caspian Seas. His parents were peasant farmers who lived in a predominantly agricultural area. From the days of his youth and continuing through his tenure as party leader in Stavropol and Politburo member in Moscow, Gorbachev has been closely associated with Soviet agriculture. Gorbachev, an agricultural economist, understands the root causes of the problems underlying Soviet agriculture, but he also has a clear vision of what will be required to correct these problems—namely, radical economic reform.

Industry

By the mid-1970s, the Soviet Union's simple growth formula that produced major economic gains in the post–World War II era—ever-increasing inputs of capital and labor—was simply no longer feasible. During the 1970s and early 1980s, the Soviets experienced stagnation in steel output, a precipitous increase in the cost of energy and other raw materials, a sharp decline in investment, a significant decline in labor force growth, and a decline in productivity. Problems in the energy, steel, and construction materials sectors, coupled with occasional transportation bottlenecks, restricted industrial growth during the 1981–84 period to only about half the target growth rate. Attempts to increase the quantity and quality of industrial output and make more efficient use of available resources were frustrated by a relatively backward technological base, inflexible production processes, a cumbersome, inefficient system of planning and management, and a distorted system of incentives.

Many of the economic problems of the Soviet Union are endemic to the structure of its economic system, which insulates managers and workers of state-owned enterprises from the competitive pressures of the marketplace. Soviet plant managers not only are told by government officials what to produce and how to produce it, but they have little discretion over decisions concerning product prices, sources of raw materials, plant and equipment, technology, and international marketing. Since the 1930s, all of these decisions have been controlled by government ministries in conjunction with the state planning commission, Gosplan. Enterprises have virtually no competition because imports are discouraged and many goods and services are in excess demand, thus providing sellers with enormous market power. It is almost impossible to be fired from one's job, and the concept of bankruptcy is completely unknown.

Management

In a system in which product output, factor inputs, technology, new investments, and environmental controls are all determined by Moscow bureaucrats, it is not surprising that Soviet managers have little or no incentive to improve product quality, reduce product costs, conserve on the use of energy and raw materials, and improve efficiency and productivity. The entire system is biased towards meeting the output quotas mandated by the state, with only limited attention devoted to quality and cost.

Inefficient management, the results of past investment mistakes, and numerous economic disincentives have all contributed to widespread shortages of energy, raw materials, and intermediate goods as well as transportation bottlenecks. Central planners can mandate the solution of a problem in a particular industry, but this creates problems for other industries. When production managers are confronted with bottlenecks that may or may not be within their realm of control, they often respond by producing substitute products that consumers do not want or by lowering the quality of their products. In either case the result is an excess supply of unwanted products on store shelves.

It is not easy to motivate Soviet managers and workers with financial incentives if there is nothing for them to buy with their increased earnings because high-quality consumer goods and services are in short supply. The shortages in consumer goods are in turn the result of production bottlenecks and inefficiencies. Soviet reformers have their work cut out for themselves. What would you do if you wanted to change all this? As Gorbachev seems to understand quite well, you must change the system, and not merely treat the symptoms.

Plant and Equipment

As a result of cutbacks in the rate of investment in plant and equipment in some civilian industries, the rate of depreciation of equipment now exceeds the rate of investment. This failure to modernize some key industries has in turn contributed to the severity of a number of other major economic problems including production bottlenecks, shortages of consumer goods, and poor product quality. The primary cause of this problem was the allocation of exceedingly large amounts of investment resources in the late 1970s and early 1980s to military hardware, energy development, and major construction projects rather than to the modernization of existing civilian plants.

The machinery required for industrial modernization is produced in the machinery and metalworking sector, which is also the primary source of production of military hardware and consumer durables. In the near term, the Soviet military establishment is well positioned to accommodate the possible shifts in machinery demand required by industrial modernization in the Soviet Union.

The Soviets have been allocating 40 percent of all of their capital investments to the development of oil and gas reserves. Until 1986, crude oil production had been declining in spite of the heavy investment in exploration and development. In a nonmarket economy, politics is often a more important determinant of resource allocation decisions than economics. Political expediency may dictate the allocation of resources to projects that have little or no economic benefit.

Technology

In spite of the fact that it invests a large share of its GNP in research and development, and graduates more engineers each year than do countries in the West, the Soviet Union continues to suffer from a technological gap with the West. Although the Soviets are particularly skilled at basic research, science, and mathematics, they seem to experience consistent problems in transforming basic research into nonmilitary products and applications. Even though the Soviets have achieved significant technological breakthroughs in military and aerospace research and engineering, few of these achievements seem to have spilled over into the industrial sector of their economy. Some of their most notable technological deficiencies include computer hardware and software, process control systems, and energy-related equipment.

As recently as 1982, I was surprised to discover the dearth of so-called decision support systems or computer-based planning software systems in the Soviet Union. Systems that had been available in the United States since the early 1970s to support long-term planning and budgeting were not available in the Soviet Union.

At least part of the problem lies with the fact that Soviet enterprises operate as monopolists with virtually no competition from domestic suppliers, foreign vendors, or customers. The pressure to innovate comes from governmental bureaucrats for whom technological innovation is only one of many government objectives. Enterprise incentives are usually tied to meeting production targets. Because the penalties for failing to meet targets are usually severe and the rewards for success are relatively small, few managers are willing to take the risk of experimenting with innovative methods that might lead to failure. Another important reason for the Soviets' persistent technological gap is the fact that research and development is usually organizationally separated from prospective producers and users of new technologies. The Soviet system of rigid prices often fails to provide the proper signals and rewards for product innovation and quality improvements.

Firms find it more profitable and less risky to stay in a rut. Lastly, these systematic barriers to innovation also impede the rapid and efficient assimilation and diffusion of technologies imported from abroad, thus reducing the potential payoff of these technologies.

Energy

Because 60 percent of the hard currency earnings of the Soviet Union comes from petroleum-based products, the Soviet economy recently suffered a twofold loss—two straight years of declining oil production in 1984 and 1985, followed by a precipitous drop in the price of crude oil in early 1986.

However, overall energy production actually increased in 1985 as a result of strong performances in the coal, natural gas, and electric power sectors. Natural gas production increased by nearly 10 percent and electric energy output increased by nearly 4 percent. In addition, coal production increased by 13 million tons.[2]

At the time of the Chernobyl nuclear plant disaster near Kiev in April 1986, the Soviet Union was generating 11 percent of its electric power from nuclear plants, and it had hoped to double that amount by 1990. With forty-six nuclear plants in operation and seven under construction, the Soviet Union was second only to the United States in terms of its commitment to nuclear power. Prior to the Chernobyl accident, the Soviet Union was trying to reduce its dependence on fossil fuels, which are located far from its largest urban population centers and are increasingly difficult and expensive to recover. Obviously, the Chernobyl nuclear accident clouds the future of the Soviet nuclear power program with uncertainty.

Finance and Banking

Since the 1930s, the Soviet Union has survived with a truly primitive monetary system in which state-owned enterprises receive literally all of their operating funds from the state monopoly bank, Gosbank.

Until recently, Soviet enterprises could receive no funds whatsoever from either private or international sources. Unlike the situation in China and Hungary today, in the Soviet Union there are no commercial banks or capital markets. Furthermore, the ruble is tightly controlled and not easily convertible into other currencies, thus making foreign trade even more difficult than it might otherwise be. Until 1987, both international finance and international trade remained highly centralized in the Soviet Union. Whereas Hungary and Poland now have access to outside funds through the World Bank and the International Monetary Fund, the Soviet Union does not participate in these international financial institutions. If Gorbachev wants to make the Soviet Union a competitive force in the global economy, he must come to grips with the gross inadequacies of the Soviet monetary system.

Commerce

Inconsistencies between supply and demand of consumer goods have persisted in the Soviet Union for decades, but they seem to have worsened in recent years. Many of the products produced by Soviet enterprises are of poor quality, obsolete, and essentially unsalable. As the standard of living has improved, consumers have become more sophisticated and will no longer settle for inferior products. Given the lack of high-quality consumer goods, material incentives to motivate factory managers and workers meet with only limited success. Why work hard to earn more rubles if there is nothing to buy?

With only a limited number of consumer goods available, Soviet citizens save a huge portion of their meager salaries. The state provides them with almost everything they need to live on either free or very cheaply, and everything else is simply unavailable in Soviet stores. Even though the Soviet Union produces 1.3 million cars per year, a potential buyer may have to wait up to three years to purchase one of the better models, and the waiting list includes between two and three million people. There is a shortage of garages to protect cars from vandalism and the weather. Garages are often located so far from the owner's flat that the owner must take a bus home after parking the car. Furthermore, it has become a real status symbol to own a foreign car such as a Volvo or a Mercedes.

Shortages of consumer goods, including food, clothing, and durable goods, have become so widespread that Soviet consumers spend significant percentages of their lives waiting in lines to buy such goods. It has been estimated that Soviet citizens spend sixty-five billion person-hours shopping each year. This is equivalent to the full-time employment of thirty-five million people. Eighty percent of this time is spent shopping for food, and this does not include the time spent in finding a store that stocks the particular item in the first place.[3]

One result of these shortages of consumer goods is an extensive black market, which employs over twenty million people and generates annual sales of $7.3 billion, according to the Soviet newspaper *Izvestia*. Until May 1987, virtually any service worth having, such as auto and home repairs, could only be obtained on the black market. These services can now be provided legally by private individuals.

To satisfy its increasing domestic needs for consumer goods as well as agricultural commodities and technology, the Soviet Union has become increasingly dependent on imports from the West.

Political Structure

The political legacy of the Brezhnev era, which began in 1964 and lasted until November 1982, was a very stable government without visible pressures for change and without any serious threats of political disintegration. The entire period was characterized by a high degree of political conservatism in which the political elites who controlled the party, the KGB, and the military seemed to have an overwhelming desire for political stability and security at any price.

The Soviet leadership moved away from Stalin-like purges and police-state tactics towards a relatively inflexible political oligarchy. The influence of professional experts and technocrats increased substantially. These same professionals were increasingly motivated by professional achievements and personal materialism. Only a limited amount of political and cultural dissent was tolerated in the 1970s and early 1980s. For all practical purposes, the Soviet Union remained a closed society.

U.S. journalists often referred to the aging political power structure in Moscow as the Soviet gerontocracy. Most of the party and government leaders who were still around in 1985 when Gorbachev came into power were not only old, but they were very old. With few exceptions, most of Brezhnev's political cronies not only fought in World War II, but they also remembered Stalin's purges in the 1930s. These two experiences alone go a long way towards explaining the conservatism and aversion to risk of Brezhnev and his associates.

Under Brezhnev the military expanded its powers, attained a higher degree of professional autonomy, and had a greater voice in military-related issues. The military's subordination to the civilian political leadership remained unquestioned, however, and its role in influencing civilian affairs was limited. Its success in achieving its resource allocation goals during the Brezhnev period was less a result of independent political power than the result of a "symbiosis of views" between the political and military leadership.[4]

The key players in the Soviet political system in the 1970s and early 1980s were the bureaucrats who controlled the major ministries, subministries, state committees, and state-owned enterprises. Not unlike their counterparts in other parts of the world, their overriding concern was not political ideology but rather protecting their own political turf. Given the rigidities of the political system, the initial Soviet delay in responding to the April 1986 nuclear accident at Chernobyl was hardly surprising. The structure of the system virtually precludes a quick response to anything.

But as early as May 1985 in a speech in Leningrad, Gorbachev signaled his intentions to shake up the leadership of the Communist party and the Soviet government. "We must, of course, give a chance, as it were, to all cadres to understand the demands of the moment and this stage, and to adjust," he said. "But those who do not intend to adjust and who, moreover, are an obstacle to the solution of these new tasks, simply must get out of the way, get out of the way and not be a hindrance."

By the end of the twenty-seventh party congress, barely a year later, Gorbachev had achieved a shake-up in the top Soviet leadership ranks that was unprecedented in such a short period of time. What Gorbachev achieved in his first year had taken Stalin, Khrushchev, and Brezhnev several years to accomplish. Not only did he take control of the Politburo and the Secretariat of the Central Committee of the Communist Party but also the Council of Ministers, which carries out the decisions made by the party. Furthermore, more than thirty of the eighty or so heads of ministries or state committees were retired or removed from office. An umbrella state farm–industry committee resulted from the merger of five ministries and a state committee. What is even more impressive than the changes at the top, where Gorbachev would be expected to bring in his own people, has been the shake-up of the vast state machinery below.

Gorbachev has far more political clout than most U.S. Sovietologists ever dreamed would be the case. His political influence is by no means limited to the central party apparatus and the large national ministries, but also extends to far-flung republics, oblasts, and cities. Gorbachev's rapid inroads into the vast bureaucracy seem to be the result of a combination of incredible political savvy, superb timing, some rather good luck, and the political groundwork that had been laid by his mentor, Yuri V. Andropov. Few Americans realize the extremely important role played by Andropov in paving the way for radical reform.

Foreign Affairs

The international environment into which Gorbachev entered in 1985 was dominated by two overriding themes. First, U.S.–Soviet political relations were at an all-time low. Second, Soviet influence abroad had been slipping throughout the decade of the 1970s and continued to do so in the 1980s. The intervention of the Soviet Union in Afghanistan in 1979, the declaration of martial law in Poland in 1981, President Ronald Reagan's anti-Soviet rhetoric, and the downing of the Korean Air Lines Flight 007 in 1983 all contributed to a rapid deterioration in U.S.–Soviet relations in the 1980s. Indeed, relations between the two superpowers seem to be based on a never-ending cycle of fear and distrust of each other combined with a heavy dose of tough talk and macho pride.

The Soviet Union was also confronted with pressures for increased independence on the part of its Eastern European allies. Yugoslavia, for example, split with Moscow in 1948. Although it still has a communist government, it rejects the rigidity of Soviet foreign policy, experiments with decentralized management of factories and other enterprises, and trades freely with the West. Albania, another communist country, also remains unaligned with the Soviet Union.

Since the 1960s Romania in foreign affairs, and Hungary in economic policies, have steadily tested and stretched the limits of acceptable Soviet-bloc behavior. Romania has demonstrated occasional independence in foreign policy by denouncing Soviet interference in Czechoslovakia in 1968 and Afghanistan in 1979. Furthermore, Romania does not allow Soviet troops to be stationed within its territorial boundaries, and unlike the Soviet Union, it maintains diplomatic relations with Israel. Hungary though remaining a member of the Council for Mutual Economic Assistance (CMEA) and the Warsaw Pact, has been experimenting with Western-style management practices since the 1970s. Of course, the influence in Poland of the independent trade union, Solidarity, has not gone unnoticed in Moscow. More recently, the East Germans have been visibly increasing their ties to the West German government in Bonn.

In Western Europe, the Soviets' anti-Euromissile campaign was a complete disaster. Instead of wedging the NATO nations away from the United States, Moscow's hard-line position served to consolidate the Western allies in Europe. Furthermore, communist parties are shrinking all over Western Europe—particularly in France, Spain, and Italy.

In other parts of the world, Soviet influence is also on the wane. In Afghanistan, the war has dragged since late 1979. What was intended as quick and decisive surgery has become the Soviet equivalent of Vietnam. The presence of Soviet troops in Afghanistan, an intensely Islamic country, has also reduced the influence of the Soviet Union in the Middle East. Indecisiveness during the 1982 Israeli invasion of Lebanon was also a setback for the Soviets in the Arab world. During the war between Iran and Iraq, the Soviets have shipped arms to both sides.

Although Moscow can take some pleasure from the advancing communization of Ethiopia, its overall influence in Africa is minimal and is limited to Angola and Mozambique, in addition to Ethiopia.

In Latin America only Cuba remains solidly in the Soviet bloc, and it represents a huge financial drain on the Soviet economy. In Nicaragua, the Soviets have acted cautiously. Although they have strengthened ties with the Sandinistas by providing desperately needed oil and increasing the flow of arms, the Soviets have refrained from actions that could provoke direct military intervention on the part of the United States.

In the Far East, Laos and Vietnam are considered members of the Soviet bloc, but China has steered an independent course of Moscow since the early 1960s. Although Sino–Soviet relations in the late 1960s and 1970s were characterized by open antagonism, confrontation has been averted and more recently relations have shown signs of improvement.

For the Soviets the phenomenal economic success of Japan since the end of World War II must be a source of considerable frustration. Although the Soviet Union and the United States continue to spend hundreds of billions of dollars each year on conventional and nuclear arms, the Japanese—with only minimal defense expenditures—have become an undeniable economic force throughout the world. Although the Soviet Union and Japan were industrialized at about the same time and both suffered tremendous losses during World War II, the Japanese have rebounded to become an economic force second to none. In the meantime the Soviet Union has continued to lose credibility as a model for economic development throughout the world. The traditional Soviet claim that their economic development model is a viable one for Third World countries has fallen on deaf ears in one country after another—Taiwan, India, Indonesia, Argentina, Mexico, and Brazil, to mention only a few. But the biggest blow of all must be Deng Xiaoping's visible success as he continues to distance himself from the ideology of Marx, Lenin, and Mao.

The fundamental problem that Gorbachev faces in the field of foreign affairs stems from the fact that in a closed society such as the Soviet Union, the whole concept of "foreign policy" represents a contradiction in terms. It is extremely difficult to formulate and implement a viable foreign policy for a country that insists on such tight controls on the flow of literally all information, people, trade, and capital into and out of the country. To have stable diplomatic and economic relations between two countries necessitates a certain degree of openness and flexibility in relations between the two countries—something that has never existed in the Soviet Union. If Gorbachev wants the Soviet Union to become a major force in international economic and political relations, he has no other choice than to open the door to the Soviet Union.

Military Affairs

Gorbachev's inheritance not only included the world's second largest economy, albeit somewhat ailing, but a military force that is second to none. Since the 1960s and 1970s, the Soviet military might has been built up through a massive commitment of the country's best human and technical resources. Soviet military expenditures grew in constant rubles by nearly 50 percent between 1965 and 1975. Although the growth rate slowed in the mid-1970s, the Soviets were still able to sustain military spending at very high levels, thus enabling them to procure massive quantities of military hardware. The share of GNP devoted to military activities increased in current ruble prices from between 12 and 14 percent in the early 1970s to between 15 and 17 percent in the early 1980s as the growth in military spending continued to exceed the rate of growth of the overall economy.[5] Table 1–1 provides some information on the extent of the Soviet military buildup (compared with U.S. figures) during the 1974–85 period.

The military consistently takes priority over civilian industry for raw materials and equipment, as well as top technicians and highly

Table 1–1
*Procurement of Selected Weapons Systems by
the United States and the Soviet Union, 1974–85*[a]

	US	USSR
ICBMs and SLBMs	1,050	3,500
Surface-to-air missiles[b]	11,700	105,000
Long- and intermediate-range bombers	8	400
Fighters	4,050	7,800
Helicopters	2,050	6,500
Submarines	44	110
Major surface combatants	98	90
Tanks	8,400	27,000
Artillery	2,200	22,000

Source: Central Intelligence Agency and Defense Intelligence Agency, *The Soviet Economy under a New Leader*. A report presented to the Subcommittee on Economic Resources, Competitiveness, and Security Economics of the Joint Economic Committee of the U.S. Congress, Washington, D.C., 19 March 1986, p. 6.

[a]The numbers represent gross additions to weapons inventories and do not reflect retirements because of obsolescence or SALT restraints.

[b]Does not include naval or portable SAMs.

skilled workers. All of this takes its toll on the agricultural and consumer sectors of the Soviet economy, which must compete with the military for scarce resources. Thus we see that the combined effects of increased military spending and shortages of food and consumer goods all add to the pressure for economic reform.

Culture

To understand the Soviet culture it is necessary to have at least a cursory knowledge of Soviet history. Most people find it difficult to fathom the tyranny perpetrated by Stalin in the 1930s, 1940s, and after World War II. But Ivan the Terrible in the sixteenth century, Peter the Great in the eighteenth century, and Nicholas I in the nineteenth century each exhibited behavioral patterns that were all too similar to the style of Stalin in the bloody purges of the 1930s. Although Peter the Great is best known for opening Russia to the West and introducing a modern army and state administration, he also introduced measures to improve the efficiency of authoritarian controls, some of which are still in place in Moscow today. He established the first police administration, instituted censorship, and introduced the practice of issuing internal passports to prevent Russians from traveling away from their permanent homes without special approval.

Although Soviet leaders no longer engage in mass terror as a means of controlling, manipulating, or changing society, their treatment of political dissidents is not fundamentally different from that of the czars. The Soviet practice of putting dissidents in mental hospitals can be traced back to the early nineteenth century, when an eminent scientist was branded insane for an essay he had written condemning Russia as backward and for advocating westernization and Catholicism.

One of the fundamental differences between Russians and Americans is in their attitudes towards power and authority. Americans have an intense distrust of authority and shy away from Big Business, Big Labor, and Big Government. The Russians have a tremendous respect for bigness and power. The sheer size of the Kremlin walls and the massive buildings built during the Stalin era all connote power and authority. Although the Russian people feared Stalin, they nevertheless respected him for his power and his authority. Long before Lenin and Stalin came to power, the Russians had been subjected to five centuries of authoritarian rule from Ivan the Great and Ivan the Terrible forward. Furthermore, they have no experience whatsoever with Western ideas such as common law, habeas corpus, political debate, and the decentralization of political power.[6]

Another persistent theme of Soviet culture is a strong aversion to risk. To minimize their personal economic risk as well as the risk of outside military invasion, the Soviets have paid dearly in terms of personal freedom and liberty. In the Soviet Union it is very difficult to become wealthy—legally, that is. But because everyone is guaranteed a job, free medical care, a free education, and low-cost housing, there is very limited personal financial risk. In the United States it is possible to make a lot of money and many people manage to do so. But it is also possible to go bankrupt in the United States and end up in the "poor house" with no income and no health insurance.

A long history of invasions by everyone from the Mongols and Napoléon to Adolf Hitler has made the Russians particularly paranoid about the possibility of foreign invasion. To ensure political stability, they have been willing to put up with what in the United States would be considered a broad range of human rights violations including arbitrary arrests, police controls, censorship, labor camps, and enforced intellectual conformity. Most in this country abhor these practices, but the Russians reply that these are no worse than what they consider to be U.S.-style human rights violations—unemployment, drug addiction, violent crime, political assassinations, and racial discrimination.[7]

The Soviet responses to the destruction of Korean Air Lines Flight 007 in 1983 as well as the Chernobyl nuclear accident in 1986 illustrate very well the influence of Soviet culture. In both incidents order and security seemed to take precedence over more human concerns such as health, safety, and compassion. If Gorbachev expects to reform the Soviet economic and political systems, he must confront the culture of a closed society—a truly formidable challenge.

Strengths

Although my analysis of the environment inherited by Gorbachev indicates that all is not well in the Soviet Union, the Soviets do possess some important strengths upon which they may be able to build as they attempt to achieve their ambitious long-term objectives. In spite of its limitations, the Soviet economy has managed to achieve some of the fundamental objectives of its leaders—the establishment of socialism, the transformation of a predominantly agricultural economy into a highly industrialized economy, and the buildup of a massive military capability. All Soviet citizens have access to guaranteed employment, relatively inexpensive housing, free high-quality education, free medical care, low-cost public transportation, and a pension on which to live after retirement.

Among the other Soviet strengths are an abundance of land rich in natural resources—particularly oil and natural gas. The Soviets also possess an extensive transportation network of roads, railroads, and airlines. Although somewhat obsolete, they have the necessary plant and equipment to produce durable goods on a very large scale. By any standards, the Soviet education system is first rate. The Soviets are particularly good at basic research but lack experience in developing and marketing products based on their technology. The military might of the Soviet Union is second to none.

Finally, whether by choice or not, the Soviets are highly disciplined. They have survived century after century of military defeat, occupation, and repression. They have experienced the atrocities of Adolf Hitler and Joseph Stalin. They understand what pain and suffering mean, and they are able to delay gratification almost endlessly. These are extremely important resources upon which Gorbachev may draw as he attempts to lead the Soviet Union into the next century.

Last, and by no means, least, Gorbachev shows every sign of being a very strong leader. Unlike his predecessors, he does not appear to be locked into a particular political ideology. His problem-solving management style is pragmatic, flexible, and imaginative. But these are precisely the attributes that a Soviet leader must possess to be successful in turning the Soviet Union around.

In chapter 2 I will define Gorbachev's long-term objectives and examine the strategic options available to him for achieving these objectives. In chapters 3 through 6 I will assess the impact of four specific international factors on Gorbachev's strategies—Hungary, the People's Republic of China, East–West trade, and the Reagan administration's foreign policy, respectively. I will show how each of these external forces motivates Gorbachev to pursue a strategy of radical reform and simultaneously helps create an environment conducive to the successful implementation of a radical strategy. In the final two chapters I analyze how Gorbachev is going about making the Soviet Union a more open society and implementing his strategy of radical reform.

2
Gorbachev's Strategy: Radical Reform

I n a highly pluralistic society such as the United States, whose government has no formal long-term strategic planning process, it is
difficult to make definitive statements about the nation's long-term
objectives and strategies. At the beginning of each year, the president
delivers two reports to the Congress—the State of the Union message
and the annual budget message. (The State of the Union message is
analogous to the situation assessment of a large company.) It includes
a review of the international environment and an assessment of domestic affairs. But in a large U.S. company, the budgetary process
would not begin without agreement among the senior managers on
corporate objectives and strategies. In the United States neither the
president nor the Congress produces any formal statement of national
objectives or strategies.

In the Soviet Union, the situation is quite different. Every five
years the Communist party holds a congress in Moscow of which the
twenty-seventh party congress, which began on 25 February 1986,
was the most recent. The twenty-seventh congress was attended by
five thousand delegates representing nineteen million Soviet communists, as well as by 153 delegations from 113 foreign countries. The
delegates endorsed the *Guidelines for the Economic and Social Development of the USSR for 1986–90 and for the Period Ending in
2000.* These guidelines, on which the twelfth five-year plan is based,
constitute the bulk of the publicly available information on the plan.
Details on defense spending, foreign aid, and other sensitive areas are
omitted from the public version of the guidelines. In spite of their
limitations, the guidelines do provide us with substantial information
about the sense of direction for the Soviet Union to the new millen-

ium. In addition, they also contain aggregate targets for the Soviet economy as well as descriptions of major projects. The complete five-year plan is usually not published by the Soviets. Whenever I refer to the guidelines for the twelfth five-year plan, I will use the notation "FYP12."

In attempting to define and analyze the objectives and strategies of the Soviet Union, I will draw heavily on the guidelines for FYP12 as well as speeches by Mikhail S. Gorbachev, Prime Minister Nikolai I. Ryzhkov, and other party leaders at the congress. I will also examine other speeches made by Gorbachev since he came into office as well as his actions through early 1987.

In a typical U.S. company, whether or not the strategic plan will be successfully implemented depends on the commitment of the CEO and the line managers to the objectives and strategies of the plan. The Soviet Union is no exception to this rule. Obviously it is impossible to assess in any objective fashion the true commitment of Gorbachev, party leaders, Soviet bureaucrats, and the Soviet people to the objectives and strategies of FYP12. However, I will attempt to look below the surface at possible reasons why Soviet leaders and the Soviet people may be motivated either to support or to block the implementation of the plan.

Strategic Objectives

At the beginning of his keynote speech before the party congress, Gorbachev said, "Acceleration of the country's socio-economic development is the key to all our problems," thus signaling that improving the Soviet economy was indeed his number-one objective.[1] Then with a degree of candor that is unprecedented in the Soviet Union, Gorbachev proceeded to elaborate on the nature of the Soviets' economic problems:

> Difficulties began to build up in the economy in the 1970s, with the rates of economic growth declining visibly. As a result, the targets for economic development set in the Communist Party program, and even the lower targets of the 9th and 10th year plans were not attained. Neither did we manage to carry out the social program charted for this period. A lag ensued in the material base of science

and education, health protection, culture, and everyday services. Though efforts have been made of late, we have not succeeded in wholly remedying the situation. There are serious lags in engineering, the oil and coal industries, the electrical engineering industry, in ferrous metals and chemicals and in capital construction. Neither have the targets been met for the main indicators of efficiency and the improvement of the people's standard of living.[2]

Gorbachev then called for doubling national income in the Soviet Union by the year 2000. To achieve this ambitious goal, the CIA estimates that GNP would have to grow at an average annual rate of 3.5 percent over the 1986–90 period and 5.0 percent annually between 1990 and 2000.[3] Real per capita income is targeted to increase by 2.5 to 2.8 percent during FYP12 and 3.2 to 4.0 percent over the 1990–2000 period. As can be seen from table 2–1, these targets are substantially higher than the results that were achieved during the first four years of FYP11, 1981–84.

Gorbachev's plan calls for an economic program involving strict standards of discipline, the massive replacement of obsolete plant and equipment, a dramatic improvement in technology, and increased ef-

Table 2–1

Measures of Soviet Economic Performance:
Results, 1976–84, and Targets, 1986–2000

(average annual growth rates expressed as percentages)

	Actual		Target	
	1976–80	*1981–84*	*1986–90*	*1990–2000*
GNP (CIA estimates)	2.7	2.7	3.5	5.0
Real per capita income	3.3	2.2	2.5–2.8	3.2–4.0
Industrial production	4.5	3.7	3.9–4.4	4.9–5.1
Agricultural production	1.5	2.6	2.7–3.0	—
Labor productivity				
Industry	3.1	3.1	4.2–4.6	—
Agriculture	2.8	2.7	3.9–4.2	—
Gross investment	3.7	3.8	3.4–3.8	—

Source: Ed A. Hewett, "Gorbachev's Economic Strategy: A Preliminary Assessment," *Soviet Economy* 1 (October–December 1985), p. 289.

ficiency in the use of energy and other natural resources. Without mentioning Leonid Brezhnev by name, Gorbachev was extremely critical of previous Soviet leadership.

> The inertness and stiffness of the forms and methods of administration, the decline of dynamism in our work and an escalation of bureaucracy—all this was doing no small damage. Signs of stagnation had begun to surface in the life of society.
>
> The situation called for change, but a peculiar psychology— How to improve things without changing anything?—took the upper hand. But that cannot be done, comrades. Stop for an instant, as they say, and you fall a mile behind.[4]

Throughout his opening address, Gorbachev made considerable use of terms such as *flexible prices, market forces, financial incentives, local autonomy, radical reform,* and even *private enterprise.* In his speech, Prime Minister Ryzhkov frequently used the expression *radical reform.* He argued that cost overruns, bureaucratic red tape, obsolete equipment, and a lag in applied research had combined to cripple the Soviet economy.

In his closing address to the party congress on 6 March 1986, Gorbachev said:

> To achieve the acceleration of the socio-economic development of the country means to give a fresh strong impetus to the growth of the productive forces, to scientific and technical progress and to set in motion the huge reserves of our national economy through perfecting the economic system of socialism.
>
> Yes, comrades, acceleration, radical transformations in all spheres of our life are not just a slogan but a course the party will steer firmly and unwaveringly.[5]

Against this background of overall Soviet objectives for FYP12, let us now consider some of Gorbachev's more specific objectives for the socioeconomic development of the USSR.

Agriculture

One of the most acute problems facing Soviet leaders is agriculture. Agricultural production increased by only 1.5 percent and 2.6 percent respectively during the two previous planning periods—1976–80 and 1981–84. Gorbachev took a very direct approach to Soviet agriculture in his party congress speech: "A problem we will have to solve in the shortest time possible is that of fully meeting our country's food needs."[6] He then called for a doubling of the growth rate of farm production so as "to insure a substantial increase in the per capita consumption of meat, milk, vegetables, and fruit."

The Soviets hope to achieve increases in agricultural production of approximately 3 percent annually between 1986 and 1990. To reach this goal labor productivity in agriculture must increase by 4 percent per year—substantially higher than the results for FYP10 and FYP11. Per capita meat production is targeted to increase by 17 percent per year over the next five years.

The Soviets' agricultural objectives have become more critical since the party congress. The sharp decline in the price of crude oil has made it even more difficult to finance agricultural imports to cover production shortfalls.

One of the more interesting ideas put forth by Gorbachev in support of his agricultural production targets was a system of contracting agricultural production work to "teams, groups, and families," and a more flexible approach to the marketing of surplus agricultural produce. In the latter case, collective farms and state-owned farms would be given the opportunity to use or sell, as they see fit, all of the produce harvested over and above the production targets. If these ideas seem familiar, it is because they have been successfully implemented by the Hungarians since the late 1950s and the Chinese since 1978. They have often been accompanied by disclaimers by Gorbachev assuring his comrades that "socialist economic principles" were not being compromised.

A resolution approving the party's program for FYP12 appeared to pave the way for radical agricultural reform. It called for "new far-reaching measures aimed at shaping an effective managerial mechanism . . . which will provide conditions for a broad use of incentives and profit-oriented methods" in Soviet agriculture. It also advocated a "considerable extension of the independence and initiative of collective and state farms, and other enterprises and for raising a dependable barrier to mismanagement and parasitism."[7] These are strong objectives, and Gorbachev appears to be dead serious about implementing them—but to do so will necessitate radical economic reforms.

Industry

FYP12 targets a 100-percent increase in industrial output between 1986 and 2000 to be generated by a 150-percent increase in labor productivity. In another strongly worded resolution, the party congress mandated that industrial management at all levels "must shift the emphasis from quantity indicators to quality and efficiency, from the intermediate to the end results, from expanding production capacities to their modernization, from building up fuel and raw material resources to improving their utilization, and to the crash-development of science-intensive industries." As if to underscore the sense of urgency associated with these radical industrial reforms, the resolution went on to propose the necessary structural and investment changes that would be required to achieve these ambitious industrial objectives.[8]

The stock of industrial machinery and equipment in the Soviet Union has been estimated to be twenty years old on average. In laying out his program for industrial modernization, Gorbachev has proposed (1) doubling retirement rates of capital stock to accelerate the replacement of obsolete capital by more efficient, largely state-of-the-art machinery; (2) modernizing the nation's capital stock so that by 1990 a third of it, including up to half the machinery, is new; and (3) increasing capital investment in civilian machine building over the 1986–90 period by 80 percent over that of the 1981–85 period.[9]

Consistent with Gorbachev's long-term targets, industrial output is scheduled to grow by 4.5 percent per year between 1986 and 1990, led by a 7–8 percent annual increase in production for the machine-building sector. The Soviets plan to pump 200 billion rubles ($300 billion) into the machine-building sector over the next five years. Special emphasis will be placed on the machine-tool, computer, instrument-making, electrical-equipment, and electronics industries—the same industries that have paced modernization in the West.

FYP12 assumes a 5 percent annual rate of growth in construction and housing. It also calls for total energy output over the five-year period to grow about 18 percent, with oil output increasing by 6–7.6 percent, natural gas by 31–33 percent, nuclear power by 235 percent, and coal by 7.6–10 percent.[10]

Overall investment in Soviet industry is scheduled to increase by

3.4–3.8 percent according to FYP12. In apparent contrast with Gorbachev's earlier statements that the share of investment in energy would be held constant during FYP12, investment in oil exploration and development is scheduled to increase by 31 percent, in the coal sector by 27 percent, and in the electric power sector by 24 percent.[11] Those targets for energy output and investment were prepared before the Chernobyl nuclear accident.

Prime Minister Ryzhkov spoke out in favor of linking prices more closely to productive costs and consumer demand. He also suggested that incentives for workers should be improved, and that central planners should step back from involvement in day-to-day operations of enterprises. Other party leaders called for tying wages and salaries to labor productivity and measures of the quality of products produced by labor. Considerable emphasis was placed on the more efficient use of natural resources.

At the party congress, Gorbachev and others spoke of the need to "change the economic mechanism" of the Soviet Union. Such statements were frequently tempered with reassuring words to the party faithful to the effect that changing the economic mechanism did not constitute the complete abandonment of the "principles of socialism." One resolution explained that accelerating socioeconomic development "necessitates a deep-going restructuring of the economic mechanism, the shaping of an integrated, effective, and flexible system of management based on the principle of democratic centralism and allowing for a fuller utilization of socialism's possibilities."[12]

U.S. economists are absolutely correct when they claim that Gorbachev's industrial targets are unattainable without radical economic reform. But no one understands that fact better than Gorbachev himself.

Technology

Much has been said about the absolute necessity of improving Soviet technology—particularly in such areas as computers, high-tech machine tools, automated equipment, and robots. For example, Prime Minister Ryzhkov said that

[i]t is no secret, however, that although we possess noteworthy research and development results and advanced ideas we often lag

behind in the development of progressive technologies, including even some that were born in our country.

A new retooling of the national economy on the basis of achievements of the scientific and technological revolution is a task of truly historic significance.[13]

Ryzhkov proposed doubling the level of automation in the Soviet economy and trebling the number of industrial robots over the next five years. The closing resolution of the party congress came on even stronger in its advocacy of an improved technological base for the Soviet Union:

> The party regards as the main lever for the intensification of the economy, a cardinal acceleration of scientific and technological progress, a broad introduction of new generations of machinery and of fundamentally new production techniques that make for the highest possible productivity and effectiveness.
>
> The foremost task set by the congress is that of carrying out a deep-going technical reconstruction of the economy on a basis of up-to-the-minute achievements in science and technology.
>
> Each industry, enterprise and association must have a clear programme for the continuous modernisation of production.
>
> And those managers who substitute showy postures and half-hearted decisions for the real thing, and who distort the very idea of technical reconstruction, must be called strictly to account.[14]

The resolution went on to make a number of very specific suggestions for improving Soviet technology in such fields as engineering, computers, energy, metallurgy, and chemicals.

> Engineering, which must attain the highest possible technical standards in the shortest possible time, is called upon to play the leading role in accelerating scientific and technological progress.
>
> A most important task is to develop and start up the mass production of up-to-date computers.
>
> There must be a radical reconstruction of the fuel and energy complex; the Energy Programme must be fulfilled.
>
> Much remains to be done in advancing metallurgy and the chemicalisation of the economy, in meeting the demand for new structural and other progressive materials.

There is little doubt that one of Gorbachev's primary objectives is closing the Soviet Union's technological gap with the West—particularly with regard to computers, process control equipment, and robotics.

Commerce and Trade

The development of consumer goods and services as well as international trade were also among the topics receiving special emphasis in FYP12. The plan includes a comprehensive program for increasing the output of nonfood consumer goods by at least 80–90 percent and more than doubling the value of services to the population. Textile and shoe production are expected to increase dramatically over the next five years.

Soviet authorities acknowledge that some consumer goods such as fashionable knitwear items and leather footwear for the younger generation are still in short supply. Light industrial factories are being given greater latitude to adjust quality, style, and prices to reflect market conditions. Gorbachev even raised the issue of the need for more flexible prices at the party congress. "Prices must be made more flexible, price levels must be linked not only with the outlays but also with the consumer properties of the goods and the degree to which products meet the needs of society and consumer demand."[15]

By providing manufacturers of consumer goods with increased flexibility to make their own product-mix and pricing decisions, Soviet leaders hope to stimulate improvements in technology and materials. For example, some textile mills have begun using shuttleless equipment, which should allow them to double labor productivity and improve working conditions. High-speed automatic machines are also being introduced at knitwear plants, and semiautomatic machines and new technologies are being installed at shoe factories. Furthermore, enterprises in the consumer goods sector are now able to retain a portion of their profits for investment in modernization. They can also receive bank loans for up to six years to finance the speedup of retooling.

Under FYP12 the Soviets will open a number of shops and boutiques to sell fashionable consumer goods at higher prices. French designer Pierre Cardin signed an agreement with the Soviets in 1986 to design men's and women's clothes for the Soviet fashion market. Plans call for Cardin to design two collections each year for manufacture in the Soviet Union as ready-to-wear garments.

Manufacturers of consumer goods for export are now allowed to dispose of part of their hard currency earnings as they see fit—a concept that has been used quite successfully by the Hungarians and the Chinese.

With regard to the service sector, Gorbachev has approved of legalizing some routine services in private hands that were previously illegal. The government is also providing loans to these private businesses.

To meet the Soviet Union's needs for imports of foodstuffs, consumer goods, and technology, FYP12 calls for increased trade as well as scientific and technical cooperation with captialist nations, Third World countries, and CMEA countries. Concerning trade relations with the West, Gorbachev had this to say.

> We are prepared to compete with capitalism exclusively in peaceful creative activities. Therefore we are for the development of political dialogue and interaction with capitalist states, for the large-scale development of mutually beneficial trade, economic, scientific, technical and cultural relations, and are ready to develop such relations on a stable long-term basis. But these relations must be honest and genuinely mutually advantageous, without any discrimination. Attempts to use trade as a tool for interfering in our domestic affairs are futile. We do not need such trade. We can do without it.[16]

In a meeting with U.S. Secretary of Commerce Malcolm Baldrige on 20 May 1985, Gorbachev was somewhat more blunt. He attributed the unsatisfactory state of U.S.–Soviet trade and economic ties to "the U.S. Administration's policy of discrimination against the Soviet Union, attempts to interfere in the Soviet Union's internal affairs and to use trade as a means of political pressure."[17]

The Soviet leader has consistently advocated improved trade relations with the United States as a strategy for raising the level of trust between the two superpowers, with the aim of eventually reducing the arms race and improving U.S.–Soviet political relations.

> Obviously, it is high time to unfreeze the potential of Soviet–American cooperation, and to freeze—or, to be more precise—to curb

the arms race and the escalation of hostility. In this respect, business ties between both countries can play a role. There exist possibilities for that, but only on the basis of equality and mutual benefit, without any discrimination whatsoever. The main goal is to restore the climate of mutual trust in relations between our countries.[18]

Putting aside political rhetoric, Gorbachev's real objective concerning international trade appears to be nothing short of the complete internationalization of the Soviet economy.

Domestic Politics

From the very outset, Gorbachev began selling his radical program to the Soviet people. He seemed to understand that to achieve his economic, social, and military objectives he would need the enthusiastic support not only of senior party leaders but also the support of factory managers and middle-level party officials as well. To obtain their political support he began taking his program directly to the people. He visited factories, hospitals, and schools—shaking hands and hobnobbing with ordinary citizens. As he worked the crowds in places far away from Moscow, he consistently emphasized three themes—stepped up production, labor and management discipline, and increased initiative and incentives. In stark contrast to his three aging predecessors, Gorbachev came across as open, energetic, and hard-working. Not only has Gorbachev introduced a more streamlined style into Soviet domestic politics, but he seems to be highly skilled in the use of television and the mass media to reach the Soviet people. He has rejected the usual effusive personal tributes so cherished by most Soviet leaders in the past.

He has communicated the message to party leaders that the cronyism and the corruption of the Brezhnev era must give way to the practical, problem-solving orientation of the new breed of Soviet leaders. He has put together an aggressive political campaign that includes firing corrupt and incompetent officials, intimidating potential adversaries, and putting together a network of protégés of his former mentor, Yuri V. Andropov. In his first year in office he concentrated on procedural matters such as increased discipline and new personnel. He has now turned to the difficult long-run issues laid out in FYP12.

Gorbachev summarized his domestic political objectives in his

closing speech before the party congress by calling for the removal of
all impediments to social and economic progress and by "strengthening discipline and order and creating organizational, moral and
material prerequisites for an all-out promotion of creative activity,
bold quest and socialist enterprise." According to Gorbachev,

> [t]he style needed today is concreteness, efficiency, consistency, the
> unity of word and deed, the choice of the most effective means, a
> careful consideration of the people's opinions and a skillful coordi-
> nating of efforts of all public forces.
>   It is necessary completely to overcome inertness, formalism, ap-
> athy, the habit of drowning a living cause in idle and endless roun-
> dabout talk, attempts by some people to "get onto the bandwagon
> of reconstruction."
>   In the final analysis, the success of our entire effort . . . will be
> determined by a conscious participation of the broadest mass of the
> people in Communist construction.
>   Everything depends on us, comrades. The time has come for
> vigorous and concentrated action.[19]

In many of Gorbachev's speeches, he frequently makes use of the
terms *democratic centralism* and *socialist self-government*. Although
the precise definition of these terms remains illusive, they have been
used to justify a number of different reforms ranging from the decentralization of government to participatory management of enterprises
to the release of Soviet dissident Andrei D. Sakharov from exile. Gorbachev appears to be committed to making the Soviet Union a more
democratic state. How far he is prepared to go remains a matter of
speculation. Will he eventually permit opposition political parties and
free elections as we know them in the United States? Only time will
tell.

Foreign Policy

Gorbachev has become increasingly specific about his foreign-policy
objectives. To help him design and implement foreign policy objectives and strategies, he has turned to Eduard A. Shevardnadze, the
former party leader of the Soviet republic of Georgia—a region known
for its free-wheeling lifestyle, corruption, and illegal free enterprise.

Shevardnadze was named foreign minister as well as a full member of the Politburo. Like most of the other Gorbachev appointees, Shevardnadze is relatively young, tough on corruption, but flexible on economic experimentation.

Just prior to the November 1985 Geneva summit meeting, Gorbachev outlined the basic principles of Soviet foreign policy—"peace, peaceful coexistence, equality, and mutually beneficial cooperation." In Gorbachev's words, "the Soviet Union seeks neither foreign territory nor foreign resources. We have enough of everything. Besides, the Soviet people know the horrors of war and its tragic aftermath only too well from their own bitter experience."

To no one's surprise, Gorbachev has had only warm things to say about the Soviets' socialist allies. "A basic principle of our Party and State is to preserve and strengthen in every way the fraternal friendship with our closest friends and allies—the countries of the great Socialist Community."[20] No doubt the leaders of Hungary, the German Democratic Republic, and Poland—the more independent Eastern European allies of the Soviet Union—breathed a sigh of relief when Gorbachev told the party congress that "complete unanimity among Communist parties does not exist always and in everything. . . . We do not see the diversity of our movement as a synonym for disunity." This statement was widely interpreted in Eastern Europe to mean that not only was Gorbachev tolerant of the increasing independence of Eastern European nations, but that he seemed to be encouraging it.

With regard to relations with capitalist nations, Gorbachev has said that "we will firmly follow the Leninist course of peace and peaceful coexistence. The Soviet Union will always respond to goodwill with goodwill, to trust with trust. But everyone should know that we shall never relinquish the interests of our Motherland and those of our allies."[21]

Soviet relations with Western Europe have suffered as a result of the war in Afghanistan, Poland's crackdown on the Solidarity labor movement, and the Soviets' unsuccessful attempts to divide the NATO members over deployment of cruise and Pershing missiles. In his first foray into Western Europe in October 1985, Gorbachev offered to negotiate arms pacts separately with France and Great Britain, Western Europe's two nuclear powers. Although his offer was declined,

Gorbachev had, nevertheless, signaled his intentions to cultivate improved relations with the NATO countries.

In 1986 Gorbachev became increasingly vocal in his advocacy of the concept of Europe for Europeans. He called for reductions in Soviet and U.S. troops in Europe.

Gorbachev's approach to Third World nations has been subdued. According to Gorbachev, the Soviet Union has always supported "the struggle of the peoples for liberation from colonial oppression. Today our sympathy is with the countries of Asia, Africa, and Latin America, which are following the road of consolidating their independence and social rejuvenation." He added that "for us they are friends and partners in the struggle for a durable peace, for better and just relations between nations."[22]

A recurring theme at the party congress was that the Soviet Union "has profound sympathy for the aspirations of peoples who have experienced the heavy and demeaning yoke of colonial servitude."[23] This is a far cry from the bombastic speeches of Brezhnev before the 1976 and 1981 party congresses in which he extolled the virtues of Soviet client states in Africa and Southeast Asia and heaped praise on radical socialist solutions to economic development problems in the Third World. Conspicuously absent has been any mention of the military role in preventing the export of what the Soviets call "counter-revolution."[24] In his party congress speech, Gorbachev omitted any separate discussion of the Third World altogether, failed to mention a single Third World client by name, and gave no special recognition to "socialist-oriented" countries.

Francis Fukuyama has suggested three reasons why the Soviets began backing away from their Third World empire in the 1980s. First, the cost of supporting these clients has become prohibitively expensive. In addition to the ever-increasing subsidy to Cuba (estimated to be $5 billion annually), Soviet adventurism in the 1970s added new multibillion-dollar obligations to countries such as Vietnam, Ethiopia, Afghanistan, and Angola. The cost to the Soviet Union of supporting its socialist clients (including Eastern Europe) increased from $21.8 billion in 1970 to $46.5 billion in 1980. Second, in the early 1980s, the Soviets began to recognize the deleterious consequences of their Third World activism on broader East–West political relations—particularly on U.S.–Soviet relations. Third, most of Moscow's Third World clients did not fare very well either economically or politically during the 1970s.[25]

Today the Soviets seem to be much more interested in developing their own economy, cutting their losses in the Third World, and developing trade relations with the stronger Third World nations such as Argentina, Brazil, and India.

As for the "bleeding wound," Afghanistan, Gorbachev has called for the withdrawal of Soviet troops in the "nearest future" at the request of the Afghan government. Referring to the Soviet troops, Gorbachev has said that "we have agreed with the Afghan side on the schedule for their phased withdrawal as soon as a political settlement is reached that insures an actual cessation and dependably guarantees the non-resumption of foreign armed interference in the internal affairs of the Democratic Republic of Afghanistan."[26] By the end of 1986, the Soviets had withdrawn six regiments from Afghanistan.

Gorbachev has shown a strong interest in improved relations between the Soviet Union and the People's Republic of China (PRC), noting that the possibility exists "despite the distinctions in the approach to a number of international problems, of promoting co-operation on a basis of equality without affecting third parties." Furthermore, "there are huge potentials for such co-operation because they are consistent with the vital interests of both countries, for the peoples of which the dearest things—socialism and peace—are indivisible."[27] A new Sino–Soviet trade agreement and increased trade attest to Gorbachev's seriousness about improved relations with the Chinese.

Since the 1950s, the United States has assumed that Moscow's foreign-policy objectives and strategies were set permanently in concrete. Brezhnev's leadership did little to dispel this view. The Soviets were seen as aggressive, complacent, and firmly committed to the deployment of military power in pursuit of global dominance. Afghanistan and Poland were viewed as irrefutable evidence of the Soviets' inherently expansionist nature.

To achieve his objective of revitalizing the Soviet economy, Gorbachev needs a stable international environment—particularly a stable relationship with the United States. He must avoid another major round of the arms race that would tie up enormous amounts of scarce resources needed to strengthen the civilian economy. This economic explanation may provide at least part of the rationale for what appears to be a major shift in Soviet foreign policy under Gorbachev.

Another important theme of Gorbachev's foreign policy is the complete repudiation of the Leninist doctrine of an inevitable, final, physical battle between capitalism and communism. Gorbachev has stated repeatedly that this doctrine is suicidal and has been rendered obsolete and inoperative by weapons technology. On the day of his election he said:

> We value the successes of détente achieved in the 1970s and are ready to take part in carrying on the process of establishing peaceful, mutually beneficial cooperation between nations on the principles of equality, mutual respect, and noninterference in internal affairs.
>
> Never before has so terrible a threat hung over mankind as now. The only reasonable way out of the existing situation is the reaching of an agreement by the opposing forces on the immediate termination of the arms race; the nuclear arms race on earth and the prevention of an arms race in space. We need an agreement on an honest and equitable basis without attempts at "outplaying" the other side and dictating terms to it. We need an agreement which would help all to advance toward the cherished goal: the complete elimination and prohibition of nuclear weapons for all time, toward the complete removal of the threat of nuclear war. This is our firm conviction.[28]

In early 1986 Gorbachev became increasingly active in his proposals covering arms control. On 15 January 1986, he proposed a three-stage arms-control process beginning with a moratorium on nuclear testing and eventually leading to a complete ban on all nuclear weapons by the year 2000.

Stage 1. Over a five- to eight-year period, the proposal called for each side to reduce by 50 percent the number of nuclear weapons that are capable of reaching the other's territory. It renounced the development, testing, and deployment of space-based weapons. U.S. and Soviet medium-range missiles would be removed from Europe and the British and the French would agree not to increase their nuclear arsenals. The proposal also called for a complete moratorium on nuclear testing. The Soviet Union extended its own self-imposed moratorium of 6 August 1985 for another ninety days.

Stage 2. Starting in 1990, other nations would also stop testing nuclear weapons and freeze their nuclear arsenals. Both the United States and the Soviet Union would continue reducing the number of missile warheads and bombs capable of reaching the other's territory until their level had reached six thousand on each side. The remaining medium-range nuclear weapons would also be eliminated. Short-range tactical weapons with a range of less than 642 miles would also be eliminated.

Stage 3. Finally, between 1995 and 2000, all remaining nuclear weapons would be eliminated, with "a universal accord that such weapons should never again come into being."

To promote this proposal in the United States, the Soviets took out a one-page advertisement in the *New York Times* on 5 February 1986.

Throughout the party congress Gorbachev reiterated his theme that the two superpowers share a common problem of survival, and that this places an enormous responsibility on the shoulders of the respective leaders.

> The character of present-day weaponry leaves no country with any hope of safeguarding itself solely with military and technical means, for example, by building up a defense, even the most powerful. To ensure security is seen increasingly as a political problem. . . . The highest wisdom is not in caring exclusively for oneself, especially to the detriment of the other side. . . . Without being blind to social, political and ideological differences, all have to master the science and art of restraint and circumspection on the international scene.[29]

During the remainder of 1986, Gorbachev continued to echo the foreign-policy proposals that had been set forth at the party congress and in the 15 January nuclear disarmament statement.

It may well be that international trade rather than arms control that is the driving force of Soviet foreign policy. Whether dealing with Eastern Europe, Western Europe, the Third World, China, Japan, or the United States, the really important factor for Gorbachev is the potential for bilateral trade and technology transfer. I believe that the primary aim of Gorbachev's foreign policy is to support his objective of integrating the Soviet Union into the global economy. This is the overriding foreign-policy issue, and it takes precedence over political ideology and arms control. If one wants to predict how the Soviets will relate to a specific country, it is best to examine the country's trade and technology potential.

Defense

Of all the strategic objectives of the Soviet Union, none is more difficult to define and analyze than their military objective. The reasons are twofold. First, because of their penchant for secrecy, the Soviets do not publish data on military outlays or the size of their military arsenal. Second, none of the organizations (such as the CIA and the DIA) that routinely forecast future Soviet defense strategies and expenditures have any definitive methods for incorporating the effects on Soviet military policies of U.S. foreign-policy changes. Will any of Gorbachev's arms reduction proposals be implemented—partially or otherwise? Obviously, the answer to this question depends, in part, on the response of the Reagan administration to Gorbachev's arms control initiatives. Prior to Reykjavík, the administration had systematically ignored most of Gorbachev's peace proposals.

In spite of his aggressive advocacy of arms control, there is little evidence to suggest that Gorbachev is likely to call for the unilateral disarmament of the Soviet Union any time soon. Indeed, nothing could be further from the truth. One of Gorbachev's strongest statements about the importance of defense was made at a celebration of Lenin's birthday in 1983, two years before he was named general secretary.

> The might of the defensive alliance of the Warsaw Treaty countries safeguards peace and the gains of socialism. And as long as the situation requires, the peoples of the socialist community will continue, as before, to do everything necessary to make their defense stronger, and even more effective. The Soviet armed forces, supported by the love of the entire Soviet people and the concern of the CPSU and the Soviet state, are safeguarding vigilantly the peaceful life of the Soviet people, of the entire community of the fraternal

socialist countries. Those who are fond of adventures should not forget this.[30]

Concerning the importance of military parity with the United States, the Soviet party congress said that

> the establishment of military–strategic parity between the USSR and the USA, the Warsaw Treaty Organization and NATO was an historic accomplishment of socialism.
>
> It strengthened the positions of the USSR, the countries of socialism and all progressive forces, and dashed the hopes held by imperialism's aggressive circles of winning a world nuclear war.
>
> Preservation of this balance is a serious factor of safeguarding peace and international security.[31]

This statement is particularly noteworthy when one considers the Soviets' view of the Reagan administration's foreign policy. In their view Reagan would deny them the right to military parity with the United States.

The party congress also addressed the issue of Soviet military preparedness.

> One of the most important tasks in the future as well should be an all-round improvement of the combat preparedness of the armed forces, the upbringing of the fighting men of the army and navy and all Soviet people in the spirit of vigilance and constant readiness to defend the great gains of socialism and the maintenance of the armed forces at a level that rules out strategic superiority of the forces of imperialism.[32]

Many Americans believe that Soviet military interests dominate economic and foreign-policy priorities. However, during his first two years in office, Gorbachev may have managed to reverse these priorities—a truly amazing accomplishment, if indeed it is so. Two points are clear. First, under Gorbachev military leaders have been accorded a much lower profile than was the case near the end of the Brezhnev era. Second, many of the Soviet military leaders have been much more subdued in their policy utterances since Gorbachev came to power.

Undoubtedly, the Soviet military establishment will derive both direct and spillover benefits from Gorbachev's industrial modernization program. Furthermore, there is bound to be continued tension between military and civilian economic planners as they compete for scarce resources. Whether Gorbachev is able to achieve his economic targets may depend on the degree of flexibility he can retain concerning his military objectives. If he is forced into a corner by Soviet military leaders, his economic objectives are likely to suffer.

Former Under Secretary of the Air Force Townsend Hoopes has summarized Gorbachev's arms control objectives as follows.

> The Gorbachev proposals on arms control give substantial evidence of serious, perceptive analysis, based on objective realities and combined with a readiness for major compromise. They reflect, above all, a keen awareness that the superpowers (and the world) now stand on the edge of a new divide: Either they will promptly stop making more (and more accurate) weapons of mass destruction and acknowledge that they share a common problem of survival, or the arms race will be inexorably extended into space, bringing greater uncertainty and danger of war to all concerned.[33]

Culture

The Soviet Union is essentially a risk-free society with a highly centralized inflexible economy and a tightly controlled government. This combination has taken a heavy toll on the lives of the Soviet people in the form of declining life expectancy for men, rising infant mortality rates, increasing alcoholism, and increasing crime, corruption, and cynicism. Against this background, the party congress dealt with a number of social and cultural objectives. In broad terms the party congress called for "raising the well-being of the Soviet people to a qualitatively new dimension, ensuring such a level and structure of consumption of material, social and cultural boons as will meet the aim of moulding a harmoniously-developed, spiritually-rich individual to the fullest degree possible." On a more specific level, the party congress came out vigorously against hard drinking and alcoholism, parasites, pilferers of socialist property, and bribery. It also proposed increased benefits for mothers and children. With regard to cultural development, the party called upon writers and artists to "create works that will be worthy of the greatness of the Party's and the people's innovative undertakings, and that will truthfully reflect the life of Soviet people, in its diversity and motion with a high degree of artistry."

The party congress was characterized by an openness that is unique in modern Soviet history. Delegates were encouraged to discuss and debate various proposals openly. Even before the party congress began, writers, artists, and academics were becoming more vocal in their public criticisms of Soviet life. I believe that one of Gorbachev's fundamental objectives is not only to make the Soviet Union a more open society, but also to reshape the culture.

Ten Fundamental Objectives

Based on his actions as well as his words during his first two years in office, General Secretary Gorbachev appears to have embarked on a strategy to make the Soviet Union a more open society. This strategy is based firmly on ten fundamental strategic objectives:

1. *Economy:* To strengthen the Soviet economy and make significant improvements in the quality of life of the Soviet people.

2. *Agriculture:* To become self-sufficient in agricultural products and foodstuffs.

3. *Technology:* To reduce the technological gap between the Soviet Union and the West—particularly with regard to computers, automatic machines, and robotics.

4. *Consumption:* To produce world-class consumer goods for domestic consumption and export abroad.

5. *International Trade:* To integrate the Soviet economy into the global economy.

6. *Democratization:* To encourage democratic principles and socialist self-government in the Soviet Union and Eastern Europe.

7. *Foreign Policy:* To strengthen the Soviet Union's political and

economic relationships with such countries as West Germany, Japan, China, Israel, India, Mexico, Argentina, and Brazil.

8. *Third World:* To reduce the cost to the Soviet Union of its relations with Third World nations such as Afghanistan, Ethiopia, Angola, Mozambique, and Cuba.

9. *Arms Control:* To reduce the level of tension between the Soviet Union and the United States and negotiate a comprehensive arms control agreement with the United States by 1990 covering conventional forces, nuclear weapons, and space weapons.

10. *Culture:* To change the culture of the Soviet Union in such a manner that in exchange for more personal freedom individual citizens will be encouraged to assume more risk and responsibility for their individual lives.

Strategic Options

Sovietologists have suggested three distinctly different strategic options from which Mikhail Gorbachev may choose in attempting to achieve his strategic objectives—conservative, liberal, and radical.

Conservative Strategy: Discipline

Even after two years of substantial evidence to the contrary, many in the United States feel that little has changed in the Soviet Union and that it is unlikely that any significant changes will occur by the year 2000. According to this pessimistic scenario, the Soviet economy, political system, and foreign policy will remain virtually unchanged in the foreseeable future. The approach taken by East Germany in the 1950s and 1960s is seen as the socioeconomic, political model that Gorbachev will emulate in the 1980s.

The Soviet economy will continue to be highly centralized, rigid, and tightly controlled. The state will own the means of production and all property income will revert to the state. Because private enterprise will not be permitted, individual incomes will be limited to wages and salaries. Economic administration will continue to be hierarchical, with decision making centralized at the top in Moscow. The production and distribution of goods and services will be planned in detail by Gosplan.

Prices, wages, and industrial production quotas will be set by the state. Investment decisions, major resource allocation decisions, research and development strategies, and foreign-trade deals will also be state controlled. Military spending will continue to increase and shortages of consumer goods will persist.

To achieve the FYP12 targets, a conservative strategy will require sweeping personnel changes and stern labor disciplinary policies. By mid-year 1986, Gorbachev not only controlled most of the key positions in the Politburo, the Council of Ministers, and the central committee, but he had replaced a substantial number of officials at all levels of government throughout the entire nation. Both the party and the government now appear to be under Gorbachev's effective control.

Given the absence of positive incentives to motivate workers to increase productivity under this scenario, Gorbachev will impose rigorous standards of discipline on managers and workers alike. Such disciplinary actions will include criminal penalties for lateness to work, absenteeism, drunkenness, and corruption. From a political standpoint Gorbachev may find it necessary to increase the power of the KGB; discourage contacts with the West; reimpose the iron curtain; reinstate a xenophobic nationalism; and tighten ideological, political, and social discipline. Emphasis will be placed on intensifying production as a means of achieving socialist ideals. Political dissent will be illegal and punishable by imprisonment. Religious freedom will be minimal and Jewish emigration will be held to a trickle.

The Soviet Union will maintain tight political, economic, and military control over Eastern Europe. If an Eastern European country deviates significantly from the Soviet party line, its people will risk the kind of harsh treatment received by the Hungarians in 1956, the Czechoslovakians in 1968, and the Poles in 1981. The Soviets will continue the war in Afghanistan and increase their military support to the Afghan government. Not only will Soviet adventurism be continued in Third World countries such as Angola, Nicaragua, and Cuba, but it will be increased overall in Africa, Asia, and Latin America. Relations with Western Europe, China, and the United States will remain strained, and military spending will increase at an annual rate of 5–10 percent over FYP12.

A conservative strategy will mean that the highly centralized, tightly controlled economic system and the authoritarian, repressive government of the Soviet Union will essentially remain unaltered. Foreign policy will follow closely the Brezhnev model of the late 1970s and early 1980s. If Gorbachev opts for a conservative strategy, then it will truly be business-as-usual in the Soviet Union.

There is little evidence to suggest that Gorbachev is following the conservative East German approach to economic and political development. Although he has made sweeping personnel changes in the party, the government, and the management of the economy, and has taken severe disciplinary action against alcoholism, crime, and corruption, most of his other actions represent a direct challenge to the highly centralized, tightly controlled economic system and authoritarian government.

Those who argue that Gorbachev is following a conservative strategy also claim that the goals and objectives of FYP12 are unattainable with such a strategy. Does this mean that Gorbachev has deliberately developed a strategy that is doomed to failure at the outset? Or is he simply stupid or perhaps a pathological liar?

Liberal Strategy: Partial Reform

Most Sovietologists feel that Gorbachev will follow what I will call a liberal strategy. According to this scenario, Gorbachev will not only make personnel changes and stress discipline, but he will also implement a limited number of organizational and policy changes as well. Under the liberal strategy, the overall economic and political system will still remain virtually intact.

Typical of the organizational changes Gorbachev has already made is the consolidation of the activities of five ministries and a committee dealing with agriculture into a new superagency called the State Committee for the Agro-Industrial Complex. Gorbachev's investment policies appear to be heavily skewed towards computers, high technology, and the modernization of industrial plants and equipment rather than towards new construction projects (as was the case in the past). The consumer sector also stands to benefit from the investment policies that would be implemented under a liberal strategy. This strategy calls for some experimentation with the use of financial incentives to motivate agricultural and industrial workers and does not preclude the limited use of private ownership in the service sector as well as small family plots of land for farmers.

But the policy changes of a liberal strategy do not approach the degree of economic reform that has been achieved by the Hungarians and the Chinese. Such policy changes mostly represent efforts to fine-tune the existing economic system without actually changing the system itself.

The common theme underlying each of these examples of partial economic reform is the assumption that if a single part of the system is fixed, then the entire system will benefit as well. But everything is related to everything else in the Soviet economic system. Fixing one part of the system may very well aggravate other parts of the system. It is virtually impossible for central planners to anticipate all of the possible consequences of a series of small changes. Cynics are understandably pessimistic about the likelihood that partial reforms will produce any significant long-term benefits to the Soviet economy.

Unless the Soviets are willing to consider major structural changes in the economic mechanism similar to those implemented by China and Hungary, then their economy is likely to continue to stagnate. Anything short of the Hungarian type of market-oriented socialism will be inadequate to deal with the myriad of economic problems faced by the Soviets.

The liberal strategy differs from the conservative strategy in that it assumes a modest increase in political flexibility and ideological tolerance. Although the Marxist-Leninist ideological model will remain firmly in place, it would not be nearly so rigid as in the conservative strategy. The liberal strategy represents a step in the direction of increased political and economic freedom, but a rather small step.

Among the primary beneficiaries of a more liberal foreign policy on the part of the Soviets would be their Eastern European allies. Countries like Hungary, East Germany, and Poland would be permitted to continue some of their experiments with economic reform provided they did not deviate too far from Marxist-Leninist ideology.

Although this strategy does assume some improvement in relations with the United States and the West, the arms race between the two superpowers is assumed to continue. Soviet relations with China will improve and the two nations will become important trading partners. There will be a gradual shift in Soviet support away from very poor Third World nations (such as Ethiopia and Angola) towards increased contacts with more affluent Third World countries (such as Argentina, Brazil, and some of the countries in the Pacific Basin).

Some argue that the liberal strategy is the most likely scenario for Gorbachev to follow, but they also point out that it is incapable of achieving the economic targets of FYP12. To these cynics anything short of radical reform will be inadequate to reach Gorbachev's economic targets, but in their minds radical reform is simply not politically feasible at this time.

Radical Strategy: Market Socialism

To achieve his overall objective of making the Soviet Union a more open society, Gorbachev has formulated and is in the process of implementing a strategy of radical reform consisting of ten specific strategies:

1. *Economy:* Decentralization of decision making of state-owned enterprises including such decisions as product mix, prices, output, wages, employment, investment, research and development, domestic and international sales and marketing, and incentives. Creation of new financial institutions to finance the expansion of Soviet enterprises. Authorization of private enterprises in the service sector of the economy.

2. *Agriculture:* Decentralization of state-owned farms and strengthening of agricultural cooperatives. Greater use of market incentives and an increase in the number of private farms.

3. *Technology:* A substantial increase in the commitment of resources to education and research and development in high technology fields—computers, process controls, robotics, genetic engineering, and space research. Creation of joint ventures with Western high-tech companies. Increased purchases of Western technology from such countries as West Germany, Japan, Israel, and Brazil.

4. *Consumption:* Increased investment in the manufacturing of consumer goods. Importation of high-quality consumer goods from the West.

5. *International Trade:* Decentralization of foreign trade to individual enterprises with the authority to trade directly with Western companies. Encouragement of joint ventures with the West. Participation in international trade and financial institutions.

6. *Democratization:* Decentralization of the Communist party, the Soviet government, and the Soviet economy. Increased democracy in the workplace. Greater freedom of political dissent. Improved possibilities to emigrate from the Soviet Union.

7. *Foreign Policy:* Encouragement of increased political independence for Europe. A major effort to increase bilateral trade with Japan and China. The establishment of diplomatic relations with Israel and China.

8. *Third World:* Development of a face-saving strategy to get out of Afghanistan. Concentration of political and economic relations on the more affluent Third World nations that offer the greatest promise for trade and technology.

9. *Arms Control:* Reduction in the level of anti-U.S. rhetoric and pursuit of a strategy aimed at signing a major arms control agreement with the United States in 1990.

10. *Culture:* Increased freedom of expression in speech, the press, literature, art, drama, movies, and religion. Permission for firms to go bankrupt and to fire incompetent employees. Tough disciplinary actions for alcohol and drug abuse, bribery, theft, and corruption.

When Deng Xiaoping assumed the political leadership in China in 1978, he did not stand up in Tiananmen Square in Beijing and publicly denounce Marxist-Leninist-Maoist ideology. Rather he quietly and systematically began implementing a form of market-oriented socialism that included the well-known "Responsibility System" and "Open-Door Policy," both of which represented radical departures from traditional communist ideology. Nearly ten years later, Deng has not abandoned Marxist-Leninist ideology in his public statements, even though China's economic system has shed itself of many of the communistic underpinnings on which it was previously based. Whenever Deng speaks of the Chinese economic reforms, he refers to them as either extensions or modern interpretations of the ideology of Marx, Lenin, and Mao. In Hungary, János Kádár followed a similar path to market socialism even earlier than China.

But in February 1986, when Gorbachev failed to denounce Marxist-Leninist ideology in his party congress speech, most people in the United States concluded that radical reform was out of the question in the USSR during the 1980s. According to the conventional wisdom, nothing has changed in the Soviet Union and nothing is likely to change anytime soon.

In what follows, I will show that Gorbachev is pursuing a strategy of radical reform in the areas of economics, culture, domestic politics, and foreign policy. In addition to the internal forces described in chapter 1, I will show that Gorbachev has also been influenced by Hungary, China, international trade, and the foreign policy of the Reagan administration. But unlike Khrushchev and Brezhnev, each of whom tried and failed in their attempts to reform the Soviet economy, Gorbachev has decided to confront the culture of the Soviet Union. He is the first Soviet leader since Stalin who has understood that it is impossible to change the Soviet economic and political systems without coming to grips with the fact that the Soviet Union is a risk-free society. To implement a strategy of radical reform one must take on the Soviet culture. And that is precisely what Gorbachev is doing.

He is implementing a uniquely Soviet style of reform in which many of the old rules have already been tossed aside in favor of practical, realistic solutions to some very difficult social, economic, and political problems. No, it is not business-as-usual in the Soviet Union these days, and the people in the Soviet Union and Eastern Europe understand that fact very well. We hope to shed some light on the changes that are taking place in the USSR and perhaps contribute to a better understanding of the significance of these changes to the Soviet Union, the United States, and the rest of the world.

Part II

The International Environment

3
The Hungarian Connection

U nder Soviet leader Gorbachev there is increasing evidence that the Soviets are paying close attention to what is happening in Hungary today. At the Moscow party congress in February 1986, Gorbachev challenged Soviet industrial leaders to emulate the economic reforms of Hungary.

Since the 1950s, the Hungarians have been quietly moving towards a less-centralized, market-oriented economic system. Unlike the situation in 1956, when the Soviets resorted to force to snuff out Hungarian initiatives, this time around the Soviets appear to be motivated by a desire to emulate some of Hungary's economic successes. They seem to be much more interested in learning from the Hungarians than in trying to control them.

As evidence that the Hungarians do indeed have Gorbachev's attention, consider the following sequence of events. First, former Soviet leader Yuri V. Andropov, who was the Soviet ambassador to Hungary during the 1956 revolution, maintained his Hungarian connection and strong interest in economic reform throughout his lifetime. Second, as is well known, Gorbachev was the protégé of Andropov. In 1983, for example, Gorbachev visited Hungary and had nothing but praise for the highly successful Hungarian agricultural policies. Third, the Soviets are very much aware that the Hungarians enjoy a quality of life that is without equal in Eastern Europe. Fourth, shortly after Gorbachev came to power in 1985, a delegation of very high-level Hungarian government officials, enterprise managers, and academic leaders was invited to Moscow to meet with their Soviet counterparts to discuss the experiences of Hungary with economic reform. Their agenda included such topics as alternative management systems, finance and banking, planning and control, efficiency, motivation, human resource development, and strategies for development.

The Hungarian Alternative Socialist System

On 12 April 1985, the Chicago Council of Foreign Relations cosponsored a seminar in Chicago with the Hungarian Chamber of Commerce on "Investment in Hungary: Opportunities for American Business." The following excerpt from the announcement of the seminar accurately portrays what is happening in Hungary today.

> Hungary offers unique opportunities for both investment and trade in Eastern Europe. The *Hungarian alternative socialist system* has produced both a more prosperous and varied economy and a more inviting business environment than most other Eastern European countries. The Hungarian government is now placing a new emphasis on joint-venture programs with U.S. firms and inviting greater participation in both general trade and investment.

Since 1968 the large state-owned firms in Hungary have become highly decentralized and have increasingly turned to the marketplace for incentives and improved efficiency. The goals and objectives of the general managers of Hungarian firms are amazingly similar to those of their U.S. counterparts. Hungarian managers are devoting substantial energy to market-driven strategic planning. Indeed, László Kapolyi, the Hungarian minister of industry, has said that "the number one challenge facing Hungarian managers today is to improve their international marketing strategies so that Hungary can compete more effectively in the international marketplace." In response to this challenge, the Hungarian Chamber of Commerce is aggressively seeking U.S. investments in Hungary and is encouraging joint ventures between Hungarian firms and U.S. and Western European companies.

Basically, free enterprise is permitted for small firms in Hungary, and the size limitation has been increased from twenty to one hundred employees. A variety of small private shops flourishes in Budapest—grocery stores, butcher shops, florists, laundromats, beauty shops, restaurants, and bars. Unlike the empty shelves seen in the large state-owned stores in Moscow, the shelves in Budapest's markets are well stocked with fresh meat, eggs, fish, and produce.

Today the Hungarians enjoy a relatively free lifestyle that includes fine wines and brandies as well as excellent restaurants. They not only have their own traditional folk music but Western tourists are surprised to find a flourishing night life in Budapest that includes modern jazz, discos, and exotic nightclubs such as Club Havana and the Moulin Rouge. The Hilton Hotel has a plush new gambling casino that caters only to foreign visitors—one of many clever devices conceived by the Hungarians to attract much-needed hard currencies. In August 1986, the first formula-1 grand prix automobile race ever held in a communist country took place in Budapest.

The Evolution of Economic Reform

The 1956 Revolution

Few Westerners realize that when the Hungarian revolution was crushed in November 1956 by Soviet tanks and troops, the initial seeds were sown for a thirty-year trek towards economic reform in Hungary. At least two thousand Hungarians died in the short-lived revolution and another 200,000 fled to the West. At that time János Kádár, the first secretary of the Hungarian Socialist Workers' Party (HSWP), was perhaps the most hated man in the world in the eyes of several hundred thousand Hungarians who were bitterly opposed to the communist regime in Hungary. And in the Western press words like "traitor," "tyrant," and "Soviet agent" were used to describe Kádár. Thirty years later János Kádár is still first secretary of the HSWP—only today Kádár is without a doubt the most respected person in Hungary and even attracts praise from the same Western newspapers that called him a "traitor" in the 1950s.

Between 1949 and 1979 Hungary enjoyed unprecedented economic growth. The economy grew at an annual rate of 5.9 percent. Furthermore, between 1967 and 1973 the average annual growth rate was close to 7 percent. This period was characterized by a rapid rise in the standard of living, increased production of agricultural products and consumer goods, and balanced trade flows between Hungary and the rest of the world.

Many of these economic achievements are directly linked to some of the new economic policies that were introduced by the Kádár government on the heels of the 1956 uprising. The compulsory delivery of agricultural products by Hungarian farmers was abolished in 1957. As a result of this new policy, farm families were given fewer quotas to meet and much more control over their time and labor. Not only was this the key to the Hungarian agricultural success, but it paved the way for industrial profit incentives, a development process based on broad societal cooperation, and the end of government-imposed centralized planning. However, it was not until 1968 that the seeds of economic reform that had been sown in 1956 really began to take root and provide a solid foundation upon which the dynamic reforms of the 1980s now rest.

The 1968 Economic Reforms

Hungary is a small country with 10.58 million inhabitants who live in a geographical area about the size of the state of Indiana. It is poor in natural resources—particularly energy-related resources such as coal, oil, and natural gas. Today nearly half of its national income is derived from international trade.

In the 1950s, as Hungary gradually evolved from a predominantly agricultural economy to a more industrialized economy, it employed an economic model that closely resembled that of the Soviet Union in the 1930s and the 1940s. However, by the mid-1960s it was apparent to Hungarian economists and government officials alike that the Hungarian economy was very dependent on a high-growth global economy and the availability of low-cost energy resources and other raw materials. It became increasingly obvious that if the Hungarian economy was to remain a viable force in international trade, on which it was highly dependent, then it must become more flexible. Taking these complex factors into consideration, the central committee of the HSWP began exploring ways to change the economic mechanism in Hungary as early as 1966. This led to the comprehensive economic reforms of 1968.

Prior to 1968 managers of Hungarian state-owned enterprises had very little control over which products they produced, how they were produced, the prices that would be charged for their products, or how they would be marketed, either domestically or internationally. All of the planning for the state-owned firms was highly centralized, top-down planning imposed on the enterprise managers from the appropriate government ministries. Hungarian managers had no responsibility whatsoever for sales and marketing. They simply produced the goods according to the plan and turned them over to another government bureau to distribute. Under such a rigid, inflexible system, there were few incentives for innovation or the efficient use of scarce natural resources. Thus Hungary found it increasingly difficult to compete in an open economy with an economic system designed for a tightly controlled closed economy.

With the economic reforms of 1968, Hungarian managers were given considerably more freedom and flexibility to decide which products to produce, how to produce them, where to sell these products, and which raw materials to use in producing them. The production targets of the National Planning Office became much more flexible and less detailed. Managers had the freedom to assess consumer needs and market opportunities and to match the skills, resources, and production of their respective enterprises with market demand.

Thus, with the introduction of the 1968 economic reforms, the Hungarian alternative socialist system was officially launched with the full participation of the HSWP. It would face many challenges during the 1970s, both from government bureaucrats and from a very turbulent international economic environment. There would be rocky waters ahead, but the principal direction of the Hungarian economic system would always be the same—towards more decentralized, market-oriented planning.

The Agricultural Revolution

In contrast to the Soviet Union, agriculture is the foundation on which Hungary's market-oriented economy rests today. Under a system of flexible controls unlike those in any other communist country, Hungarian farms yield bumper crops and outperform the farms in the other CMEA countries. Hungary is the only net food exporter in the Warsaw Pact. Although some of the Hungarian agricultural policies have their origins in the aftermath of the 1956 revolution, most of them were initiated since the early 1970s. As an alternative to Soviet-style forced collectivization, Hungarian farm families were given fewer production quotas and more control over their time and labor. Relatively autonomous cooperatives were also encouraged. Cooperative members were also provided with land that they could use as their own but could not pass on to their heirs. The state also rented equipment to them. Basically, they were permitted to manage their farms with minimal interference from the government.

Seventy-five percent of Hungarian farms are now managed by 1,360 independent cooperatives, which cultivate 80 percent of the country's farm land. There are also 130 state-owned firms that represent 20 percent of the total number of farms. The remaining 5 percent of the farms are privately owned.[1] Over 1.5 million families have small private plots of land on which they raise fruits, vegetables, and animals. On these small parcels of land, Hungarian farmers raise half of all pigs; a third of all cattle; 70 percent of the poultry; half of the grapes, fruit, and wine; and 10 percent of all agricultural products produced in Hungary.[2]

There is a very close working relationship between the private farmers and the cooperatives in Hungary. For example, nearly all of the rabbits that are produced in the country are raised by private farmers who in turn sell them to the cooperatives, which then process and prepare them for export. Most of the high-quality paprika is also produced by private farmers, then processed by the cooperatives for shipment abroad.

The result of all of this has been a dramatic increase in the quantity of and quality of agricultural products in Hungary. Today, the Hungarians not only eat very well but they also export substantial quantities of wheat, beef, lamb, rabbit, wine, and paprika. Nearly a fourth of Hungary's exports comes from its agricultural sector.

Of particular interest to the Soviets are a number of highly successful, diversified agribusinesses in Hungary. For example, a large agricultural company in Tatabánya is in four different businesses—feed, rabbits, pork, and agricultural equipment. This highly automated company employs state-of-the-art scientific methods to process farm animals and grain. The Soviets have recently purchased a number of automated poultry plants from the Hungarians, for which they paid in hard currency.

Given the magnitude of Soviet agricultural problems and the fact that Gorbachev was trained as an agricultural economist, it is not surprising that he is attracted by the results of the Hungarian agricultural reforms. He was clearly influenced by Hungarian agriculture in his 1986 party congress speech. Not only are the Soviets emulating the Hungarian agricultural reforms, but Soviet agricultural production began responding to these reforms in a positive manner in 1986.

Recent Experience

When the 1968 reforms were first implemented, it was still possible for Hungary to obtain abundant supplies of energy and other natural resources at relatively low prices. However, the 1973 and 1979–80 explosions in the international price of crude oil soon changed all of that. Between 1973 and 1980, Hungary's terms of trade deteriorated by 20 percent due in no small part to the fact that Hungary imports 45 percent of all of its energy and 80 percent of the crude oil it consumes. Although economic growth averaged 5.3 percent between 1973 and 1978, by 1978, as a result of its heavy dependence on energy imports, Hungary had accumulated an enormous foreign debt. Furthermore, by 1981 national income barely surpassed that of 1979, in sharp contrast to the 5.9 percent growth rate of the past.[3]

As previously indicated, the 1968 economic reforms reinstated the profit incentive and introduced decentralized planning and control into the large state-owned Hungarian firms. However, product pricing decisions and wage decisions remained, for the most part, highly centralized. Furthermore, there was some backsliding in the actual implementation of the reforms during the 1970s. Overly zealous ministries that had been squeezed out of the planning process began imposing increasingly restrictive information requirements on many of the state-owned enterprises at precisely the time when they needed a high degree of flexibility to respond to the deteriorating international economic environment.

In spite of some occasional temporary setbacks, economic reform continued to evolve throughout the decade of the 1970s and was greatly accelerated in the 1980s. In 1985 the National Planning Office indicated that the economic reforms were intended "to encourage autonomous, entrepreneur-type, dynamic, and innovative managers who are able to mobilize the internal resources of the economy and make enterprises, collectives, and workers interested in the improve-

ment of the efficiency of management."[4] Since 1968, economic reforms in Hungary have been concentrated in five important areas—
prices, income, and wages; management and control; foreign trade;
joint ventures; and banking and finance.

Prices, Income, and Wages. Since 1980, producer prices and consumer prices have increasingly been determined by the market. That
is, for most goods and services, enterprise managers are free to charge
within some limits what they think the market will bear. However,
the government does still control prices for certain goods and services
for which there is only limited competition. These include the price
of electric energy and the wholesale prices of some agricultural commodities such as meat, poultry, and corn.

Managers of state-owned enterprises have also been given additional authority to set wages, salaries, and bonuses of employees so
long as they are tied to profits. To encourage increased efficiency and
profitability, the government has also introduced a number of tax-
reform programs. The proportionate share of taxes on profits and
fixed assets has declined, while labor-related taxes have increased. A
personal income tax will be introduced in 1988.

Management and Control. Until recently, each state-owned enterprise
in Hungary was under the control of a particular government ministry. For example, the managing director and senior officers of a
large state-owned chemical company such as the Borsod Chemical
Complex (BVK) would be appointed by the Ministry of Industry,
which is responsible for the chemical industry. Under the new self-
management law in Hungary, the managers of state-owned enterprises are elected either directly by the employees or by employee
enterprise councils.

Most medium-sized industrial firms and some large state-owned
enterprises are now controlled by enterprise councils. An enterprise
council is composed of elected representatives of the company's employees and representatives of management. The representatives of
the employees are elected for a specified time period and are account-
able to the employees. The management representatives are appointed
by the managing director. In the case of ongoing enterprises, the original managing director would have been appointed by the founding

ministry, but all future managing directors are elected by the enterprise council. The secretaries of the company's party organization, trade union, and communist youth organization also participate in the work of the enterprise council.

The managing director is responsible for the day-to-day operational decisions of the company. The enterprise council is the strategic decision-making body of the company and exercises the property rights transferred to it by the state as well as the employees' rights with regard to the company's managing director. Among the responsibilities of the enterprise council are:

Approval of the company's annual budget, strategic plan, and financial statements;

Approval of capital budgets, major resource allocation decisions, and changes in the company's line of business;

Approval of mergers, acquisitions, or any other major corporate reorganization decisions; and

Election and evaluation of the performance of the managing director.

The enterprise council elects its own chair; the managing director is not permitted to be the chair. The Ministry of Industry retains a reserve veto over the appointment of the managing director of a company, as well as over any decisions involving the liquidation or creation of companies.

In the case of smaller state-owned companies, the managing director is elected directly by the employees of the company at the annual employees' meeting. The employees of smaller companies have powers that are similar to those of the enterprise councils of the large companies. The state still maintains direct control over a limited number of enterprises, including petroleum, aluminum, defense, public utilities, and communal and cultural services. Another important organizational structure in Hungary is the cooperative. These highly decentralized organizations are widespread in the agricultural sector and have control mechanisms that are similar to those of the state-owned companies.

By the end of 1986, nearly half of the 720 state-owned industrial enterprises were operating under some form of self-management. The Hungarian approach to self-management has not gone unnoticed by Soviet leaders. In his party congress speech, Gorbachev said that

> in developing democratic economic management principles it is advisable to extend the principle of electiveness to all team leaders and then gradually to some other categories of managerial personnel—foremen, shift, sector or shop superintendents, and state-farm department managers. Long years of experience testify that this is the direction in which we must look for modern forms of combining centralism and democracy, of combining one-man management and the principle of electiveness in running the national economy.[5]

However, the Hungarian self-management system is not without some problems. Eager to please the workers who elected them, some bosses have increased wages much faster than the growth in productivity. As a result, wages rose nearly 9 percent during the first six months of 1986, while labor productivity increased by only 3 percent.

Foreign Trade. To finance its imports of petroleum, natural gas, and automobiles, Hungary must export pharmaceutical products, busses, axles, alumina, paprika, salami, wheat, and wine. Some of the most dramatic changes in the Hungarian economic mechanism were a direct result of the very unfavorable position in which Hungary found itself following the precipitous increase in the world prices of crude oil and natural gas perpetrated by OPEC. The introduction of enterprise autonomy and foreign joint ventures; the revival of alternative sources of capital (including bonds, stocks, and associations); the legalization of small privately owned companies; the continuous adjustment of the tax system; the evolution of new forms of enterprise management and control; and the concurrent reduction in the authority of government ministries over state-owned companies have all signaled the fact that the Hungarian economy is increasingly willing and able to adapt to the requirements of a global economy.

In 1986, when the Soviets announced that seventy industrial enterprises would have the right to trade directly with Western companies rather than going through the Ministry of Foreign Trade, they were emulating a trade practice that the Hungarians had been successfully using for a number of years. Decentralized trade policies contributed significantly to Hungary's trade surpluses with the West between 1981 and 1985. Many of the new Soviet trade policies appear to be patterned after the Hungarian and the Chinese practices.

Joint Ventures. Since 1972, it has been possible for Western investors to establish joint ventures in Hungary with state-owned companies and to take profits and/or capital from the joint venture company in the currency of their choice. Furthermore, foreigners have actually been permitted to participate in the operations of these joint venture companies since 1977.

By 1987 there were seventy foreign joint ventures in Hungary, most of which had been established since 1980. Among the better-known foreign investors in Hungary are BASF, Volvo, Siemens, Furukawa, Bramac, and Schwarzkopf. West Germany and Austria are the leading foreign investors in Hungary, each having participated in over a dozen Hungarian joint ventures. Close behind is Switzerland, which in turn is followed by the United States, the United Kingdom, and Japan. In addition, companies from Sweden, Denmark, Belgium, Italy, France, and Portugal have also participated in Hungarian joint-venture companies.

The largest nonbank joint venture to date involves Hungary's largest retail chain, Skala Co-op, and ITT's Stuttgart subsidiary, Standard Electric Lorenz. The joint venture, known as Selectronic, assembles color television sets and video recorders for domestic consumption and export to the West. The initial capital base for Selectronic was over $10 million, of which 65 percent was provided by the Hungarian partner. Skala is one of Hungary's most innovative and successful companies. Its sixty-six retail stores produce annual sales of over $600 million. Two other foreign joint venture companies in Hungary are VAEV-BRAMAC and POLIFOAM. The former is an Austro–Hungarian company that produces and markets concrete tiles and was started with $6 million in equity capital. POLIFOAM on the other hand, is a Hungarian-Japanese venture that manufactures polyethylene foam sheets and has an equity base of $2.4 million.[6]

Most of the Hungarian joint-venture companies are limited liability companies whose statutory origins go back to 1935. However, a handful of the joint ventures are joint stock companies based on regulations that were first set forth in 1875.

The general rule governing ownership of joint venture companies is that the Hungarian partner must control at least 51 percent of the ownership of the company. However, the minister of finance has the authority to grant exceptions to this rule. The well-known exceptions are the Central European International Bank and Schwarzkopf Cosmetics. Six European banks own over 60 percent of the Central European International Bank and the West German company Schwarzkopf owns 51 percent of Schwarzkopf Cosmetics.

To attract more foreign working capital and technical expertise into Hungary, the regulations on joint ventures were liberalized in January 1986. Among the concessions granted to joint ventures were a reduction in the tax on net profits from 40 percent to 20 percent, five-year tax exemptions for priority fields, the possibility of Western majority ownership, and the simplification of licensing, registration, and accounting procedures. If a joint venture reinvests 50 percent of its profits back into the business, then 50 percent of the paid-in tax is reimbursed to the firm. If the reinvestment is 100 percent, then the tax refund is 75 percent of the paid-in tax.[7]

When the Soviet Ministry of Foreign Trade first announced the legalization of foreign joint ventures in 1986, it was obvious that the regulations on which the Soviet joint ventures are based are very similar to those in Hungary. Once again the Soviets appear to have been using Hungary as a kind of laboratory testing ground to evaluate economic reforms before implementing them in the Soviet Union.

Banking and Finance. Perhaps the single most important economic reform in Hungary to date has been the changes made in the money and banking system that have made it possible for Hungarian firms to compete in the international marketplace. Most of these changes were implemented either in the late 1970s or the early 1980s.[8]

The National Bank of Hungary is the central bank of Hungary and carries out the usual functions related to control of the money supply and foreign exchange. Until recently, it was also responsible for a variety of other financial activities that are usually carried out by commercial banks, investment banks, merchant banks, and other financial institutions in less-centralized economies. However, many of these noncentral bank activities have been spun off by the National Bank of Hungary and are now being implemented by other banks in the country. For example, the National Savings Bank handles credit transactions for the general public.

Founded in 1971 to finance large centralized investments of the state, the State Development Bank has recently diversified into several new fields, including issuing and distributing industrial bonds, providing venture capital to new firms, and actually organizing new ventures. Since 1982, it has been possible for Hungarian companies, cooperatives, and banks to issue bonds to finance their growth and development. Companies and cooperatives cannot issue such bonds without the participation of a bank. Thus far, the State Development Bank has handled 60 percent of these transactions. The arrival of industrial bonds in Hungary has also necessitated the organization of a bond market in Budapest, which makes it possible for investors to buy and sell bonds in an orderly fashion. Interest rates for these bonds are, of course, determined by the bond market according to the laws of supply and demand. In 1984, Skala Co-op raised $10 million in extra capital on the Budapest bond market in conjunction with the State Development Bank.

The 1980s have witnessed the creation of a number of relatively small, innovation banks in Hungary that not only provide capital for new ventures but actually help organize them. The State Development Bank was the first bank to begin implementing these new venture capital activities. It owns a 20-percent share of the equity in VAEV-BRAMAC and a 26-percent interest in POLIFOAM.

In 1982, Hungary obtained membership in the World Bank and the International Monetary Fund, thus further strengthening its ties with the international marketplace. The Budapest Credit Bank, the first and only commercial bank, opened in 1985. It holds deposits for local-council-managed firms, industrial and trading cooperatives, public utility companies, and small private companies as well. When it makes commercial loans, the Credit Bank focuses primarily on the profitability of the particular deal or venture. New York–based Citibank now has an office in Budapest.

The Agrarian Innovation Bank, which opened in early 1987, was organized as a shareholder company with shares owned by state-owned enterprises and cooperatives. Shareholders receive credit concessions as well as special assistance with other banking services. All of these banking and financial activities have served to help mo-

netize the Hungarian economy and make it more flexible and responsive to changes in the international economic environment.

One area where the Soviet economic reforms have lagged significantly behind the Hungarian reforms is finance and banking. However, Soviet trade officials seem to be fully cognizant of the fact that
they must make some significant moves in the direction of monetizing
the Soviet economy if they want to be successful in the international
marketplace. Soviet trade officials have expressed an interest in Soviet
membership in the International Monetary Fund, the World Bank,
and the General Agreement on Tariffs and Trade.

Decentralized, Market-Oriented Planning

Thus, in less than twenty years, the Hungarian economy has moved
quite systematically away from a system of highly centralized, state-
owned enterprises towards an approach to management that permits
the general managers of companies to make their own decisions about
production, product mix, marketing, pricing, research and development, sources of funding, wages, bonuses, and international joint ventures. According to Miklos Pulai, deputy chair of the National Planning
Office and one of the principal architects of the Hungarian economic
reforms, "Most of the power and control mechanisms of the National
Planning Office have been delegated to the managers of the state-
owned companies as a result of the 1984 economic reforms." The
National Planning Office no longer concerns itself with detailed plans
of particular companies. Today it is more concerned with national
trends, forecasts, and plans, as well as with the overall structure of
the Hungarian economy.

The Hungarian alternative socialist system is a unique amalgam-
ation of economic ideas drawn from the Soviet Union, Yugoslavia,
Austria, Western Europe, Japan, and the United States. It is truly a
mixed economic system. Only the state can create large companies,
own them, and liquidate them. Although foreign companies are allowed to participate in joint-venture companies with the Hungarian
government, private Hungarian citizens are not permitted to own
shares of state-owned companies at present. Long before the Soviets
began introducing Hungarian-like reforms in their economy, the
Chinese were making frequent visits to Budapest. There is no doubt

whatsoever that Deng Xiaoping has been positively influenced by the philosophy and political style of Hungarian leader János Kádár.

Although many of the state-owned enterprises in Hungary have become increasingly market-oriented and profitable, some relatively inefficient companies (including several steel producers) are being heavily subsidized by the state, thus raising the effective tax rate of the more efficient enterprises, which must finance these subsidies. This problem has weakened Hungary's competitive position abroad because insufficient funds have been available to invest in the modernization of those companies that have the potential to compete in the Western international market. To deal with this problem, Hungary finally enacted a tough bankruptcy law in September 1986 and began applying it to financially strapped enterprises almost immediately. Obviously, the Soviets have the same problem as the Hungarians concerning state subsidies of inefficient enterprises. They too are in the process of enacting and implementing a bankruptcy law similar to the Hungarian law.

Many sectors of the Hungarian economy are highly competitive. For example, there are over twenty-five hundred firms in the construction industry alone, of which less than forty are owned by the state. Josepf Kiss, general manager of Alba Regia, one of the largest state-owned construction companies, has indicated that 90 percent of his company's business is generated from competitive bidding. Less than 10 percent of the company's projects are actually mandated by the state.

There is vigorous competition in Budapest between private taxi companies and the state-owned taxi company. They compete on the basis of service. The private taxi drivers take considerable pride in their promptness in responding to customer calls. Budapest has three first-rate international hotels—Hilton, Hyatt, and Intercontinental—each of which is owned by the Hungarian government, financed by private Austrian capital, and managed by a U.S. hotel chain.

On my most recent trip to Budapest, in December 1986, the streets were jammed with Christmas shoppers. The elegant pedestrian mall on Váci Street and the boutiques were all decorated for Christmas. The electronics stores were filled with imported stereos, VCRs, and home computers. There was little evidence in the private retail sector that 1986 had not been a good year for the Hungarian economy.

During the same week that McDonald's announced that it would open its first restaurant in Budapest in 1987, Soviet television aired a documentary depicting a McDonald's restaurant in New York as efficient and well-managed, and offering excellent food and service.

Despite overregulation, one of the major successes of the Hungarian economic reforms is the tremendous growth and vitality of the private sector. Nearly 400,000 people are now employed in about thirty-five thousand private businesses and company-based working groups. Although the private sector accounts for less than 5 percent of the Hungarian work force and less than 20 percent of GNP, private businesses are an important competitive force in the Hungarian economy. In many industries, the private firms set the norm in terms of efficiency and prices. As the Hungarian economy becomes more market oriented, it is impossible for the larger, state-owned firms to ignore the smaller, more efficient private firms. In this regard, it is interesting to note that the first private restaurant opened in Moscow in the fall of 1986. Furthermore, private enterprise in the service sector became legal in the Soviet Union on 1 May 1987.

It has been estimated that 70 percent of the Hungarian work force holds a second or third job. These second jobs take a variety of different forms, ranging from the production of certain goods and services in the home to moonlighting at factories at night and on the weekends.

For example, on a recent visit to the Remix Manufacturing Company in Szombathely, I was surprised to find twenty to thirty people working at the factory on a Saturday morning when the rest of the factory was obviously closed. Upon inquiring about the matter, I learned that the group of workers was a private business under contract with Remix to work at nights and on weekends. I was struck by the efficiency level of the workers in the group. These so-called work partnerships have become quite popular in Hungary. They represent a novel attempt to deal with chronic labor shortages, underutilized plant capacity, and low employee morale in state-owned enterprises.

However, second and third jobs appear to be a mixed blessing. On the one hand they provide Hungarians with an opportunity to not only increase their incomes but also to gain some experience as entrepreneurs and risk-takers. On the other hand, the efficiency of the Hungarian workers is likely to suffer simply because they are exhausted from the burden of carrying two or three jobs. They have less time for their families, and this can lead to long-term social problems as well.

One reason why so many Hungarians have more than one job is that salaries are low. But salaries are low because productivity is low—about one half that of Austria. There is also substantial over-employment in the state-owned companies, thus reducing productivity and holding salaries down. Breaking out of the mold of what had once been a risk-free society is not easy, but the Hungarians seem to be aware of the costs and the benefits of this process. With increasing consistency they seem to be opting for less regulation and less control from the government in favor of more flexible, market-oriented alternatives.

In spite of some public resistance, Hungary is actually starting to develop a wealthy class that can afford luxurious trips abroad, West German cameras, Pierre Cardin clothes, and Rosenthal china. Although the Hungarian press often refers to an "antirich" mood, Hungarians are beginning to accept the notion that "he who works better lives better." Increasingly, wages and salaries in factories are tied more closely to job performance.

By Western standards, many of the so-called wealthy Hungarians would be considered to be at best middle class. Most of the rich Hungarians are professionals, skilled workers, or entrepreneurs who work very long hours to earn their money. Their lifestyles are totally dependent on the level of their work. Whenever there is a lapse in the amount of effort that they put into their jobs, there will be a corresponding decrease in their standard of living. There are virtually no idle rich in Hungary and it is still relatively difficult to accumulate wealth and to pass it on to one's heirs.

Strategic Challenges

Although the Hungarian people enjoy the highest degree of economic freedom in Eastern Europe, their per capita GNP stands at the average for countries in the Eastern bloc. East Germany and Czechoslovakia have the highest per capita GNP followed by the Soviet Union, Hungary, and Poland. Bulgaria and Romania have the lowest income levels. However, the East Germans and the Czechs do not possess the degree of economic and political freedom that the Hungarians enjoy.

Between 1980 and 1983, the Hungarian economy was almost at a standstill, with industrial production growing at less than 1 percent. The average Hungarian worker received no wage increases during this period. In 1984 the Hungarian economy began to respond to the combined effects of the austerity programs initiated in 1983 as well as the economic reforms. Hungary made significant progress in reducing its foreign debt in 1984 and 1985. After experiencing a $1.6 million hard currency trade deficit in 1978, Hungary chalked up five consecutive trade surpluses with the West between 1981 and 1985—a development that did not escape the attention of the Soviet Union.

As a result of bad luck and some long-term structural problems, the Hungarian economy turned in a lackluster performance in 1986—reduced economic growth, a hard currency trade deficit, and the highest per capita foreign debt in the Eastern bloc.

What caused this setback? Normally agriculture is the mainstay of Hungarian exports to the West. Agricultural exports were adversely affected by a variety of different factors, most of which were beyond the control of Hungarian farmers. Two consecutive summer droughts, an extremely cold winter, the EEC's temporary ban on fresh-food imports following the Chernobyl nuclear accident, and declining world prices for agricultural products all took their toll on the value of agricultural exports in 1986. In addition, the Ministry of Agriculture reported that 70 percent of Hungary's arable land is threatened by a steady decline in the quality of soil. The primary cause of this problem is acid rain.

In May 1986, Hungary was hit by a dozen major industrial fires, one of which virtually wiped out the entire semiconductor industry in four hours. The decline in the price of crude oil did little to help the Hungarian economy, because Hungary purchases most of its oil from the Soviet Union through long-term agreements in which the negotiated price is based on a five-year average. However, Hungary's Middle Eastern clients, who are dependent on oil revenues, found it necessary to reduce their consumption of Hungarian-made products. The severe winter caused Hungary to import more crude oil for which it had to pay in hard currencies.

Hungarian textiles and manufactured goods, though cheap by

Western standards, were undercut by a flood of low-priced goods from the Far East. In his June 1986 visit to Budapest, Gorbachev put additional pressure on the Hungarians to improve the quality and quantity of their exports to the Soviet Union in exchange for Soviet energy and raw materials.

The Hungarian economy also suffers from some serious structural problems—government subsidies to inefficient state-owned enterprises. Not only do these protected enterprises continue to ring up substantial financial losses, but they are unable to compete effectively in the international marketplace. State funds that should be allocated to plant modernization and capital improvements for enterprises that have the potential to be successful in the export market are frittered away on inefficient, unprofitable enterprises.

The slumping economy has also widened the gap between affluent and less-fortunate Hungarians. There continues to be an acute housing shortage in Budapest, with over sixty-thousand people on the waiting list for housing. Some young couples have to wait over ten years for a flat of their own. At the same time in the Rózsadomb section of Budapest, overlooking the Danube River, Hungary's new rich are building opulent three-story homes and driving expensive Western automobiles. Particularly squeezed by the slow growth of the economy are unskilled workers, teachers, and pensioners.

One result of the economic reforms is that the Hungarian people have come to expect a rising standard of living. Not only have many Hungarians traveled to the West, but Vienna television has helped influence their taste for expensive Western consumer goods. Along with rising economic expectations comes a lot of psychological pressure to earn enough money to have a well-furnished flat, a new automobile, designer clothes, and occasional trips to Vienna, Paris, and London. Few Hungarians receive enough income from a single job to be able to afford these luxuries. Therein lies the rationale for second and third jobs. But all of this economic pressure is producing disastrous social consequences (divorce, broken homes, alcoholism, drug abuse, and crime), and the highest suicide rate in the world—43.5 self-inflicted deaths per hundred thousand people, one-third more than Denmark, the country with the second highest suicide rate.

Not only are Hungarian officials concerned about these social problems, but undoubtedly Soviet officials are pondering them as well.

They appear to be part and parcel of the hybrid form of capitalism and socialism that has evolved in Hungary since 1956. The Soviet Union and the rest of Eastern Europe do not merely recognize the pitfalls of the Hungarian approach—they hope to avoid them as well.

The Hungarians will face a number of major strategic challenges if they want to solve their social problems and get their economy back on an track that leads to economic growth and trade surpluses with the West. But these are precisely the same kinds of challenges that the Soviets face as they open their economy to the international market. Six of these challenges are described below.

International Marketing

Hungarian enterprises are now attempting to compete in three quite different markets—domestic, CMEA, and international. The domestic market is a relatively sheltered market in which some state-owned firms have a high degree of monopolistic control, thus enabling them to cover up inefficient operations by charging high prices in the domestic market. CMEA, the Eastern European equivalent of the European Economic Community (EEC), also represents a relatively protected market that usually takes the form of large-scale contracts with the Soviet Union and other Eastern European countries.

But neither the domestic market nor CMEA are sources of hard currency, which is necessary to pay for the importation of consumer goods and technology from the West. This is the reason for the heavy emphasis that is being placed on trade with Western Europe, Japan, and the United States. Until recently, not unlike the Soviet Union, most Hungarian companies were required to use specialized trading companies to market their products in the West. However, by 1984 over two hundred Hungarian firms were authorized to deal directly with Western trading partners.

In 1978, the United States granted Hungary most-favored-nation status. Today the United States is Hungary's ninth largest export market, as well as its fourth largest Western market. Among the products that Hungary exports to the United States are textiles, medical equipment, pharmaceuticals, busses, light bulbs, truck tires, paprika, and wines.

Even though the Hungarians export to 143 countries and import from 103 countries, the greatest single obstacle to increased Hungarian exports to the West is the relative inexperience of Hungarian managers in Western marketing practices. Because they previously had no responsibility for international marketing, Hungarian managers simply lack the know-how to plan, organize, promote, and implement deals with the West. There is a definite need for improved management education in general in Hungary, but particularly in the area of international sales and marketing. In response to this problem, Skala Co-op, the large retailer, hired a recent Hungarian graduate from an MBA program in the United States to plan and coordinate its new management development program—the first in Hungary. Increasingly, Hungarian managers are going to graduate schools of business for executive education either in Western Europe or the United States. More and more U.S. and Western European academics are being invited to lecture at institutions such as Karl Marx University on Western-style management practices. Several institutions in Budapest are seriously considering creating a graduate school of business to offer an MBA degree to Hungarian managers—the first in Eastern Europe.

Some Hungarian companies have begun advertising their products in Western European trade journals. Thus far the Hungarians have had only a modicum of success with either joint ventures with the United States or exports to the United States. They might do well to emulate the Chinese in this regard. China has retained a U.S. public relations and advertising agent to represent it in the United States. The results have been very impressive.

Some critics of the Hungarian experiment claim that the Hungarian economy is being held back today by political ideology. In my opinion, nothing could be further from the truth. The Hungarians have taken all of the right steps to make their economy a decentralized market-oriented economy. Their real problem today is not Marxist-Leninist ideology but inexperienced management. They have a very serious management problem, not an ideological problem. Until they come to grips with this fundamental issue, the Hungarian economy is likely to continue to flounder.

As one Hungarian cynic put it, "Hungary is playing on the world's stage and everyone is watching, but it may not have the right script." I believe Hungary does have the right script, but its players need more training and experience.

As for the Soviets, they will face exactly the same management problems as the Hungarians as the Soviets begin to decentralize their economy and enter the global marketplace. Where will Soviet managers learn how to compete in the international market? Certainly not in Red Square.

Organizational Development

Most of the large, state-owned companies in Hungary were originally organized as highly centralized functional organizations. Even with the recent economic reforms, there have been few changes in the organizational structure of most enterprises. The usual corporate functions of finance, marketing, manufacturing, and research and development remain highly centralized even though many of the firms are attempting to operate on a worldwide basis.

Consider the case of the Borsod Chemical Complex (BVK), the second largest chemical company in Hungary, which produces two hundred different products, employs sixty-five hundred people, and has annual sales of $250 million. In a multiproduct company such as BVK, functional resources must be shared. The production manager is responsible for manufacturing all two hundred products, and the marketing manager is in charge of marketing the entire product line.

Suppose that the general manager of BVK observes that a particular product is performing poorly. Sales are down, costs are up, and profits are plummeting. The general manager asks the marketing manager about the problem, and the marketing manager suggests that the problem lies in the quality of the product and the relatively high cost of producing it. The production manager, on the other hand, feels that the product is basically a good product and that production costs are reasonable. He feels that the problem is primarily a marketing problem—that the marketing manager is not pushing the product in the marketplace. Finally, the chief financial officer feels that both the marketing manager and the production manager are to blame. He argues that manufacturing is inefficient and that the marketing manager is spending too much on promotion. Neither the marketing manager, the production manager, nor the chief financial officer is willing to assume overall responsibility for the profitability of the particular product. Therein lies the problem of attempting to manage a large, multiproduct firm with a centralized, functional organization.

Introduction of additional products imposes a second dimension on a company's management system, namely, a product dimension. As BVK discovered, with each addition to its product line, increased stress was placed on its single-dimension, functional organization. With the company attempting to compete in the domestic, CMEA, and Western international markets with two hundred products in its market line, coordination of the interdependent financial, marketing, and production activities became increasingly difficult as the company's product line continued to expand. To overcome some of the limitations of its centralized functional organization structure and to be able to respond more effectively to the competitive forces of the international marketplace, in 1985 BVK began experimenting with a participatory planning management system known as the *strategy matrix*.[9] The strategy matrix is used by such firms as IBM, Burroughs Wellcome, Shell Oil, and Dow Chemical to balance the profitability requirements of individual products against the limited supplies of critical functional resources. The strategy matrix makes extensive use of management teams to overcome some of the frustrations traditional hierarchical organizations experience in coping with interdependent products. It is being used by several Hungarian firms as they evolve from highly centralized functional organizations into less-centralized, multiproduct organizations.

In most cases, the decentralization of large state-owned enterprises was initiated by the government itself. But the government has only limited experience with modern theories and practices of organizational development. As a result, some of the attempts at reorganization and decentralization have met with limited success. Not unlike international marketing, the problem of organizational development can only be solved with improved management education and practical experience.

Like the Hungarians, the Soviets have virtually no experience with modern approaches to organizational development in a decentralized, market-oriented economy. They must be watching the Hungarians struggle with this problem with great interest.

Financial Management

Previously, financial management was a relatively unimportant responsibility of senior managers of Hungarian companies. The principal source of funds for operations and expansion was the National

Bank of Hungary. That is, the National Bank would allocate funds
to a particular firm according to the state plan. Corporate finance
consisted primarily of budgeting and accounting. There was no need
for a treasurer for there were no funds to manage. Financial management as we know it in the United States did not exist in Hungary
until recently.

Today Hungarian firms have access to a variety of alternative
sources of public and private funds including the National Bank of
Hungary, the State Development Bank, a number of Hungarian merchant banks and innovation banks, as well as international lending
agencies such as the World Bank. It is possible for Hungarian firms
to sell industrial bonds on the open market and to obtain funding
directly from Western joint-venture partners. They can also use retained earnings generated by the business as a source of funds.

Hungarian firms may soon have another source of capital available to them. The inside betting is that the Budapest Stock Exchange,
which closed in 1946, will reopen before 1990. One senior government official has outlined the steps that will be required before the
Stock Exchange can reopen. These include tax reform, changes in the
monetary system, increases in the degree of autonomy of state-owned
firms, and making shares of these firms available to employees. If you
issue shares to employees, what do you do if the employees want to
transfer the ownership of their shares to someone else? At that point
you need a stock market. In April 1987 the Polish government announced that it would open a stock market in Warsaw.

In a relatively short period of time, financial management has
become very important to Hungarian companies. Although the National Bank of Hungary, the Ministry of Finance, and the National
Planning Office have some sophisticated financial experts, this expertise has not filtered down to many enterprises. Improved management
education is the key to improved financial management. Financial
management is a field in which neither Soviet government officials
nor Soviet enterprise managers have much experience. This is another
area where the Soviets have a lot to learn from the Hungarians.

Technological Development

Due to the continuing and often widening gap in technological development between Hungary and the West, a large proportion of

Hungarian industrial production is unsuitable in terms of quality and product design for export to the West at profitable prices. This problem is also a carryover from the excessive centralization of industry in the past. Hungarian managers previously had little or no incentive to develop innovative new products or more efficient production processes. With the new decentralized, profit-oriented management systems, the way is paved for increased creativity and innovation within Hungarian firms.

Hungary has recently embarked upon a dual strategy for improving its technology. On the one hand, it is actively seeking to purchase Western technology, particularly in the areas of industrial processes, computers, and robotics. The effectiveness of this strategy is constrained by U.S. bans on the export of technology to Eastern European countries. However, many Hungarian firms use industrial processes licensed to them by West German, Austrian, U.S., and Japanese firms. Although one sees relatively few U.S.-made computers in Hungary, there is no shortage of Japanese and West German models.

Hungary has been criticized for having made relatively poor use of the technology that it has imported from the West. Despite the economic reforms, the technology gap between Hungary and the West was not narrowed significantly in the 1970s. This is yet another example of a problem with origins in inexperienced management and continued state subsidies for inefficient, unprofitable enterprises. As long as the state continues to subsidize these ailing enterprises, there is little incentive for the management to get its act together and either acquire or develop modern technology to improve efficiency.

The other strategy employed by the Hungarians to strengthen their technological position calls for the development of their own technologies. They have achieved some degree of success recently in developing computer hardware and software. Their success with computers is due in part to the high priority given by the Hungarian government to popularizing the use of microcomputers in homes, schools, and businesses to raise the level of computer consciousness and help bridge the East–West gap in computer technology. As a result of this effort there are already five major manufacturers of computers in Hungary as well as dozens of smaller, privately owned manufacturers. At the retail level, hundreds of computer outlets have sprung up recently in response to the growing thirst for computer equipment in Hungary. Hungary is second only to East Germany among CMEA countries in the production of computers. In addition, there is also a profitable new computer-related business in Hungary, namely, exporting computer software to the West.

Public Policy

There is little opposition to the economic reforms in Hungary either by members of the Politburo or the central committee of the HSWP. However, there is considerable debate over the future direction of the reforms. Most enterprise managers, both public and private, are pushing for fewer government regulations and an even more market-oriented economy. Their voice is the Hungarian Chamber of Commerce. On the other hand, the trade union leaders are concerned about low wages and the widening gap in income between the rich and the poor. They also express fears about unemployment, if the government vigorously enforces the new bankruptcy law and reduces subsidies to unprofitable state-owned companies.

The debate over the future direction of the reforms is confounded by the pending retirement of aging János Kádár. Kádár's successor—whoever that might be—must soon come to grips with three public policy issues—state subsidies for unprofitable enterprises, a wages and incomes policy, and tax reform.

If the economy is to resume its growth path of the 1970s, the state must discontinue its present practice of subsidizing inefficient enterprises and use its limited resources to support those enterprises that can compete effectively abroad. Furthermore, people must be paid better if they work more efficiently in state-owned enterprises. Hungarian managers must be given more freedom in this regard. In 1985, taxes on private enterprises were increased by 31.5 percent even though their income increased by only 13.2 percent. Business leaders feel that the present tax system inhibits profit-making and encourages corruption. A progressive income tax and a value added tax are expected to be implemented in 1988.

Political Reform

Although Hungary does not have the highest per capita income in the Soviet bloc, most would agree that the Hungarians enjoy the highest overall standard of living in Eastern Europe. This is due to the fact that not only do they have more economic freedom than any other country in the Eastern bloc, but they also enjoy the highest degree of political freedom as well.

Hungary stopped jamming Western radio broadcasts in 1964, and Austrian telecasts from Vienna are accessible all over Hungary. There are fifteen hundred magazines and newspapers in Hungary, most of which are free of any direct government control. Most of the major Western European newspapers, including the *Financial Times* and the *International Herald Tribune,* are now available to foreigners and Hungarians alike in the hotels of Budapest. Bookstores offer a broad range of U.S. and Western European books.

There is also considerable religious freedom in Hungary. In the Catholic and Baptist churches I have visited in Budapest, there were standing-room-only crowds attending the Sunday morning worship services. In September 1985, U.S. evangelist Billy Graham preached to a crowd of fifteen thousand at the Budapest Indoor Stadium.

Hungarians can legally come and go as they please. It is possible to obtain a passport in a relatively short period of time, leave the country, and return. Some Hungarians who immigrated to the United States in 1956 are now returning to Hungary. They find that their U.S. Social Security checks go much further in Hungary than they do in the United States. Hungarians and Austrians can travel freely between their two countries without a visa. Visas are not required for travel in either direction between Hungary and China, Finland, India, and Sweden. The only restriction on international travel is the amount of hard currency that can be taken out of the country at one time.

What seems to be happening in Hungary is that increased economic freedom breeds increased political freedom. That is, the economic reforms have created expectations for additional freedom— social, religious, cultural, and more recently, political freedom as well. Under János Kádár, these expectations for greater political freedom are gradually being realized in a number of different areas.

For example, in the 1985 elections for the Hungarian Parliament, 352 of the 387 seats were contested by rival candidates. The remaining thirty-five seats were reserved for senior party officials, who are always elected unopposed. However, five high-ranking members of the central committee actually lost their parliamentary seats to so-called "independent" candidates who opposed the official candidates nominated by party selection committees. Nearly thirty of these independent candidates were elected in all.

In the past, the Hungarian Parliament has not been a particularly important political institution because it typically meets only three or four times a year for a total of eight days to rubber-stamp party decisions. (Approximately 850,000 people belong to the party—8 percent of the population.) Recently the government has been trying to give the Parliament additional powers. However, it is likely to be some time before it will be allowed to initiate laws on its own or to challenge decisions of the Politburo or the central committe.

The party is also gradually introducing democratic principles into other facets of Hungarian life. Decentralized economic planning, enterprise councils, cooperatives, and private enterprise are all examples of steps taken by the party to make economic decision making more participatory in Hungary. Local party committees and local governments are also being given more power in Hungary.

All of this must provide food for thought for Soviet leaders as they open the doors to their closed society.

The Rest of Eastern Europe

I believe that the evidence supports the view that Hungary has had a positive influence on the strategic thinking of Soviet leader Gorbachev. But Hungary is by no means the only Eastern European country that has influenced the Soviet Union.

The Soviet Union has on at least three occasions made it abundantly clear—Hungary in 1956, Czechoslovakia in 1968, and Poland in 1981—that it will not tolerate challenges to communist rule in neighboring Eastern-bloc countries. But during the years of Brezhnev's aged and indecisive leadership, more independent economic and political trends did emerge in Eastern Europe. Despite the four decades in which the six European members of the Warsaw Pact and CMEA have operated under essentially the same Soviet-model political system, there are still enormous differences among the six countries. Czechoslovakia and East Germany, which have the strongest economies in the Eastern bloc, have virtually no Western debt and send most of their exports to the Soviet Union and other CMEA countries. The most repressive of the Eastern bloc countries is Romania, which maintains a relatively independent foreign policy and has been granted most-favored-nation status by the United States. It has resorted to an extreme austerity program to reduce its debt to the West, and this has resulted in cutbacks in energy imports to the point where streets are dark and apartments are cold. Poland has a powerful church, private farmers, a volatile political opposition, and a huge foreign debt to Western banks. Bulgaria also permits some private agriculture and is trying to attract tourists to its seashore.

Other than Hungary, East Germany and Poland have probably had the greatest influence over Gorbachev's long-term plans for the Soviet Union. I now turn to these two countries.

East Germany

Since its creation by the Soviet Union out of the ashes of World War II, the German Democratic Republic (GDR), or East Germany, has had the reputation of being a model Soviet clone with a repressive, Stalin-like government and economic system. With the strongest economy in Eastern Europe, the GDR is considered to be Moscow's most important military ally as well as a critical source of technology. During the early 1980s, the GDR's army was significantly modernized and is now the best equipped in the Warsaw Pact. The GDR has achieved a relatively high degree of economic success (by Eastern European standards) through the use of stern discipline and a highly centralized Socialist economic system. This is why many Sovietologists believe that Gorbachev will follow the East German model for economic development. For the reasons stated previously, I believe that Gorbachev will reject the conservative, inflexible East German approach in favor of the Hungarian model.

Up until a decade ago, the GDR was considered to be a diplomatic pariah and was shunned by the West. In the 1980s, under Socialist Unity party leader Erich Honecker, the GDR began to carve out a more independent niche by maintaining a dialogue with the West—particularly with the Federal Republic of Germany (FRG, or West Germany). The GDR began playing host to a number of high-level Western dignitaries, and along with Hungary, it became the foremost proponent of détente with the West among the Warsaw Pact countries. Although once regarded as a hard-line Stalinist state, the GDR has aligned itself increasingly with independent-minded Hungary in making the case that small European countries might be able to play a special role in reducing East–West tensions. What has emerged is a region of common interests that links the GDR, Hungary, Romania, and Bulgaria. The common interests are to increase trade with the West, continue economic reform, encourage private enterprise, rekindle détente, and deemphasize military alliance obligations.

As evidence of rapprochement between the GDR and the FRG, in 1983 and 1984 the Bonn government approved two private bank credits worth $730 million to the GDR, and in return the GDR made it easier and less expensive for West Germans to visit friends and relatives in the East. In addition, in 1984 a record forty thousand East Germans were allowed to emigrate westward—the largest number permitted to do so since the Berlin Wall was erected in 1961.

In 1983, cynics claimed that the détente between the GDR and the FRG was motivated primarily by U.S.–Soviet political considerations. At that time the Bonn government was in the process of deciding whether or not to deploy U.S. medium-range missiles. As long as Bonn had not irrevocably committed itself to the deployment of these missiles, improved relations between the two Germanies could be used as an instrument to encourage the FRG to reconsider its position to accept additional nuclear weapons. However, in 1984 after Bonn had committed itself to deployment of the missiles, Erich Honecker announced his intentions to visit Bonn. Under apparent pressure from the Soviets the trip was postponed.

The primary forces drawing the GDR and the FRG together are economic rather than political. After the Soviet Union, the FRG is the GDR's most important trading partner. West German subsidies, private investment, bank loans, and outright gifts have contributed to the GDR's unique prosperity among Warsaw Pact countries. The GDR also enjoys a unique relationship with the EEC. Because of a legal loophole in the Treaty of Rome, the GDR is a de facto member of the EEC. As a result of this anomaly, the GDR is permitted to export to the FRG and other EEC countries without having to pay import duties. No other Eastern European country enjoys such a privileged position with Western Europe. Another force that furthers a common identity between the countries is West German television, which saturates most of the GDR.

If Gorbachev opts to emulate the socioeconomic, political model of the GDR, which will he emulate—the rigid one of the 1950s and 1960s, or the more flexible one of Erich Honecker in the 1980s? I think the answer is clearly the latter alternative.

Poland

Prior to the 1986 party congress in Moscow, there was understandable apprehension among Soviet bloc leaders as to Gorbachev's likely reaction to the economic reforms of Hungary and Poland as well as the increased political independence of the GDR and Romania. Would Gorbachev feel political pressure to seek greater conformity among his Warsaw Pact allies or would he encourage independence?

To the surprise of most Western pundits, it was neither János Kádár nor Erich Honecker who attracted the most attention among the Warsaw Pact leaders attending the party congress, but rather Polish leader General Wojciech Jaruzelski. Not only did Jaruzelski make a surprise visit to Vilnius, the capital of Lithuania, which was for centuries a cultural center of the old kingdom of Poland, but he emerged as the party leader closest to Gorbachev in age as well as outlook. Gorbachev's pronouncements on economic reform were widely interpreted as tacit approval of the Hungarian and Polish economic reforms.[10]

In an interview with *New York Times* foreign correspondent Flora Lewis, Jaruzelski indicated that his primary interest was neither communism, nor East–West antagonism, nor other global issues, but, "Polishness, Polish pride, Polish patriotism, Polish pain, Polish emotion."[11] Jaruzelski went on to say that he liked Gorbachev as a human being and particularly appreciated his "respect for Poland."

Not only has the government of General Jaruzelski released the last of the Polish political prisoners, but it is encouraging the start-up of private businesses, many of which have been organized by former Solidarity activists who lost their jobs during martial law. Some of the energy previously dissipated in the Solidarity movement is being channeled into private enterprise. Young Polish engineers are financing new businesses with venture capital obtained from Solidarity sympathizers who fled to the West but who have been lured back home by high-tech business opportunities.

Financed by a $3,000 investment from a Swedish businessman in 1983, Inter-Design is typical of the private firms that have emerged since the mid-1980s. It produces microcomputers and process control devices for Eastern Europe, the Soviet Union, and China, and computer software that it sells for hard currency in Sweden through a Swedish–U.S. firm. According to its president, Leonard Zabielski, the firm is extremely profitable and employs nearly thirty people, most of whom are highly motivated, top-flight electrical engineers attracted by "good pay, hard work, and extremely interesting projects."

None of this should come as a complete surprise, because an IBM PC/AT that costs $5,000 in the United States sells for $30,000 on the Warsaw black market. President Reagan's technology embargo against Poland and a stiff business income tax levied by the government in the fourth year of operations are the two biggest obstacles to Inter-Design's future success. However, private businesses are subjected to much lower tax rates than are state-owned companies.

Two engineers, both of whom were Solidarity activists, started a thriving electronic auto alarm business in 1984. Their only reliable source of high-quality electronic chips is the Sunday Morning Market, which operates in the wee hours each Sunday morning near a sports stadium in Warsaw. Several hundred vendors sell, among other things, a wide variety of electronic devices and components.

Biala Dalia, a private up-scale restaurant in the village of Konstancin near Warsaw, which caters to Polish yuppies and Western tourists, epitomizes the new entrepreneurial spirit. When asked how the restaurant (which opened in 1985) was doing, a waiter responded, "It's flourishing. It has to."

And how does the Jaruzelski government cotton to all of this? It loves it. Much of the resurgence of the private sector is attributable to the three-year tax exemption granted to new businesses by the government. Over the long run, the government hopes to gain much-needed tax revenues and generate new sources of foreign currency to help pay off Poland's $35 billion foreign debt. Successful Polish entrepreneurs have neither the time nor the energy to engage in anti-government political activities.

General Jaruzelski's strong personal relationship with Soviet leader Gorbachev has provided the Polish government with increased confidence to pursue Hungarian-like reforms with more vigor. Lately, some party leaders have advocated the use of the private sector to inject new vitality into Poland's lagging economic reform movement, which has been bogged down in a sea of bureaucratic inertia. "Our management systems must become more compatible with those of the West, if we are to compete successfully in the international market-place," said Wieslaw M. Grudzewski, deputy minister of scientific and technological progress.

Under a 1987 austerity program initiated by the government, many party leaders will have to give up their chauffeur-driven automobiles, stop making expensive junkets to the West, and spend more time in their offices. A stock market will soon be opened to sell shares in some state-owned companies.

Jaruzelski is seeking input on government policies from a broad range of people by creating a consultative council of prominent individuals from all walks of life—an idea traceable to the days of Solidarity. Although Solidarity's political influence has been reduced, it remains an important cultural force.

The biggest impediment to further reforms is the never-ending feud between the Catholic church and the government. On 31 August 1986, nearly fifteen thousand Poles attended an outdoor Mass at St. Stanislaw Kostka Church (where pro-Solidarity priest Rev. Jerzy Popieluszko is buried) to celebrate the sixth anniversary of the Gdańsk Agreement. The Mass consisted of a two-hour diatribe against communism and the Soviet Union without any constructive suggestions for healing Poland's severe economic and political wounds. Recently Primate Józef Cardinal Glemp ended negotiations with the government over the controversial, Western-supported fund to aid private farmers. Perhaps one reason why the church and the Polish government have so much trouble getting along is that they are too much alike—rigid, hierarchical, and authoritarian.

While the church and the state continue their battle, the Polish people are quietly getting their act together. The new breed of entrepreneurs is telling the church and the government that "it's high time we put aside ideological and political differences and get on with the job of rebuilding Poland."

Not unlike the GDR, Poland is an important political, economic, and military ally of the Soviet Union. There is no doubt whatsoever that Gorbachev understands full well the significance of the Solidarity movement in Poland as well as the disastrous economic and political consequences of martial law. If the government of any Eastern European country is either unable or unwilling to respond constructively to rising public expectations for greater economic and political freedom, then a clash between the government and the people is inevitable, as was the case in Hungary in 1956, in Czechoslovakia in 1968, and in Poland in 1956, 1970, 1976, and 1981. Gorbachev has little desire to see such conflicts replicated either in Eastern Europe or the Soviet Union. Indeed, that is why he is pursuing a strategy of radical economic, political, and cultural reform.

What about the Soviets?

Hungary is a very small, relatively homogeneous country with a population of only 10.58 million, compared with the Soviet Union, which has 280 million people spread over fifteen heterogeneous socialist republics. Is the Hungarian experience merely a special case, or will it be emulated by the Soviet Union and its Eastern European allies? In varying degrees, Bulgarian, Czechoslovak, East German, Hungarian, Polish, Romanian, and Soviet managers are all singing the same tune: "The old ways don't work anymore." Increasingly, they are turning to the marketplace for solutions to their economic problems. Hungary has taken the largest steps towards the market, but the Soviets are moving very strongly in the same direction under Gorbachev.

Has Gorbachev been influenced by the Hungarian connection? I believe that the evidence clearly suggests that the answer is "Yes." Repeatedly I have cited examples in which Gorbachev's actions were virtually identical to those of the Hungarians. In the remaining chapters, I will present further evidence that Hungary is one of the most important factors drawing Gorbachev towards radical reform.

To what extent is the Hungarian economy directly influenced by Moscow today? According to Miklos Pulai, deputy director of the State Planning Office in Budapest, "The Soviets no longer make any direct suggestions about the Hungarian economy; the two countries are major trading partners, however, and do exchange information." As noted previously, Hungary is dependent on the USSR for energy and natural resources. On the other hand, the USSR purchases over half of the machine tools produced in Hungary.

What about the future direction of the Hungarian economic reforms after János Kádár steps down? Will Gorbachev have any influence over the reforms in the future?

Most of the party leaders with whom I have met in Budapest and in Warsaw feel that Gorbachev's strong commitment to economic reform will greatly increase the self-confidence of the leaders of all of the Eastern European countries to become more bold in their support of economic and political reform. As recently as December 1986, I found Hungarian business leaders to be very enthusiastic about Gorbachev and the positive influence that he is having in Eastern Europe. Ironically, there is a feeling in the air in Budapest these days that unlike 1956, when the Soviets suppressed the Hungarians' bid for increased freedom, the next time around it may be the Soviets who provide the leadership to save the Hungarian reforms rather than destroy them. Gorbachev's 1987 visits to Prague and Bucharest provide further credence to this point of view.

4

The New Chinese Socialism

The People's Republic of China

When Secretary of State Henry Kissinger and President Richard Nixon visited the People's Republic of China (PRC) in 1971 and 1972, respectively, China was still consumed by the disastrous Cultural Revolution inspired by Mao Zedong and was literally tearing itself apart. Few Americans would have believed the dramatic changes that would soon take place in China over the next six years. Not only would Chairman Mao and Premier Zhou Enlai both be dead, but the infamous "Gang of Four" (including Mao's widow Jiang Qing) would have been arrested; Hua Guofeng, Mao's handpicked successor, would have been pushed aside; and the preeminent leader of China would be Deng Xiaoping, who had been purged twice during the Cultural Revolution as a "capitalist-roader." No one could have predicted that U.S. anticommunist rhetoric against the Chinese would have subsided to such an extent that on 15 December 1978, President Jimmy Carter would announce the normalization of relations with the PRC, the recognition of the PRC as the sole legal government of China, and the opening of the U.S. Embassy in Beijing on 1 March 1979. Thus three decades of hostility and noncommunication between the United States and China had finally come to an end.

During the ten-year period following Mao's death, China evolved from ideological rigidity towards flexible pragmatism; from repressive totalitarianism towards reform-oriented authoritarianism; from a Stalin-like centralized economy towards a decentralized market-oriented economy; and from international isolationism to global interdependence.

What began as a very small opening in China's window to the West has been followed by the unprecedented transformation of the world's most populous country form a backward, impoverished, repressive, inward-looking dictatorship into a dynamic, increasingly democratic, outward-looking nation with one of the highest rates of economic growth in the world. Out of the political and economic ruins of the Cultural Revolution (which did not end until 1976), the triumverate of Deng Xiaoping, party chairman Hu Yaobang, and Premier Zhao Ziyang put together the socioeconomic and political miracle of the twentieth century. Since then Deng and his team of pragmatists have been sending increasingly clear signals to China and the rest of the world that the old ways don't work anymore and that it is time for practical problem solving to replace political ideology as the guiding principle by which China will attempt to achieve its ambitious economic, political, and social goals for the year 2000.

As undeniable evidence of Deng's success, China's average rate of economic growth between 1981 and 1984 was 8 percent, compared to 2.5 percent for the Soviet Union and 2.7 percent for the United States. Real gross national product increased by 12 percent in 1985, slightly down from 13 percent in 1984.

Most of the Chinese reforms are a mirror image of the Hungarian reforms. But the Chinese have taken less than ten years to replicate what required thirty years to implement in Hungary.

Just as the repressive years of Stalin in the 1930s and 1940s and the benign neglect of Brezhnev in the 1970s helped pave the way for the radical reforms in the Soviet Union under Gorbachev, so too were the disastrous social, economic, and political policies of Chairman Mao necessary precursors to the type of market socialism being practiced in China today.

The dramatic results of the Chinese economic reforms have not gone unnoticed in the Kremlin. China is too big and too important to be ignored. After over two decades of estrangement, Sino–Soviet relations appear to be on the mend. Since 1985 relations between the Soviet Union and China have been characterized by reciprocal visits by high-ranking officials, increased bilateral trade, the intensification of educational and cultural exchanges, and a significant improvement in the overall atmosphere surrounding the two countries.

The fact that China has successfully replicated the Hungarian experiment with a population one hundred times that of Hungary in less than one third the time not only validates the Hungarian experience in the eyes of Soviet leaders, but it greatly enhances its credibility.

To better understand China and its influence on the Soviet Union, I include a brief history of China prior to the time when Deng Xiaoping came to power. I then describe some of the Chinese economic, political, and cultural reforms and compare them with what is now happening in the Soviet Union under Gorbachev. I conclude with an analysis of the effects that the Chinese reforms are having on the Soviet Union in general and Sino–Soviet relations in particular.

The Reign of Mao Zedong: 1949–76

In 1911, after the collapse of the Manchu Dynasty that had ruled China since 1644, the popular Chinese leader Sun Yat-sen founded the new Republic of China. Shortly thereafter, civil war broke out and for nearly a decade China was ruled by a number of independent warlords. However, in 1927 Chiang Kai-shek emerged as a potential overlord of all China. After taking control of Sun Yat-sen's Nationalist Party, the Guomindang (Kuomintang), in 1928, with the assistance of weapons and material aid provided by the Soviet Union, Chiang Kai-shek became president of the Republic of China. Ironically, Chiang was considered to be a left-wing political force in China in the 1920s, but this was soon to change.

The Nationalist Party of Chiang was by no means the only active political force in China in the 1920s and 1930s. In 1921 the Chinese Communist Party was founded. One of its founders was a young teacher named Mao Zedong. Initially, the Guomindang tolerated the communists as part of the price of their support from the Soviets. However, it was not long before there were increasing conflicts, often quite violent, between the communists and the Guomindang. These continued until Japan invaded Manchuria in 1937. After serving as the political commissar of the Red Army, by 1936 Mao had emerged as the political and ideological leader of the Chinese communists. As a student of Marx, Lenin, and Stalin, he devoted substantial energy to writing his own theoretical and polemical works, many of which provided the ideological basis for the People's Republic of China, which he would found in 1949.

During the eight years of war between 1937 and 1945, while Chiang Kai-shek's Nationalist government was fighting against the Japanese, Mao Zedong's communists were consolidating their power base in the northwestern part of China. In spite of substantial military support from the West against the Japanese throughout World War II, Chiang's leadership of the Nationalists took the form of a series of disastrous military mistakes. His military leadership of the Chinese during the war was characterized by corruption, poor training, and malnutrition among the soldiers, as well as widespread chaos and incompetence.

When the war ended in 1945, Chiang's army was in a complete state of disarray and he was in no position to maintain the degree of control that he previously exercised over China in the 1930s. In a series of decisive, well-organized military campaigns, Mao led the Red Army into northeastern China and then central China, eventually driving Chiang to the island of Taiwan in 1949. Interestingly enough, the Soviet Union maintained diplomatic relations with Nationalist China right up to the point of Chiang's departure from Mainland China.

Rehabilitation: 1949–57

After Chiang had been unceremoniously routed from the mainland, Mao established the People's Republic of China, which was soon recognized as the official government of China by the Soviet Union. Given the fact that the United States continued to maintain its steadfast support of Chiang and refused to recognize Mao's government as the legitimate government of China, Mao had nowhere to turn but to the Soviet Union to help him rebuild China.

In 1949, China was in a state of economic, political, and social chaos after decades of imperialist exploitation by the Manchu Dynasty, the war with Japan, civil war, and the incompetence and corruption of the Guomindang government. During the so-called Rehabilitation Years (1949–57) the government of Mao inaugurated a series of programs aimed at putting China back on its feet again and curbing inflation, which had reached 4,000 percent in 1949. The government took over the Bank of China, issued a new currency, and implemented an agrarian reform program in which land was nationalized and then redistributed to peasant farmers. However, private industrialists were permitted to continue operating their own enterprises. Although there were no drastic changes in the economic system during this initial three-year period of economic rehabilitation, industrial output increased at the rate of 30 percent per year and agricultural output at 10 percent per year.

The cold war, the Korean War (1950–53), and the U.S.-led trade embargo of the PRC forced Mao even closer to the Soviets. But this unholy alliance between Mao and the Soviets was doomed to failure from the very outset because of a lack of trust between the two parties, which can be traced back (among other factors) to territorial disputes between China and Russia during the Manchu Dynasty. It should also be recalled that Stalin consistently supported Chiang and not Mao from the 1920s until 1949.

Nevertheless, the first five-year plan (1953–57) followed closely the Soviet model of economic development. Guided by Soviet technical assistance the PRC proceeded to collectivize most of the peasant farms and nationalize most of the industrial enterprises. A Soviet-style central planning mechanism was put in place that emphasized centralization and control. Not unlike the Soviet Union, the PRC gave high priority to the development of heavy industry. Profits from agriculture and industry were heavily taxed to support government investments in nearly ten thousand new industrial and mining enterprises that were established during this five-year period. Although estimates vary as to the exact rate of economic growth for the PRC during the first eight years of its existence, most would agree that it was, indeed, a period of sustained economic improvement. Substantial progress was also achieved in reaching a subsistence level of nourishment in the countryside and in raising the level of education of the Chinese people.

The Great Leap Forward: 1958–62

In spite of the success of the first five-year plan, Mao became impatient with the rate of economic development. After the death of Stalin in 1953, tensions between Mao and Khrushchev began to increase. In 1958, in complete defiance of the Soviets, Mao launched a completely new economic program aimed at accelerating the rate of economic progress—the "Great Leap Forward." Between 1958 and 1962 all sectors of the Chinese economy were exhorted to go all out to "achieve greater, faster, better and more economical results in building socialism." Mao simply was not willing to continue the Soviet-style plan of building a massive industrial base at the expense of the peasants' standard of living. He was unimpressed with the results of such policies in the Soviet Union and was concerned that some of his political power might be slipping away. His attempts to decentralize investments in agriculture and in rural light industry too rapidly, combined with a terrible drought, yielded castastrophic results. Between 1958 and 1960 grain production fell by 57 million tons to a low of 143 million tons. Not only did the Great Leap Forward produce precipitous decreases in agricultural and industrial output, but it has been admitted that as many as twenty million Chinese died during the period—mostly of starvation, disease, and malnutrition. Although the policies of the Great Leap Forward were abandoned in 1959, starvation and suffering continued for several years.

Liu Shaoqi and some of the more liberal members of the Communist party presided over the gradual recovery of the economy between 1963 and 1965. Some of the policies introduced by Liu to revitalize the agricultural sector were precursors of the agricultural reforms of the 1980s. Private plots were reintroduced to peasant farmers. In 1964 Premier Zhou Enlai urged China to pursue the "Four Modernizations" of industry, agriculture, defense, and science and technology. After falling into disrepute during the Cultural Revolution, the Four Modernizations were rediscovered in 1977 after the deaths of Mao and Zhou. One of the important lessons of this period of readjustment was that it illustrated the potential of the Chinese economy to respond quite rapidly to more liberal economic policies.

The Cultural Revolution: 1966–76

Unfortunately for the Chinese people, the "big tomorrow" promised by Mao during the Great Leap Forward turned out to be the catastrophic Cultural Revolution. Just as Mao had felt threatened by the first five-year plan, so too was his response to the policies of the 1960s. In the 1950s he used the political muscle of the party to force people to accept his policies. In the 1960s he went directly to the people, particularly the young people, to help him fight the policies of the government and the party.

The Cultural Revolution was started by Mao in 1966 as an attack on the Chinese administrative and economic systems as well as the separation of intellectuals and cadres from the harsh realities of peasant life. It soon became a reign of terror in which millions of Red Guards transferred political power from the pragmatic economic planners in Beijing to the radical elements of the Communist party and then proceeded to destroy many of the cultural traditions that were said to impede social revolution.

The Cultural Revolution was a ten-year outburst of hysterical fanaticism. Just as the Soviet people were forced to endure the atrocities of Stalin and Hitler during the 1930s and 1940s, so also were the Chinese subjected to the incredible excesses of Mao during the Great Leap Forward and the Cultural Revolution.

Between September 1966 and February 1972 all of the universities were closed. When they reopened in February 1972, admission was based primarily on political considerations rather than academic qualifications. Priority was given to the children of working-class families and peasants, many of whom had minimal academic qualifications. Over 800,000 students had to forego a college education during the Cultural Revolution. For ten years, the research and continuing education activities of colleges and universities were discontinued. Over one hundred million primary and middle-school students received inferior educations. The real tragedy was not only that a whole generation of young people lost their chances for an education, but their lives were stripped of any sense of meaning, for which they received nothing in return. They lost their youth and their hope for the future as a result of one of the greatest frauds ever perpetrated on the human race.

Throughout the Cultural Revolution, Premier Zhou Enlai served as a force for moderation in a sea of political and economic chaos. He was an alleviating influence within the party who went along with Mao's excesses to be able to limit the extent of human suffering and be in a position to rebuild something saner after the madness was over. As Mao became increasingly feeble with age, his wife Jiang Qing, with the aid of others of the so-called Gang of Four, attempted to use Mao's prestige to push back Zhou's supporters and thus ensure their own succession. However, in April 1976, shortly after the death of Zhou, tens of thousands of Chinese showed up at Tiananmen Square in Beijing carrying wreaths, memorial photographs, and posters to mourn Premier Zhou Enlai. But this massive demonstration was much more than a memorial to Zhou. It was a repudiation of the Gang of Four and a strong voice of support for Vice Premier Deng Xiaoping, who had been embattled by the radical faction around Mao. Deng was soon arrested for the second time, stripped of his power, and banished. Only this time around he was not destined to be out of Beijing very long. He was brought back the following year by some key figures in the Politburo and military high command. On 9 September 1976, Mao Zedong died and shortly thereafter his widow and her friends were arrested, vilified, and stripped of power. Hua Guofeng, Mao's designated successor, was named party chairman.

Socialism with Chinese Characteristics

On 12 August 1977, at the eleventh party congress, Hua set the stage for Chinese economic development for the decade of the 1980s by declaring that the mission would be the "socialist modernization" of the country. He reintroduced the Four Modernizations program originally proposed by Zhou Enlai in 1964. By the end of 1978, it was apparent that it was Vice Premier Deng Xiaoping and not Hua Guofeng who would lead China out of the quagmire of the Cultural Revolution and into the 1980s.

Interestingly enough, the schisms in the party that brought Deng into power in 1978 can be traced back to the beginning of the party in 1921. Although all of the groups within the party were interested in ridding the country of its weak and corrupt rulers, there were wide divergencies in opinion as to what should be instituted in their place. The group represented by Mao had a millennial view of China that attempted to meld ancient Chinese teachings about social harmony with the writings of Karl Marx and other nineteenth-century socialists. The other principal group within the party was much more pragmatic and nationalist. It viewed the party as an instrument to restore China to a place of respect in the world.

Since the early 1950s, the two most vocal opponents of Mao's egalitarian obsessions had been Liu Shaoqi and Deng Xiaoping. After the debacle of the Great Leap Forward, they temporarily seized the initiative and began implementing more practical economic policies in agriculture and in industry.

In 1966, when Mao was outvoted in the Politburo, he turned to the masses to help him oust his opponents. Two of the earliest victims of the Cultural Revolution were Liu and Deng. Liu was among the many opponents of Mao who were killed by the Red Guards. Deng, on the other hand, was dispatched to a tractor plant in Jiangxi province.

When Deng returned to power in 1978, political, economic, and social conditions were in such a state of disarray that it was hard to imagine Deng doing anything that could conceivably make matters worse than they already were. Not only was China ripe for radical reform, but Deng faced only minimal opposition to his innovative programs. Although conditions in Moscow in 1985 when Gorbachev came to power were not nearly as extreme as they were in China in 1978, the situation was, nevertheless, quite conducive to economic, political, and cultural reform. Furthermore, each day that passes provides additional evidence that Gorbachev possesses far more political clout than anyone ever imagined possible.

I will now examine some of the reforms introduced by Deng in the pursuit of his objective of making China a modern "socialist country with Chinese characteristics."

Rural Reform: The Responsibility System

When the Communist party came to power in China in 1949 its avowed objective was to improve the plight of the peasants and to solve the problems of starvation, undernourishment, and poverty. To achieve this objective the party set out to transform the countryside. During the first thirty years that it was in power, the party managed to change the Chinese countryside not once but four times. Initially, Chinese farmers were organized into cooperatives. In 1958 they were reorganized into huge communes consisting of thousands of people. These communes included income sharing and the collectivization of work, eating, and housing. Then in the early 1960s, the communes were decentralized into brigades and teams. Under the Responsibility System of Deng Xiaoping, Chinese farmers were once again told to till their family fields.[1]

Eight hundred million people live in the Chinese countryside. To avoid replicating the problems of countries like Brazil and Mexico caused by the immigration of millions of poor farmers to Rio de Janeiro, São Paulo, and Mexico City, Deng introduced his economic reforms in the countryside first. Of course, that is precisely what János Kádár did in Hungary in 1957 after the revolution. The results in China have been absolutely astonishing. Grain production increased from 315 million tons in 1979 to 407 million tons in 1984 and is targeted to reach 450 million tons by 1990. Wheat production alone more than doubled during the 1979–84 period, and China became the world's largest producer of wheat and cotton. In 1985, for the first time, China became a net food exporter and began exporting corn as well. Grain shipments to the Soviet Union have also increased.

As a result of reduced acreage, flood damage, and confusion over new reforms, grain output fell 7 percent in 1985 but held steady in 1986. However, the production of sugar cane, peanuts, and oil seeds each increased by 25 percent in 1985, and meat and egg production grew by 14 percent and 23 percent, respectively.

Rural incomes increased by 15 percent between 1978 and 1984. Although the median peasant income was only 355 yuan (about $122) in 1984, there were already many "10,000 yuan households" in the Chinese countryside.

All of this was accomplished through the introduction of the Responsibility System—a system in which collectively owned land in the countryside is assigned to individual families on a long-term basis. Each family contracts with the state to produce specified amounts of rice, wheat, tea, or cotton, depending on the growing conditions in its region. Once the state production targets have been satisfied, the families are free to keep any surplus for themselves or sell it on the open market at a higher price. If a family farm fails to achieve its production quota, then it must pay for any production shortfalls out of its own pocket. In addition to the use of Responsibility Land, peasant families may have their own private plot on which to grow fruit, vegetables, and grain for the family to eat.

The Chinese government has also inaugurated a number of other programs aimed at improving life in the countryside. These include commune-run industrial enterprises; long-term, low-interest loans; land reclamation; and farm mechanization programs.

China has also benefited from Asia's Green Revolution, which through biological science has transformed village farming not only in China but also in India, Indonesia, Thailand, and other Asian countries. A significant part of China's 1981–84 agricultural boom is attributable to hybrid rice that increases average yields by approximately 30 percent and is now planted on half of China's rice land.

In 1985 the government began shifting away from a state regulated agricultural system towards a system that permits farmers to produce whatever they want in response to government prices and local market conditions. This caused many peasants to shift out of the back-breaking production of rice and other grains and into more profitable, easier-to-produce fruits, vegetables, and cattle. Millions of peasants quit farming and went to work for booming rural industries.

As a direct result of the government's lifting of price controls on eighteen hundred food items in May 1985, more than sixty-one thousand free markets have come into existence in China—six hundred in Beijing alone. These burgeoning markets are much like bazaars and flea markets held in other parts of the world.

Not surprisingly, the Chinese agricultural reforms have been strongly influenced by the Hungarian reforms. Senior Hungarian officials report that throughout the late 1970s and early 1980s, there were frequent Chinese delegations in Budapest studying the highly successful Hungarian agricultural reforms. Just as the Chinese have learned from the Hungarians, the Soviets are now closely observing the experiences of China and Hungary in agricultural reform.

Industrial Reform: Pragmatism and Profits

To raise the level of industrial productivity, in 1978 Zhao Ziyang (then first secretary of the party in the province of Sichuan) introduced a series of industrial experiments in six state-owned enterprises in Sichuan. These experiments were amazingly similar to the economic experiments announced in Moscow in 1983 by Soviet leader Yuri Andropov. For example, the firms in the experiment were allowed to retain and distribute a portion of their profits for incentive bonuses and the expansion of production facilities. They were also permitted to retain 60 percent of their depreciation reserves for investment in plant and equipment. Under the Sichuan reforms a firm could process work from other factories once the requirements of the plan had been met and market those products manufactured by the factory that were not purchased by the state. These same firms were also authorized to export their products abroad and retain a portion of the foreign-exchange earnings. Finally, penalties could be levied on workers, managers, and party secretaries who through negligence were responsible for economic losses for the state.[2]

State-owned firms were encouraged to emulate the Sichuan reforms to such an extent that by June 1980, sixty-six hundred industrial enterprises were involved in the experiments and in 1981 a major campaign was launched to extend the Responsibility System to industrial enterprises. In October 1984 Deng announced that central planning would be curtailed and that a million state-owned enterprises would be cast loose to compete on their own in the marketplace and that extensive price subsidies would be gradually eliminated. Henceforth, factory wages and bonuses would be tied to job performance. Each production unit would be free to determine for itself its product mix, output levels, price, capital investments, raw material suppliers, and even marketing strategies. After the state is paid what amounts to a type of lease by the managers, then the managers are free to allocate the residual profits as they see fit to capital investment projects, the employees' welfare fund, employee bonuses, and wage increases. Plant foremen and section chiefs who were previously appointed by the party are now elected by the employees of the plant.

By 1986, there were almost twelve million private businesses in China—up from only 660,000 in 1980. Over fifteen million Chinese people now work in private businesses and 14 percent of all retail sales take place in private enterprises. Between 1980 and 1985 there was a 600-percent increase in retail and service shops, most of which are privately owned. Chinese entrepreneurs have opened nearly six million stores, one million restaurants, 800,000 transportation concerns, 750,000 repair shops, 640,000 service shops, and 40,000 home repair businesses.[3] Under Deng an enterprise is judged by its economic results rather than on the type of ownership system on which it is based—"It doesn't matter whether a cat is black or white, so long as it catches mice."

Not only were price controls removed for vegetables, meat, and other nonstaple farm products in 1985, but they were also eliminated for some consumer goods including bicycles, television sets, refrigerators, washing machines, and tape recorders. In 1986, price controls were lifted for another 750 consumer items. Even further reforms were mandated by the seventh five-year plan in 1986. The plan called for the removal of government at all levels from business and industry.

The point men for China's economic reforms are the professional managers who run the state-owned factories, mines, stores, hotels, and trading companies. Under Mao they simply followed the orders of party bureaucrats. With fixed wages and prices, and inferior standards of quality, the task of the manager was to achieve ever higher production goals. All of the profits went to the government to subsidize the unprofitable firms. Under the new system the general managers are responsible for the profitability of their respective enterprises. With no guaranteed customers, each manager must find reliable suppliers and pay special attention to product quality and delivery schedules. Firms can now diversify into more profitable lines. The managers can decide which employees to reward, promote, and, if necessary, to fire. They have discretion over the allocation of profits. The new breed of Chinese manager is among the strongest supporters of Deng's economic reforms.

Thus in less than ten years Deng has managed to put in place most of the industrial reforms that Hungary took nearly thirty years to implement. Gorbachev seems to be trying to accomplish the same feat in less than five years.

In 1985, overall Chinese industrial output increased by 18 percent; rural industrial production shot up by 35 percent. Output of washing machines, electric fans, and television sets increased over 50 percent, and the production of refrigerators more than doubled. Output of building materials, heavy equipment, and machinery increased on average by about 15 percent. Investment spending soared by 35 percent in 1985.

One result of the new, market-oriented socialism in China has been a dramatic improvement in the standard of living. Per capita income increased from $300 a year in 1980 to $450 in 1985, thus pulling China well ahead of India and Pakistan, which have per capita incomes of $300 and $390, respectively. Bicycles, radios, and watches, which were scarce only a few years ago, are commonplace. Television sets, washing machines, refrigerators, and other electrical appliances are streaming into the prosperous countryside. Chinese women in fur coats shop for Western-style clothes in shops alongside workers in Mao jackets.

The Open-Door Policy

Shortly after the PRC was established in 1949, the Western powers led by the United States clamped a trade embargo on China. China countered with its own closed-door policy and was forced to turn to the Soviets for technical assistance and equipment. The Korean War made it easier for Mao to convince the Chinese that the Americans, whom they had generally liked, were their enemies, and that the Russians, whom they had traditionally disliked, were their friends.

By 1960, Mao and Khrushchev had grown apart, and the Soviets withdrew their technical assistance and abandoned 161 of the 291 planned Chinese–Soviet joint projects. China then sought economic independence from the Soviet Union and the West, and embarked on a policy of "self-reliance" until 1978, when Deng opened China's trade doors to the rest of the world. He has put together an extremely effective package of foreign-trade reforms including free-trade zones, decentralized foreign trade, improved infrastructure to support foreign trade, trade fairs and exhibitions, foreign credit, and new forms of economic cooperation. By the end of 1985, Chinese trade was approaching the $60 billion mark. In less than ten years, China has moved away from a policy of isolationism towards an open trade policy.

Among the more widely acclaimed aspects of China's Open-Door Policy are the special economic zones (SEZs)—four areas on the southern coast of China that have been designated to attract foreign investments. They include Shenzhen, located on the Hong Kong border; Zhuhai, located on the Macao border; Shantou; and Xiamen. The SEZs, fourteen open cities, Hainan Island, and three river delta areas are akin to foreign-trade zones in the United States. Between 1980 and 1984 the SEZs attracted more than $1 billion in direct foreign investment. Over $700 million of that foreign investment was directed to Shenzhen. In 1985 Shenzhen's output was estimated to be close to $700 million, up from $20 million in 1979.[4]

In 1979, the foreign-trade companies in certain designated cities and provinces were given the authority to conduct foreign trade directly with foreign firms. To support China's commitment to increased foreign trade, the government has increased its investments in the construction of railroads, the acquisition of new aircraft for its airlines, the development of communications networks including communications satellites, the modernization of harbors and wharves, and the expansion of the merchant-marine fleet. China now aggressively participates in trade fairs and exhibitions throughout the world to promote the sale of its low-cost, high-quality goods.

China has abandoned its policy of not accepting aid or loans from foreign countries. In 1980 it joined the International Monetary Fund and the World Bank and now accepts loans from foreign governments as well as private financial institutions. It participates in different types of economic cooperation and exchanges with foreign countries including joint ventures, compensatory trade, licensing agreements, and sales and purchase contracts.

Major investment projects at home and abroad are directed and controlled by the Foreign Investment Commission. The Import–Export Commission is primarily responsible for drafting legislation to regulate China's imports and exports and overseeing these activities. The Ministry of Foreign Trade formulates foreign trade plans; these must be approved by the Foreign Investment Commission and implemented by the foreign-trade corporations. To attract foreign investments for economic construction and the "socialist modernization" of China, the government relies on the China International Trust and Investment Corporation (CITIC). These foreign-trade organizations operate at the provincial and municipal levels as well. The central banking functions of China are divided between the Bank of China, which handles all international financial transactions, and the People's Bank of China, which specializes in domestic financial activities.[5]

Since 1949 China has gone through several periods of expansion in capital investments followed by periods of retrenchment. Each time investments were cut back at home, imports from abroad were reduced as well. Shortly after the auspicious beginnings of China's new trade policies in 1977, Deng temporarily backed away from some foreign-trade commitments. Both in late 1979 and again in 1981, purchase commitments that had previously been agreed upon were delayed and the confidence of many foreign traders and suppliers of equipment and machinery was adversely affected. Although the economy temporarily faltered, the liberal economic policies of Deng continued, but under a tighter reign. Restrictions were placed on foreign imports in 1985 and 1986 because of balance-of-payments problems and shortages of foreign exchange to pay for those imports.

When the Chinese began pursuing trade with the United States, they realized that they did not have a good image there. To improve their image they retained the services of Ogilvy and Mather, a leading U.S. advertising and public relations firm. They also hired two lobbyists to represent them in Washington. In addition, the China United Trading Corporation (CUTC) was established in the United States. The objectives of CUTC are (1) to promote Sino–U.S. trade; (2) to assist Chinese producers in competing in the U.S. market; (3) to introduce foreign investments in China; (4) to import advanced technology and equipment; and (5) to organize joint ventures.

Since 1980, foreign investment in China has amounted to $14.6 billion, of which about $1 billion was provided by thirty U.S. companies. A dozen U.S. oil companies including Exxon, Occidental, and Pennzoil have invested heavily in off-shore exploration and drilling projects on China's southern coast. Other companies that have set up manufacturing plants in China include R. J. Reynolds, McDonnell Douglas, Otis Elevator, and Pepsico. Pepsico opened a second bottling plant in Canton on the heels of an earlier joint venture in Shenzhen. Only two U.S. companies, 3M and W. R. Grace, have been authorized to operate wholly-owned subsidiaries in China. Other U.S. companies that are actively promoting their products in China include General Foods, IBM, Coca-Cola, Procter & Gamble, Boeing, Colgate-Palmolive, and Eastman Kodak. Some smaller U.S. firms have started doing business in China. The Chinese find that the smaller companies are more flexible, can make decisions more quickly, and sometimes are willing to work on smaller profit margins. On the negative side, many small companies find the high costs of doing business in China to be unmanageable—particularly the inordinate delays that can result from attempting to cope with the Chinese bureaucracy.

Western manufacturers of nuclear power plants felt the sting of China's foreign-currency shortages in March 1986, when the Chinese dropped plans to purchase two nuclear power plants valued at nearly $2 billion, after months of bidding for the contract by foreign companies such as Siemens of West Germany, Framatome of France, and

Westinghouse Electric of Pittsburgh. The expectations of leading nuclear power plant suppliers had previously been raised by Beijing's
initial plans to build with foreign assistance between eight and twelve
nuclear reactors valued at as much as $20 billion. Insufficient foreign
currency and capital reserves were cited as reasons for not going ahead
with the nuclear projects.[6]

In 1986, U.S. businesspeople became quite outspoken in their criticisms of Chinese business practices including an inflexible bureaucracy, poorly organized support services, inefficient local employees,
soaring costs, price gouging, tight foreign-exchange controls, limited
access to the domestic market, arbitrary tax and tariff levies, and
unpredictability. The Chinese responded in October 1986 with a new
twenty-two-article investment code that promised reduced taxes, lower
land and utility charges, greater autonomy for joint ventures, access
to bank loans, and exemption from some subsidies that have forced
up labor costs.

In the past, U.S.-imposed export controls on high-technology
products were a serious impediment to U.S. firms wanting to trade
with China. Recently the Reagan administration has been bending
over backwards to ease these restrictions as Sino–U.S. relations continue to improve. In October 1986, the United States agreed to sell
China $500 million worth of radar and related equipment to mod-
ernize fifty Chinese F-8 fighters. Persistent reports that Israel has been
supplying China with military equipment may have influenced Washington to liberalize its export policies towards China. The Chinese
have shown an increasing appetite for Israeli skills in agriculture,
advanced technology, robotics, construction, and arms manufacturing. The Chinese interest in trading with Israel is particularly interesting in light of the fact that Beijing not only does not have diplomatic
relations with Israel but regularly denounces Israel in international
forums. This is seen as further evidence of China's new economic
policies, which are aimed at achieving rapid industrial development
by acquiring Western methods and technologies from any country
that is willing to trade with them. While purchasing arms and military
equipment from the United States and Israel, China has simultaneously become one of the world's leading arms exporters. In 1985
it sold $2 billion worth of relatively unsophisticated weapons to Third
World countries. But at the opposite end of the technological spec-
trum, China has entered the commercial satellite launching business.

China posted a record $7.61 billion trade deficit in 1985 as its total foreign trade climbed to $59.21 billion, up 19 percent for 1984. Bilateral trade between China and the United States in 1985 amounted to approximately $7.9 billion compared with $6.4 billion in 1983 and only $934 million in 1974. U.S. exports to China in 1985 were $3.7 billion and included such things as fertilizer, polyester fibers, computers, office equipment, industrial machinery, and process control instruments. Chinese exports to the United States came to $4.2 billion and included gasoline, crude oil, textiles, and clothing. China's principal trading partner is its island neighbor Japan. Trade between China and Japan is approximately twice as great as trade between China and the United States. Color television sets, automobiles, VCRs, and other consumer goods all contributed to China's substantial trade deficit with Japan in 1985. In 1986, China began running up substantial trade deficits with EEC countries—particularly with the FRG.

Many of the Chinese trade reforms began to show up in the Soviet Union during the second half of 1986—decentralized foreign trade activities, joint ventures, foreign credit, and new forms of economic cooperation.

Finance and Banking

Early one morning in February 1985, hundreds of residents of Shanghai stood in line for several hours to sign up for the first public offering of common stock in China since the Shanghai Stock Exchange closed in 1949. On the one hand, this public offering of stock by the Yanzhong Industrial Corporation represented a cautious step forward during a new period of corporate fund-raising mandated by reform-minded leaders in Beijing. On the other hand, it represented a step back to the past in what had been China's largest commercial and financial center before the communists seized power in 1949. Yanzhong is a diversified manufacturing company. In 1984, it had twelve plants, twenty-five hundred employees, and profits of approximately $535,000. Most of the shares of Yanzhong were bought by state-owned enterprises, collective institutions, and the Bank of China. However, a small number of the shares was made available to private individuals. The attraction of the shares lay in the initial dividend rate, which was set at 13 percent annually—twice the prevailing bank rate.[7]

Selling stock to the public is further evidence of the shift towards autonomous enterprises under Deng Xiaoping. Under the new rules in China, companies are required to pay various taxes on their profits but may keep the rest for themselves. Instead of receiving direct investment allocations from the state, enterprises finance their growth from retained earnings, bank loans, and other financial instruments including the sale of common stock. Some Chinese believe that the stock offering by Yanzhong Industrial Corporation may lead to similar stock offerings by other companies and eventually to the reopening of the Shanghai Stock Exchange. There is now a very active debate in China between those who consider a stock market to be essential to the efficient allocation of capital and those who regard a stock market as too deep a plunge towards full-scale capitalism.

Like Hungary, China has developed a complete portfolio of financial institutions and financial instruments to finance its rapid economic growth. Recent innovations include personal checking accounts, merchant banks, joint-venture banks, and multiservice money institutions. The newly created Bank of Communications in Shanghai is partially financed by private individual shareholders. The CITIC has been decentralized into a number of independent subsidiaries including a real estate company, a bank, a trading company, and a company to focus on investment and joint ventures. CITIC recently paid $256 million for 12.5 percent of the common shares of Hong Kong–based Cathay Pacific Airways—one of the best managed and most profitable airlines in the world. China made its debut into the Eurodollar-bond market in 1986 by issuing bonds in the name of the Bank of China. Chinese banks began issuing Visa credit cards in 1987.

Representatives of the Soviet Ministry of Foreign Trade have expressed considerable interest in the financial and banking reforms implemented by China and Hungary. Inquiries have been made about possible Soviet membership in the International Monetary Fund and the World Bank. Soviet officials clearly understand the importance of monetary reforms to the success of Gorbachev's economic strategies.

Law and Politics

Both the political and legal systems were in shambles when Deng Xiaoping took over the leadership of China. During the Cultural Revolution the law was interpreted by Mao and his followers as an instrument of class struggle. Many laws were either suspended outright or simply not enforced.

A new constitution went into effect on 1 January 1980. It dealt with such issues as local and national elections, criminal law, courts, joint ventures, and foreign investment. One of the aims of the new legal system was to create a national system of courts free from ad hoc local influence. It also provided a framework in which private property and land ownership could be reestablished. Above all it provided some reassurance to intellectuals and technocrats that another Cultural Revolution could not occur.

Between 1978 and 1981, the Chinese courts were kept busy reviewing and redressing legal cases that had been tried during the Cultural Revolution. The most visible display of the new legal system took place in 1981 when Jiang Qing and her three associates were tried and convicted of attempting to overthrow the government. Today, at least in theory, it is no longer possible to be sent to prison in China without a trial. However, the evolving Chinese legal system still places more emphasis on protecting the state and preserving social order than on protecting individual rights.

At the core of the Chinese political system is the chinese Communist Party (CCP), which consists of forty million members. Although eight other political parties are recognized, their influence is minimal. The National People's Congress (NPC), which meets annually, is the highest organ of state power in China. The party is decentralized down through the various levels of government—provinces, counties, cities, communes, towns, and districts. Party branches and committees operate within schools, factories, neighborhoods, and even detachments of the People's Liberation Army. At the national level, members of the party elect the central committee and nominate representatives, called deputies, to the NPC. Since 1979, a small number of deputies has been nominated from the other parties as well.

The executive branch of the NPC is called the State Council and it is the highest administrative organization in China. Local-level equivalents of the NPC and the State Council exist for all levels of government in China. The State Council consists of the premier, the vice premiers, the ministers, and the ministers responsible for the various commissions under the State Council.

The CCP still sets the ideological tone in China today. It calls for the adherence of four basic principles: (1) following the socialist road; (2) practicing proletarian dictatorship; (3) accepting the leadership of the CCP; and (4) following Marxism-Leninism-Maoist thought.[8]

For all practical purposes, China is still a single-party state. The power to set national priorities and make major policy decisions continues to reside in the hands of the CCP. However, increasingly Deng appears to be willing to consider additional political reforms to make China more democratic. The government has been given more authority to make day-to-day policy decisions. Chinese citizens can be directly elected as representatives to county and local legislative bodies. In Beijing multiple candidates are permitted to run for each seat in municipal legislative elections. Legislators have been given more authority to question and criticize administrators. Although China is hardly a liberal democracy, most of the political changes are in the right direction and are similar to those we have seen taking place in Hungary.

Deng Xiaoping inherited two unwieldly bureaucracies—the Chinese government and the Communist party. As a result of the absence of a mandatory retirement system, many officials appointed in the early 1950s were still in office—many too old and feeble to put in a full day's work. Most of the party officials were recruited on the basis of their "class background" or "revolutionary credentials" rather than on the basis of their educational and administrative backgrounds. Many of these party officials had only a primary-school education.

Under Deng, China is engaged in a program of radical reform that is at least as sweeping as anything attempted by Mao. Not unlike Mao on the eve of the Cultural Revolution, Deng is an old man who realizes that he has only limited time to chart a suitable course for China into the twenty-first century. To rejuvenate the party and the state, Deng implemented a campaign which by the end of 1985 had resulted in the retirement of a million civil servants and tens of thousands of military officers. At one meeting in September 1985, Deng announced the retirement of sixty-four members of the central committee of the CCP and ten members of the Politburo, most of whom were in their seventies and eighties and had served under Mao. In an attempt to bring new vitality to the hierarchy these old leaders were replaced by younger, better-educated, and more pragmatic leaders.

Unlike the political and economic reforms in Poland, the Chinese,

Hungarian, and Soviet reforms have all been initiated at the highest levels of government. However, all of this changed in December 1986 in China, when tens of thousands of students took to the streets in Shanghai calling for greater democracy, student rights, and increased freedom. It is unclear whether or not these demonstrations were spontaneous or whether they enjoyed the support of Deng. What is known is that Deng and General Secretary Hu Yaobang had become more vocal during the early part of 1986 in calling for increased political reform. Shortly after the end of the student demonstrations in January 1987, Hu was forced to resign and was replaced by Premier Zhao Ziyang. Although the exact reasons underlying Hu's forced resignation were not revealed, his departure has not adversely affected the economic reforms. However, anticapitalistic rhetoric did increase in 1987.

Would the Soviet government ever permit student demonstrations of this sort in Moscow? If so, how would Soviet officials respond? With rising expectations among the Soviet people for increased economic and political reforms, it is only a matter of time before Soviet leaders will have to deal with such questions. By early 1987, Soviet leader Gorbachev had begun to devote more attention to political reforms, including secret ballot and multicandidate elections. Just as was the case in China, economic reforms in the Soviet Union seem to be opening the door to political reforms.

Cultural Reforms

The single most important lesson that Gorbachev has learned from Deng is how to go about confronting the culture of a risk-free society if one wants to introduce radical economic, political, and foreign-policy reforms. This factor was the key to Deng's success, and it will be the determining factor in whether Gorbachev succeeds in the Soviet Union.

Under Chairman Mao the channels of upward mobility were choked off by abolishing the private sector and the rewards it offered. The scope of available opportunities was narrowed by doing away with such high-prestige professions as law and banking and playing down the importance of professionals in general. Distinctions of achievement such as military rank, academic titles, and degrees for students were abolished by overemphasizing political attitudes and practicing an extreme form of egalitarianism. To achieve the goals of the Four Modernizations, Deng introduced government policies aimed at making the achievement drive and innovation more respectable. He initiated educational reforms and expanded the public education system at all levels including kindergartens, primary schools, middle schools, vocational schools, and institutions of higher education. Student, faculty, and other types of academic exchange programs are strongly encouraged and supported with the United States, Canada, Japan, and Western Europe.

One measure of the success of Deng's campaign to make the Chinese more achievement oriented is that Chinese families now have substantially more disposable income to spend on consumer goods. Ten years ago a Chinese family might have had its heart set on the "four musts"—a bicycle, a radio, a watch, and a sewing machine. Today no young Chinese couple wants to be without the "eight big things"—a color television set, refrigerator, stereo system, camera, motorcycle, modern furnished flat, washing machine, and electric fan. And when the typical young Chinese woman says she is looking for a man with the "three highs," she is thinking of salary, level of education, and a height of at least 5 feet 6 inches. Under Deng political slogans about egalitarianism and continuing revolution have been replaced by the message that "It's okay to get rich!" Among the more opulent signs of Chinese affluence are women dressed in fine furs; posh golf clubs and country clubs; and Cadillac and Mercedes-Benz limousines.

Although Deng's reforms are every bit as comprehensive and radical as Mao's, Deng takes a more incremental and fragmented approach that involves the use of compromise, cooption, and preemption to deal with potential opponents. Some have described his political style as one characterized by "bobbing and weaving." Deng has displayed amazing flexibility and has consistently avoided being backed into a corner by his opponents.

Since 1949 the government has invested heavily in the improvement of the health of the Chinese people. One measure of the effectiveness of its investment in health-care services has been the sharp decline in the annual death rate from 17 deaths per 1,000 people in 1952 to 6.6 deaths per 1,000 people in 1982.

China has a very extensive three-level health-care system that is managed and financed locally. At the commune level, the so-called "barefoot doctors," who are part-time rural paramedical workers, provide preventive and primary care. The barefoot doctors are organized by the communes and financed by their welfare funds. Patients who are more seriously ill are referred to the second level of the system, which consists of commune health centers. These typically include an outpatient clinic and twenty-five to thirty beds, and serve a population of fifteen to twenty thousand people with a staff of junior doctors who have received two or three years of training after high school. County hospitals staffed by senior doctors trained in Western medicine represent the third level of the Chinese health-care delivery system. Unfortunately, China's broad-based, low-cost health-care system has been adversely affected by the fact that barefoot doctors are being lured away from medicine by farming and rural industries, both of which have become more profitable under Deng's rural reforms. The system is being further undercut by the fact that more affluent Chinese prefer and can afford private medical care.

Not unrelated to the sharp decrease in the death rate in China is the fact that China's population increased by 78 percent between 1949 and 1979 and now stands at over one billion people. Whereas Mao was ideologically opposed to birth control, Deng actively supports policies aimed at achieving a target of zero population growth by the year 2000. Among the population programs that are vigorously supported by the Chinese government are (1) education and information about the use of birth control methods; (2) free contraceptives; (3) free sterilization for men and women, and induced abortions; (4) significant material incentives to induce couples to subscribe to the official one-child policy; (5) economic sanctions to discourage couples from having more than two children; and (6) a shift in the legal age for men to marry from twenty to twenty-two.[9]

After attempting to abolish religion between 1957 and 1976, the government reversed itself in 1982 by adopting a new policy on religious freedom. It is estimated that there are three million Catholics, three million Protestants, seventeen million Moslems, a half million Taoists, and between 150 and 200 million Buddhists in China today. Before the 1982 constitution was adopted, the official position on religious freedom read: "Citizens enjoy the freedom not to believe in religion and to propagate atheism." The text of the new Constitution reads:

> Citizens of the People's Republic of China enjoy freedom of religious belief. No state organ, public organization, or individual may compel citizens to believe or not believe in any religion; nor may they discriminate against citizens who believe in or do not believe in any religion.

In 1985, the Beitang Church in Beijing was restored and reopened. It had been closed since the 1950s and was used by Maoist Red Guards as a warehouse in the 1960s. The church was restored by the Catholic Patriotic Association, the official group that has run Catholicism in China since Mao forced Chinese Catholics in 1957 to sever their ties with Rome. This was but one of several churches reopened in 1985 in Beijing, Shanghai, and Tianjin. In July 1985, the Beijing government released an eighty-four-year-old Catholic prelate, the Most Reverend Ignatius Hung, the Bishop of Shanghai, who had been imprisoned thirty years before for refusing to break ties with Rome and recognize the Patriotic Catholic Association. Following on the heels of these developments, Pope John Paul II issued a warm message of praise to the people of China. "The Church is sympathetic to the commitment to modernization and progress in which the Chinese people are encouraged. The Catholic Church looks upon China as one great family, the birthplace of lofty traditions and vital energies rooted in the antiquity of her history and culture."

In his efforts to meld a unique blend of socialism and capitalism, Deng has also encountered the dark side of both of these systems. Although the Responsibility System has brought bustling markets and new-found prosperity to the countryside, many farmers now find it necessary to spend their nights watching their fields to prevent others from stealing their crops. Collectively built dams and irrigation systems have also been dismantled by private farmers looking out only for themselves. In the cities, private enterprise has produced a black market not only for currency but for illegally imported jeans, tape recorders, and other consumer goods. The police in Shenzhen recently had to crack down on a baby-selling ring being run by peasant mothers. There is evidence of decay in the social order that can be traced to the political and economic liberalization since the death of Mao. This decay has taken the form of increases in crime, corruption, prostitution, and pornography.

By encouraging some Chinese to become rich, resentment has been created on the part of those who have been left behind. "Red-eye disease" is the term used by the Chinese to describe this form of envy of those who have prospered under the new socialism. There are even cases of poor peasants attacking or sabotaging their more affluent neighbors. Some critics argue that Deng may be setting the stage for a new outbreak of class struggle by creating pockets of wealth. Others say this is the price of progress. One can only speculate as to how long it will be before "red-eye disease" spreads across the Sino–Soviet border into the Soviet Union. What remedies will Gorbachev prescribe for this ancient disease?

The Future of Market Socialism in China

The sweeping economic, political, and cultural changes set in motion by China's leaders since 1978 have resulted in an almost total reinterpretation of the country's official communist ideology. They have peeled away, and in some cases actually repudiated, many of the familiar tenets of Marx, Lenin, and Mao that retarded the nation's ability to modernize itself. The personality cult of Mao Zedong has been scrapped and the call for class struggle has been muted. Beijing no longer advocates exporting revolution but rather encourages the importation of Western technology and expertise. The political dogmatism of the sayings in Chairman Mao's little red book has been replaced by the search for ways to rationalize dismantling the agricultural communes and cutting back central planning.

But Deng cannot afford to discard Marxism completely because that would undermine the mandate of the CCP, which has ruled since 1949. It would also be too threatening to the forty million members of the party who have made careers out of communism. While retaining the centralized party structure of Lenin, Deng has moved decisively away from the highly centralized economic planning model of Stalin and Mao and reduced many of the Marxist beliefs to mere ritual. He seems to be much more interested in seeking practical, realistic solutions to China's enormous economic problems rather than engaging in polemical discussions about political ideology.

But Deng's march towards market socialism has not been without some serious economic problems that are the result of attempts to reform a highly centralized, planned economic system based on a completely irrational pricing mechanism. These include overinvestment, shortages of foreign currency, shortages of materials, inflation, state deficits, and the allocation of resources to low-payoff projects. There have been occasional calls by conservative party members to reimpose central control and thus effectively delay or even reverse the economic reforms. But Deng has always managed to fight off these pressures to reverse the course of the reforms.

Although China does not yet have a national bankruptcy law such as the one implemented by the Hungarians in 1986, the merits of such a proposed law are now being widely debated. Several municipal governments have experimented with their own local bankruptcy laws with some degree of success in closing down poorly managed, inefficient enterprises.

China introduced a graduated personal income tax in 1987 aimed at narrowing the growing gap between the rich and the poor. The People's Bank of China has established the first Western-style graduate school of business in China. Just as was the case in Hungary, management education remains a particularly serious problem in China today. However, the Chinese have not been hesitant to send managers and students to MBA programs in the United States.

The Chinese continue to worry about the moral and social consequences of a more liberal economic system—greed, corruption, and injustice. Deng warned in 1985 that only socialism can eliminate these evils that are inherent in capitalism. The young people in China must feel considerable tension as they attempt to sort out the differences and conflicts between the ideology of the past and the new political ideas and social values associated with Western capital, technology, and consumer goods. Thus far Deng has been able to channel the energy released by the conflicts in ideology into creative, constructive activities that have been of great benefit to China.

There is still some political opposition to Deng's reforms. On the left, for those who subscribe to the egalitarianism, populism, and self-sufficiency of Mao, there is concern over inequities in the implementation of the economic reforms between richer and poorer peasants, between skilled and unskilled workers, and between coastal and interior regions. There have also been complaints that China has become too closely aligned with the United States. This caused the Chinese leaders to announce a more "independent" foreign policy in 1982 even though the Open-Door Policy remained unaltered.

The strongest opposition to Deng's reforms comes from the political center. Some party leaders are concerned about the declining influence of Marxist-Leninist ideology and Maoist revolutionary leadership; they fear this departure will lead to an increase in dissent and disunity. Opposition also comes from the military leadership, which is less than enthusiastic about rural reforms that provide incentives to peasants. Recruiting and retaining soldiers have been hampered by the Responsibility System, which has made it more attractive for peasants to work at home. Military officers are also disheartened by the slow pace of military modernization, cuts in military spending in recent years, and the low priority given by the party leadership to the purchase of sophisticated weapons abroad. Since 1979, defense spending has continued to decrease as a percentage of total budget expenditures, reflecting the reduced priority given to the military sector under Deng. With regard to defense expenditures, China appears to be much more interested in emulating the Japanese rather than the Americans or the Soviets. There is also opposition to the liberalization of the Chinese economy from the ministries of heavy industry and from the central planning bureaucrats who see their influence being threatened by consumerism and the marketplace.

Although on more than one occasion, including 1987, Deng has had to slow the pace of his reform movement, these lapses have always been temporary. Overall the direction remains the same. The Open-Door Policy and the Responsibility System remain the bulwarks of the Chinese reforms.

Three aspects of economic reform will be emphasized in China's seventh five-year plan (1986–90):

1. The vitality of state-owned enterprises will be strengthened by making them more independent and responsible for their own profits and losses. They will be given more autonomy in purchasing, marketing, personnel, finance, and materials. They

will also be encouraged to combine and cooperate with other enterprises where appropriate and enter market competition.

2. The plan calls for the further development and strengthening of markets for agricultural products, consumer goods, and production materials as well as the opening of markets for capital and technology.

3. The state will switch from a system of direct administrative control over state-owned enterprises to an indirect control system. The new administrative control system will be exercised through macroeconomic fiscal and monetary policies. The objective is to develop a "socialist commodity" economy, expand productive forces, and improve living standards.

The five-year plan calls for an annual growth rate of industrial and agricultural output of 6.7 percent over the 1986–90 planning horizon. By the year 2000, China's goal is to raise its GNP to the $1 trillion level—the equivalent of Japan's current GNP. It also hopes to increase its per capita income to $800 per year from the present level of $450 per year. To achieve these goals, China must keep a lid on its population growth. At the present its one-family-one-child policy has reduced the population growth rate to 1.3 percent a year.

China will concentrate on developing energy, transportation, and telecommunications. It plans to invest heavily in telephones, commercial aircraft, locomotives, and electric power plants with the help of Western technology and capital. The Civil Aviation Administration of China (CAAC), which regulates civilian aviation and operates China's state-owned airline, will soon give up its operations role and spin off at least four independent airlines. The new airlines include Air China, based in Beijing, which will primarily operate international routes; Eastern Airways in Shanghai; Southern Airways in Guangzhou; and South-Western Airways in the province of Sichuan. CAAC has announced commitments to purchase a substantial number of new commercial jets from Europe's Airbus Industries, Boeing, and McDonnell Douglas. The McDonnell Douglas jets will actually be assembled in Shanghai.

The central committee of the CCP continues to reaffirm China's commitment to economic modernization, while warning against corruption and other evils. The party recently called for greater freedom of expression "to encourage and support all bold explorative efforts in order to democratize our policymaking process and give our decisions a more scientific basis."

Gorbachev is now confronting many of the same political problems in the Soviet Union that Deng has faced since 1978. By his own admission, Gorbachev is experiencing substantial opposition to some of his radical policies, both from party leaders and Soviet bureaucrats. But the fact that János Kádár and Deng Xiaoping have been able to overcome enormous internal political obstacles to their reforms and have still managed to survive politically must provide some encouragement to Gorbachev.

China: Through a Jaundiced Eye

Sino–Soviet relations have improved significantly since 1960, when Khrushchev withdrew all of the Soviet engineers and technicians who had been working in China in the 1950s. As a result of border disputes and ideological differences between Khrushchev and Chairman Mao, political relations between the two countries remained in a deep freeze until 1982, when Brezhnev invited China to end their twenty-year estrangement. As recently as the period 1978–82, the Soviets appeared to be visibly concerned with Deng Xiaoping's revisionist approach to Marxist-Leninist ideology.

Although Chinese–Soviet relations have continued to improve since 1982, China has not dropped its three demands as conditions for the normalization of political relations—that the USSR withdraw its troops from Afghanistan, reduce its military presence on the Chinese border, and discontinue its support of the Vietnamese occupation of Cambodia.

Under Gorbachev the rate of improvement in Sino–Soviet relations has accelerated. In July 1985, the Soviet Union and China agreed to double trade over the next five years. Before relations began improving between the two countries in 1982, trade between China and the Soviet Union was approximately $300 million. By 1985 two-way trade was $1.8 billion and was expected to reach $3.5 billion by 1990.

The Soviets have also agreed to aid the Chinese in building seven new plants and in modernizing seventeen others in such diverse fields as electric power generation, coal mining, chemicals, transportation, and machinery manufacturing. Some of these plants to be modernized were actually built with Soviet assistance during the 1950s. The Soviets have also indicated they plan to sell the Chinese two nuclear plants worth $2 billion and large amounts of timber. The Chinese in turn will provide the Soviets with food, agricultural products, textiles, and light industrial goods. China has also increased its political contacts and trade relations with Eastern European countries. In September 1986, General Wojciech Jaruzelski visited Beijing—the first Polish head of state to visit China in twenty-seven years. His visit was followed one month later by a visit by the GDR's Erich Honecker. Exports to China have recently become an important source of hard currency for Poland. China's message to the Soviet bloc is that trade and economic likages can be rebuilt, but that China will remain staunchly independent and defend its territorial boundaries.

At the Soviet party congress, Gorbachev effusively praised the ability of the Soviet Union and China to "cooperate on an equal and principled basis." In his 1986 Vladivostok speech, Gorbachev became even more specific about Soviet relations with China:

> [T]he Soviet Union is prepared—at any time and at any level—to discuss with China questions of additional measures for creating an atmosphere of good-neighborliness. We hope that the border dividing (I would prefer to say linking) us will become a line of peace and friendship in the near future.
>
> [W]e have similar priorities as China—those of accelerating social and economic development. Why not support each other, why not co-operate in implementing our plans whenever this will clearly benefit both sides? The better the relations, the more we shall be able to exchange our experience.

Gorbachev went on to say that the Soviet Union would withdraw six regiments from Afghanistan and that it was considering the withdrawal of its troops from Mongolia, which borders China. Gorbachev proposed a joint Soviet–Chinese space exploration project as well as a joint project to exploit the Amur River on the Chinese–Soviet border. He also indicated his positive response to a Soviet–Chinese rail-way plan.

In September 1986, Deng Xiaoping said, "If the Soviet Union can contribute to the withdrawal of Vietnamese troops from Cambodia, this will remove the main obstacle in Chinese–Soviet relations. Once this problem is resolved, I will be ready to meet Gorbachev."

There is little doubt that the Soviets are impressed with the results of the Chinese reforms. They appreciate the fact that the Chinese have replicated many of the Hungarian reforms in a country that contains one-fifth of the world's population and that this incredible feat has been accomplished in less than ten years. The Soviets see in China mounting evidence that the Japanese model of trade and economic development is transferable to different countries and different cultures.

Under Mao, China became the largest risk-free society in the world. But Deng has introduced a variety of economic, political, and social reforms that have increased the amount of personal risk assumed by individual Chinese. Contrary to the initial fears of Soviet leaders, the results of the reforms have been extremely positive for the entire country. Deng has shown that it is possible to implement radical reforms without causing the expectations of the people to exceed the ability or willingness of the government to deliver on the next round of reforms. Is Gorbachev paying attention to what is happening in China and Hungary? You bet he is!

5
The Globalization of the Soviet Economy

I n no other area are Gorbachev's reforms more sweeping than in the field of international trade. His fundamental objective is to strengthen the Soviet economy and reduce international political tensions through a strategy of increased global interdependence based on bilateral trade between the Soviet Union and the rest of the world. To achieve his goal of integrating the Soviet economy into the global economy, Gorbachev has centralized Soviet foreign-trade policy while simultaneously decentralizing foreign trade.

The relatively poor performance of the Soviet economy is obviously an important force motivating Gorbachev to pursue a strategy of international trade and tension reduction. The Soviets must increase their exports to the West to finance their much-needed imports of consumer goods, technology, and foodstuffs. Gorbachev also seems to have learned from Japan that the rules of international politics have changed, and that the number of nuclear warheads in a nation's arsenal is not nearly such an important measure of political power as it once was. Economic clout has become a more important indicator of political influence than military might. International trade has replaced the arms race as the driving force of international politics.

What is particularly striking about the dramatic changes in Soviet trade policies is their strong similarity to the trade reforms instituted by the Hungarians and the Chinese in the late 1970s and early 1980s. Just as in Hungary and China, some twenty-one Soviet ministries and seventy state-owned enterprises can now trade directly with the West. Foreign companies may own up to 49 percent of the equity in Soviet joint-venture companies. Repatriation of profits, reinvestment tax incentives, third-country operations, and expropriation protection are all part of the package. These joint ventures may own assets; but they may not own land or buildings, which they must lease from the government.

The Soviets settled czarist debts to the United Kingdom in 1986 to facilitate entry into the Eurobond market; sought observer status in the General Agreement on Tariffs and Trade (GATT) as well as formal ties with the EEC; cooperated with OPEC to drive up oil prices; and expressed interest in the International Monetary Fund, the World Bank, and Chinese-like "special trade zones." The simultaneous publication in December 1986 of a special issue on U.S.–Soviet trade in *The Journal of Commerce* and the Soviet *Ekonomicheskaya Gazeta* provides even more evidence of the increased importance of foreign trade to the Soviets—not to mention the four-page advertisement on Soviet trade and joint-venture opportunities that appeared in the *International Herald Tribune*.

Soviet Trade Needs

As a result of a sharp decline in commodity prices and crude oil prices, overall Soviet trade declined by 8 percent in 1986 to 130 billion rubles or $196.5 billion, of which 67 percent was with socialist countries. To make up for shortfalls in the production of agricultural commodities, the Soviets import substantial quantities of agricultural products from the West—particularly grain. Limited supplies of high-quality consumer goods have also caused the Soviets to turn to the West.

With priority being given to modernizing Soviet factories, the Soviets are increasing their imports of machinery and equipment—particularly machine tools, energy-related equipment, and computers. In 1985, Soviet orders included a $1.3 million contract for microcomputers and printers from Japan and a $4 million order from a U.S. company to modernize a shoe factory. To produce a new model of the Moskvich car, the Soviets have ordered machinery from Western suppliers to modernize a manufacturing plant. These equipment orders include a $58 million contract with Renault in France. The largest contract awarded in 1985 was with an Italian firm for a $1 billion turnkey project in the steel industry. To close their technological gap with the West, the Soviets are implementing a unique Western buying strategy combined with an internal development and educational program.

To finance their imports the Soviets depend heavily on the export of natural resources. Minerals, ores, and metals account for over 60 percent of the value of their exports. Eighty percent of the value of their exports to the West and 40 percent of their exports to Eastern Europe are in the form of energy—primarily oil and natural gas. Lower international oil prices and the falling U.S. dollar have made it more difficult for the Soviets to obtain hard currency to finance imports.

The Soviets must either reduce imports, increase exports, or borrow more money from the West to finance their hard-currency imports. Given the ambitious objectives of FYP12 for increased availability of high-quality consumer goods, modernization of Soviet factories, and improved technology, the only area where it may be feasible to reduce imports is agriculture.

Arms sales to the Third World are Moscow's second largest source of hard currency after oil (table 5–1). Because the economies of several of the Soviets' Middle Eastern clients are dependent on the price of oil, Soviet arms sales to the Third World decreased in 1985. The Soviets also sell diamonds and gold to generate hard currency, but both of these markets have been depressed by large South African sales.

In the short run, the Soviets may also finance their trade deficit by borrowing more money from the West. In 1984, the London-based, Soviet-owned Moscow Narodny Bank issued $50 million in Eurobonds in what is believed to be the first such issue to foreign investors since the revolution in 1917. In 1986, for the first time, the Soviet Union participated directly in a Eurobond offering of its own. Syndicated Western bank loans to the Soviets jumped to $2.3 billion during the first six months of 1986, up from $1.5 billion for the entire year in 1985 and $100 million in 1983. Because the Soviet Union maintains relatively large hard-currency deposits in Western banks, it can substantially increase its borrowing should the need arise.

To increase their exports to the West, the Soviets must increase the quantity, quality, and manufacturing efficiency of the goods that they produce. Therein lies a major reason why Gorbachev has opted for radical economic reform. If the Soviets want to compete effectively

Table 5–1

*Estimated Value of Soviet Military Deliveries
to Foreign Countries, 1974–85*

(billions of U.S. dollars)

Recipient	1974–79	1980–85	1974–85
Six Warsaw Pact countries	8.7	9.8	18.5
Syria	4.5	10.3	14.8
Iraq	6.0	8.2	14.2
Libya	5.4	5.8	11.2
Vietnam	2.1	4.9	7.0
India	2.0	4.8	6.8
Algeria	1.6	3.6	5.2
Cuba	1.3	3.9	5.2
Ethiopia	1.5	2.6	4.1
Angola	0.7	2.8	3.5
60 other countries	7.7	11.3	19.0
Total	41.5	68.0	109.5

Source: Central Intelligence Agency and Defense Intelligence Agency, *The Societ Economy
under a New Leadership.* A report presented to the Subcommittee on Economic Resources,
Competitiveness, and Security Economics of the Joint Economic Committee of the U.S.
Congress, Washington, D.C., 19 March 1986, p. 7.

in the international marketplace, they really don't have any other
alternative.

Trading Partners of the Soviet Union

Eastern Europe

The Soviets' principal trading partners are still the six Eastern European members of the Council for Mutual Economic Assistance
(CMEA)—Bulgaria, Czechoslovakia, the German Democratic Republic, Hungary, Poland, and Romania.[1]

Since the early 1970s, the Soviets exercised substantial economic
leverage over their Eastern European allies by offering them long-term
contracts for oil and gas at below the market price. However, as the
market price for crude oil plummeted in 1985 and 1986, their socialist allies became increasingly unhappy with the fact that they were
locked into contracts for oil priced considerably above the world
market price. Economic tensions were further exacerbated when the
EEC temporarily cut off agricultural imports from Eastern Europe

in 1986, fearing radioactive contamination from the Chernobyl accident.

At a CMEA meeting in Havana a year before Gorbachev came to power, Moscow warned that it could not afford to continue permitting Eastern European countries to receive more in Soviet oil and other goods than they export to the Soviet Union. A U.S. State Department study estimated that between 1970 and 1984, Hungary received $21.2 billion in Soviet trade subsidies; Bulgaria, $31.3 billion; and the GDR, $58.3 billion. The CMEA nations were told to balance their trade accounts with Moscow, improve the quality of their exports, begin repaying their foreign debts, and increase their investments in Soviet oil and mining development. The decrease in the price of oil has reduced the Soviets' bargaining power with its Eastern European allies, thus making it more difficult to extract economic concessions. Another source of tension between the Soviets and their Warsaw Pact allies is the question of defense costs, which the Eastern Europeans would like to see reduced. Thus trade with Eastern Europe represents an important force pushing the Soviets towards radical economic reform.

Western Europe

Western Europe is the target of a diplomatic offensive aimed at strengthening the Soviet Union's political and economic ties with the countries of the EEC. So important is Western Europe as a source of technology, consumer goods, and foodstuffs that Soviet trade officials recently met with EEC officials in Brussels in January 1987 to explore the possibility of establishing formal ties between the EEC and the Soviet Union. The Soviets view the EEC countries as much more reliable trading partners than the United States because they impose fewer political and legal barriers to Soviet trade than is the case with the United States. Increased trade with the EEC is an integral part of Gorbachev's strategy to reduce Western Europe's military dependence on the United States. By appealing to European pride, Gorbachev not only hopes to increase Soviet imports from Western Europe, but he also hopes to create a market niche for Soviet exports as well. Unlike the United States, which seems to be primarily interested in increasing its exports to the USSR, the Soviet Union is interested in serious two-way trade with Western Europe.

Far East

The Soviets are also devoting increased attention to trade with China, Japan, and the other countries in the Pacific Basin. The recently concluded Sino–Soviet trade agreement calls for doubling trade between the two countries by 1990. The Soviets expect to sell the Chinese two nuclear power plants and plan to provide technical assistance to help the Chinese modernize plants built by the Soviets in China during the 1950s. In return, they will receive a variety of agricultural and light industrial goods from China.

Soviet leader Gorbachev has also been wooing the Japanese. He is obviously impressed with the Japanese model for economic and political success. Manufactured products (including seamless pipe, trucks, and bulldozers) have constituted the bulk of Japan's exports to the Soviet Union. Japan has maintained a positive trade surplus with the Soviets since 1975. In July 1985, the two nations agreed to renew a previous economic pact and to bolster trade. Obviously, the Soviets view the Japanese as a potential source of sophisticated technology.

United States

The withdrawal of the Soviet Union from the U.S. wheat market in 1986 sent two messages to trade officials in Washington. U.S. agriculture is no longer a low-cost producer and cannot compete in the world market even with subsidies from the Reagan administration. The Soviets will no longer passively accept the discriminatory trade restrictions imposed on them by the United States. Instead, they will turn to less hostile, more competitive nations who view trade as a two-way street rather than merely as a means of financing their own trade deficits.

The Soviets' temporary retreat from the U.S. grain market could not have come at a more inopportune time for the U.S. economy. Once the biggest single positive contributor to the nation's trade balance, U.S. agriculture has run up the first string of monthly farm-trade deficits since the 1960s. The 1986 U.S. trade deficit reached a record high $170 billion. Intense foreign competition, decreased demand for U.S. farm products, and severe import restrictions imposed by Third World nations straining under huge debts to U.S. banks have all aggravated the problem. As a result, during the first half of the 1980s, 2.3 million manufacturing jobs disappeared in the United States. Particularly hard hit were smokestack industries.

Clearly, the United States needs to improve its competitive position, and the Soviet Union offers some unique advantages as a willing trading partner. As can be seen in table 5–2, for over ten years the United States has enjoyed a trade surplus with the Soviets. However, this surplus shrank in 1986 because the sharp drop in the price of oil has reduced the foreign currency available to the Soviets to buy U.S. goods. Increased U.S.–Soviet trade has a favorable impact on U.S. employment. Economists estimate that as many as forty thousand new jobs are created by each $1 billion in increased trade. Before President Reagan imposed sanctions against the Soviet gas pipeline in 1982, Caterpillar had 80 percent of the Soviet market for heavy-duty earthmoving equipment; Komatsu of Japan had only 20 percent. As a result of the sanctions, Komatsu now has 80 percent of the market, and nearly fifteen thousand jobs were lost at Caterpillar. The pipeline was completed ahead of schedule.

The Soviet Union offers the United States a virtually untapped

Table 5–2
U.S.–Soviet Trade between 1974 and 1986

(billions of U.S. dollars)

	Exports	Imports	Total
1974	.607	.350	.957
1975	1.833	.254	2.087
1976	2.306	.221	2.527
1977	1.623	.234	1.857
1978	2.249	.540	2.789
1979	3.604	.873	4.477
1980	1.510	.463	1.973
1981	2.339	.387	2.726
1982	2.589	.248	2.837
1983	2.002	.367	2.369
1984	3.283	.602	3.885
1985	2.423	.443	2.866
1986	1.248	.606	1.854

Source: Data from U.S. Commerce Department, 1986.

consumer market of 280 million people as well as a highly concentrated market for large-scale industrial contracts. It also has vast reserves of hydrocarbons and energy, which make it an increasingly attractive trading partner as the U.S. supply of crude oil continues to tail off.

To finance their imports from the United States, the Soviets must sell more to the United States. There is no doubt whatsoever that Soviet trade officials understand the significance of the fact that the U.S. market is the largest market in the world in terms of purchasing power. If the Soviet Union aspires to become a global economic power, then it must be able to compete in the U.S. market. But to compete effectively in the U.S. marketplace, the Soviets must produce higher-quality goods more efficiently—which can only be accomplished through radical economic reform.

U.S.–Soviet Trade Relations

In 1985 U.S. exports to the Soviet Union were $2.4 billion, 1 percent of total U.S. exports; U.S. imports from the Soviet Union were $440 million, 2 percent of Soviet exports to the West. As Gorbachev pointed out to a group of U.S. business leaders in Moscow in December 1985, "American imports from the Soviet Union are roughly equal to U.S. imports from the Ivory Coast." Grain accounted for 70 percent of U.S. exports to the Soviet Union in 1985 and fertilizers and petroleum products were 70 percent of Soviet exports to the United States. With the Soviets' retreat from the U.S. grain market in 1986, total two-way trade between the two countries dropped below the $2 billion mark—the lowest level since the 1980 grain embargo imposed by President Jimmy Carter in retaliation for the 1979 Soviet intervention in Afghanistan.

The history of U.S.–Soviet trade relations has followed an erratic pattern based on the ups and down of U.S.–Soviet political relations. Most Americans are surprised to learn that in the 1920s, nearly 40 percent of U.S. industrial exports went to the Soviet Union at a time when the United States did not even recognize the Soviet Union as a country. However, throughout the 1920s and the 1930s, there were frequent threats on the part of the U.S. government to cut off all trade with the Soviets. The Export-Import Bank of the United States was established in 1934 by the Roosevelt administration to enhance trade with the Soviet Union. However, the Export-Import Bank Act of 1945 prevented the bank from financing exports to the USSR unless the president determined that such trade was in the national interest. In 1948 all trade with the Soviets was cut off when the U.S. Commerce Department temporarily suspended all export licenses.

At the height of the cold war in 1951, the U.S. withdrew most-favored-nation status (MFN) from the Soviet Union. The loss of MFN by the Soviets put them at a serious competitive disadvantage. It increased the duty on goods imported from the USSR by as much as 23 percent on machine tools, 34 percent on binoculars, 63 percent on watches, and 78 percent on alcoholic beverages. Throughout the period between 1950 and 1970, trade flows were reduced to a trickle. However, in October 1963, in spite of considerable political opposition on the part of Congress, the Kennedy administration announced the first major grain sale to the Soviet Union. No additional grain was sold to the Soviets until 1971.

Instead of subjecting the Soviet Union to more stringent trade controls during the period of détente, which began in 1972, the Nixon administration not only liberalized trade restrictions but actively promoted Soviet trade through subsidized export credits and other interventionist measures. The 1972 U.S.–Soviet trade agreement called for expanded trade and mandated most-favored-nation tariff treatment, which required congressional approval. In 1972 President Nixon determined that trade with the Soviets was indeed in the national interest and between 1972 and 1974 the Export-Import Bank granted approximately $500 million in credits to the Soviets to purchase U.S. exports. In this same year the U.S.–USSR Joint Commercial Commission was established and the so-called North Star Consortium (involving Tenneco, Texas Eastern, and Brown and Root) was organized to study and discuss the development of a major Soviet gas pipeline involving financial and technical support from private U.S. companies.

At the time the Trade Act of 1972 was negotiated, U.S.–Soviet nonagricultural trade was miniscule, amounting to no more than $200 million annually. In spite of numerous political obstacles that were soon to emerge, trade between the United States and the Soviet Union gradually inched its way up, reaching a record of $4.5 billion in 1979 before the bottom fell out in U.S.–Soviet political relations and trade plunged to under $2 billion in 1980.

The years 1974–82 were an extraordinary period of U.S. government vacillation, ambiguity, and uncertainty that resulted in equally erratic U.S.–Soviet trade flows. Two pieces of legislation passed by Congress in 1974 and 1975 (the Jackson–Vanik Amendment to the Trade Reform Act of 1974, and the Stevenson Amendment to the Export-Import Bank Act of 1974, respectively) may have done more to chill U.S.–Soviet relations than either the Soviet intervention in Afghanistan or the declaration of martial law in Poland. The Jackson–Vanik Amendment linked MFN status for the Soviet Union and Export-Import Bank financing of U.S.–Soviet trade to Soviet emigration policies—particularly to policies affecting Soviet Jews. Under this amendment, the Export-Import Bank was not permitted to participate in U.S.–Soviet trade so long as the Soviets denied its citizens, particularly Jewish citizens, the right to emigrate or imposed more than a nominal penalty on any citizen as a consequence of his or her desire to emigrate. The Stevenson Amendment placed additional restrictions on the bank in terms of its participation in U.S.–Soviet trade even if the Jackson–Vanik Amendment did not apply.

The heart of the matter is Jewish emigration—one of the most volatile and politically sensitive issues dividing the two superpowers. In 1979 Jewish emigration increased dramatically, reaching an all-time high of 51,320. It then trailed off sharply in the 1980s and in recent years has sometimes dropped below one thousand emigrants per year. The United States has consistently denied MFN status to the Soviet Union since 1974. Furthermore, the substantial increase in Jewish emigration from the USSR in 1979 went totally unnoticed by President Jimmy Carter, who was preoccupied with events in Iran and Afghanistan. This failure on the part of the United States to respond to a relaxation in Soviet Jewish emigration policies angered the Soviet leadership and caused them to harden their position. The official Soviet view is that Soviet emigration policies are an internal matter and should be of no concern to the United States. However, in 1987 the number of Soviet Jews allowed to emigrate to the West increased significantly.

Between 1974 and 1982 the whole fabric of détente gradually came unraveled. Charges and countercharges were hurled back and forth with increasing frequency between the two superpowers on such topics as Angola, Afghanistan, Poland, Aleksandr Solzhenitsyn, Andrei Sakharov, the Soviet natural-gas pipeline to Western Europe, and the arms race. Soviet confidence in the integrity of business deals with U.S. companies was severly shaken in 1978 when President Carter revoked a license to Armco, Inc., to build a $400 million specialty steel plant in the Soviet Union. Carter also restricted the sale of oil and gas equipment to the Soviets after the Soviet intrusion in Afghanistan in 1979. By 1982 the level of trust between the two superpowers had reached a new all-time low and East–West trade had suffered accordingly.

The number of U.S. supporters of Soviet trade had dwindled to a handful of large U.S. companies such as Occidental Petroleum, Pepsico, and Control Data. Also interested were major agricultural producers who had become somewhat dependent on Soviet grain purchases; the purchases were not only revived by détente, but managed to be sustained throughout the 1970s until the 1980 grain embargo. The cancellation of the North Star Consortium by the U.S. government, the grain embargo, and President Reagan's 1982 gas pipeline sanctions sent a clear signal to the Soviets that they could not count on U.S. companies to honor their contractual commitments. As a result of these setbacks and the hard-currency crunch that they experienced during the 1980–81 period, the Soviets began to reassess the benefits associated with U.S. trade. They were also disappointed in the benefits realized from Western technological imports. Heightened political tensions and bankers' fears of being overexposed closed many loan windows that had previously been open to the East. All of this resulted in the Soviets' increasing their trade with Western Europe and Japan.

On 18 June 1982, U.S.–Soviet trade relations hit a near-term nadir. On that day President Reagan extended his order prohibiting the direct import of oil and gas equipment for use on the Soviet gas pipeline to include sales by overseas subsidiaries of U.S. companies and, more importantly, by foreign companies producing such equipment under U.S. license. Then, on 13 November he reversed himself and rescinded the June order. Three days later a trade delegation of 250 distinguished U.S. business leaders visited Moscow. The meeting was considered so important by the Soviets that it took place even though they were mourning the death of Brezhnev. It was the only major meeting not canceled by the Soviets during Brezhnev's funeral.

Although a new five-year grain agreement was negotiated in 1983, there were no major breakthroughs in U.S.–Soviet trade during the Andropov–Chernenko period. The Reagan administration continued to hammer away on the human rights and Jewish emigration issues with the Soviets always turning a deaf ear to such subjects.

Although 1985 produced several signs of a gradual thaw in U.S.–Soviet economic and political relations, total trade between the two nations actually decreased by $1 billion. The Caterpillar Tractor Company announced a new contract to sell two hundred tractors and thirty-nine pipelayers to the Soviet Union for about $80 million. It was Caterpillar's largest sale to the Soviets since the lifting of restrictions imposed by the Reagan administration in December 1981 on the export of goods for building the gas pipeline. In September 1985 U.S. Secretary for Housing and Urban Development Samuel R. Pierce, Jr., led a twenty-member U.S. delegation to Moscow to sign an agreement to implement eighteen housing and construction projects between 1985 and 1989.

One result of the Reagan–Gorbachev summit in November 1985 was that Pan American World Airways and the Soviet airline, Aeroflot, began flying again between the Soviet Union and the United States in April 1986. Service between the two countries originated in 1968. Pan Am discontinued its Moscow service claiming that it was unprofitable. In 1979, President Carter barred Aeroflot's flights to New York as part of a sanctions package protesting the Soviets' involvement in Afghanistan. Aeroflot's twice weekly flights to Washington were canceled in December 1981 by the Reagan administration in response to martial law in Poland.

In November 1985 U.S. banks began lending money to the Soviets again after a five-year hiatus. First National of Chicago, Morgan Guaranty, Bankers Trust, Irving Trust, and a subsidiary of the Royal Bank of Canada agreed to lend the Soviet Union up to $400 million at relatively low interest rates to purchase U.S. and Canadian grain. Given the Soviet Union's very favorable debt payment record in the past, U.S. banks are expected to lend the Soviets even more money in the future.

At a meeting of 415 U.S. business executives in Moscow in December 1985, Gorbachev said:

> In our dangerous world we simply cannot afford to neglect—nor have we the right to do so—the stabilizing factors in relations con-

cerning trade and economic and scientific and technological ties. If we are to have genuinely stable and enduring relationships capable of ensuring a lasting peace, they should be based, among other things, on well-developed business relations.

In this day and age each country and nation—the smallest as well as the biggest one—regard independence as their highest value and spare no effort to defend it. And yet we are witnessing the growing interdependence of states. This is a natural consequence of the development of the world economy today and at the same time an important factor for international stability. Such interdependence is to be welcomed. It can be a powerful incentive in building stable, normal and, I would even venture to say, friendly relations.[2]

With the liberalization of Soviet foreign-trade policies and the announcement of the new joint-venture law that went into effect on 1 January 1987, several U.S. firms have already signed joint-venture agreements. Monsanto will jointly own and operate a herbicide plant in the Soviet republic of Kazakhstan; Occidental Petroleum will be involved in a project to extract oil from previously developed oilfields in the Volga region; and SSMC (formerly Singer Sewing Machine) will produce sewing machines in Belorussia. In addition to the seventeen Pepsi-Cola bottling plants already located in the Soviet Union, Pepsico plans to open a hundred Pizza Huts as well. Coca-Cola plans to follow suit in 1987, and McDonald's is negotiating to franchise fast-food restaurants as well.

Technology Transfer

U.S. critics of U.S.–Soviet trade, such as former Assistant Secretary of Defense Richard N. Perle, claim that the only reason the Soviets are interested in trade with the West is to obtain U.S. technology to achieve military superiority over the United States. It is a myth that we have the power to deny the Soviets access to Western technology. How else do the Soviets gain access to our technology, when we read of sensational cloak-and-dagger arrests in Vienna or Stockholm in which U.S. agents have caught someone in the act of buying U.S. technology to ship to the USSR? It is virtually impossible for the United States to police the trade policies of neutral countries such as Austria, Finland, and Sweden. It is even more difficult to monitor technology shipped to the Third World. Countries such as Brazil have developed their own sophisticated technology and are anxious to make it available globally. Through Soviet-owned companies and representatives in the United States, Japan, and West Germany, it is easy for Soviet technicians to observe, use, and evaluate technology in a completely open and legal manner.

A 1987 study by the National Academy of Sciences has concluded that the Reagan administration's much-publicized effort to crack down on the diversion of technology to the Soviet Union has essentially failed and is costing the United States economy over $9 billion a year. The report points out that many types of high-tech equipment that are restricted by export controls (such as memory chips and personal computers) are in fact readily available in the Soviet Union and Eastern Europe.

The Soviets are often depicted by the Pentagon as incompetent kulaks, incapable of doing anything worthwhile, who must either buy or steal all of their technology from the West. Nothing could be further from the truth. The National Economic Achievement Exhibition in Moscow provides impressive evidence of the Soviets' achievements in science and technology. Some of the best mathematicians and scientists in the world are Soviets. The Soviets have state-of-the-art technology in medicine, lasers, space technology, steelmaking, eye films, and power engineering. The United States is already benefiting from Soviet technologies such as coal gasification, welding, electromagnetic casting, and metallurgical processes. Soviet-bloc countries hold over five thousand U.S. patents for their inventions. Interestingly enough, some Soviet technology is actually being used by U.S. Defense Department contractors to develop U.S. weapons systems as well as President Reagan's Strategic Defense Initiative (SDI).

The extent to which the Reagan administration is prepared to go to block the shipment of U.S. technology to the Soviets can be illustrated by two actual case studies—multibillion-dollar Dresser Industries and tiny Columbus Instruments.

Dresser Industries

The most widely publicized episode involving the Pentagon's efforts to block the sale of U.S. technology to the Soviets involved Dallas-based Dresser Industries.[3] Dresser is one of the world's leading suppliers of energy-related products and services. In the summer of 1982,

Dresser was the centerpiece in a global showdown involving the president of the United States, the leaders of the EEC countries, and the Soviet Union.

In September 1981, Dresser France, a wholly owned subsidiary of Dresser Industries, received an order from the Soviet Union to produce twenty-one of 120 mainline compressors to be installed in the trans-Siberian pipeline system. The pipeline was to provide natural gas from Soviet gas fields to Western Europe including West Germany, France, Italy, Austria, Belgium, Holland, and Switzerland.

On 31 December 1981, President Reagan extended export controls so that no gas pipeline equipment or technology could be exported from the United States to the Soviet Union for use on the pipeline project. However, Dresser France was unaffected by these sanctions, because they applied only to future shipments of equipment and technology from the United States, and Dresser France already possessed the necessary technology to fulfill its contractual obligations to the Soviets. But on 18 June 1982, the Reagan administration went one step further and prohibited users of U.S. technology abroad, whether subsidiaries of U.S. companies or licensees, from shipping equipment intended for use on the Soviet pipeline. Immediately, Dresser Industries instructed Dresser France to discontinue all production on the compressor contract and to refrain from shipping any completed products to the Soviet Union.

However, on 22 July 1982, the French government announced that it had instructed French companies to comply with their contracts to produce and deliver pipeline equipment to the Soviets despite the U.S. sanctions. The French claimed that the U.S. embargo had caused "undue commercial damage to European companies and harmed cooperation between the United States and its allies." West Germany, Italy, and the United Kingdom, each of which had companies with contracts with the Soviets involving U.S. technology, promptly sided with France in the pipeline dispute. Then on 12 August, the EEC issued a formal protest against the pipeline sanctions calling them "unacceptable under international law because of their extraterritorial aspect." The statement went on to say that

[m]any companies interested as subcontractors, or suppliers of components, have made investments and committed productive capacities to the pipeline project, well before the American measures were

taken. Though they may use no American technology, they will suffer complete loss of business if the European contribution to the project is blocked. Some of these companies may not survive.

In the meantime, the Reagan administration justified its single-minded, hardline anti-Soviet position by arguing that (1) the pipeline would make Western Europe too dependent on the Soviets for energy; (2) the Soviets must pay a price for the imposition of martial law in Poland in December 1981; and (3) the pipeline would generate $10 billion per year in hard currency that the Soviets could use for military purposes.

Ironically, in the midst of the pipeline controversy and in response to pressure from U.S. farmers, President Reagan lifted the embargo on grain sales to the Soviet Union that had been imposed by President Carter following the Soviet intrusion into Afghanistan.

The French government was so outraged by all of this that on 23 August it ordered Dresser France, under threat of criminal sanctions, to resume immediate production of the pipeline compressors and to ship three units that were already completed to the Soviet Union immediately. Failure to comply with the French order would have subjected the management of Dresser France to severe fines and imprisonment. After a series of legal moves and countermoves by the U.S. and French governments, Dresser France shipped the three completed compressors to the Soviet Union on 26 August. The Reagan administration then placed Dresser France on a denial list, which prohibited it from doing business with the United States.

Then on 13 November 1982, President Reagan quietly rescinded his 18 June order, thus ending one of the most ill-conceived maneuvers in the history of U.S.–Soviet diplomatic relations. But the damage had been done, and the wounds would take a long time to heal. As for the Soviets, the pipeline was actually completed ahead of schedule.

Columbus Instruments

In response to the nation's staggering 1986 trade deficit, President Reagan has embarked on a public relations campaign to promote international competitiveness. In the meantime the administration continues needlessly to harass small U.S. firms that export high-tech goods to the Soviet bloc, even though our trade deficit in electronics equipment soared in 1986. Consider the case of Columbus Instruments, a tiny company located in Columbus, Ohio, with annual sales of $1.7 million, which specializes in equipment used with animals in medical research laboratories.[4]

On 30 May 1985, Dr. Jan Czekajewski, President of Columbus Instruments, shipped $228,000 worth of lab-animal research equipment to Helsinki, Finland, where the company's representative planned to take it to Moscow to be demonstrated in a scientific medical symposium. Included in the shipment were five 1984 Apple IIe computers, one Rockwell AIM-65 computer, and a clone of an IBM PC-XT made in Taiwan and sold under the trade name "Super Computer." The total value of the computers was about $10,000, and none of them represented state-of-the-art technology. Given the computers' relatively low level of sophistication and the fact that they were an integral part of the physiological equipment for animal studies, Dr. Czekajewski did not apply for an export license.

Two days later U.S. Customs Agents, as part of the Reagan administration's vaunted Project Exodus to stop shipment of militarily strategic items to the Soviet bloc, seized the equipment at New York's Kennedy Airport. On 3 June 1985, eight U.S. Customs Agents descended upon Columbus Instruments and searched the premises for over six hours, taking with them files pertaining to shipments to the Soviet Union and Eastern Europe. Ten days later, they returned for a second day-long sweep accompanied by TV crews from the local television stations who had been alerted to the critical leak of militarily sensitive technology narrowly averted by the Customs Service. The hysterical news reports which followed depicted Columbus Instruments as a high-tech conduit to the Soviet Union. One television news program showed a map of the world with a red arrow connecting Columbus, Ohio, to Moscow. The headline of a local newspaper read, "Illegal Shipments to Soviets Suspected."

One month later two Columbus Instruments officials were subpoenaed to appear before a federal grand jury, but the subpoena was canceled just prior to their appearance. On 5 October 1985, the U.S. Commerce Department finally got around to decontrolling routine laboratory equipment containing nonstrategic microcomputers. All of the computers included in Columbus Instruments' original shipment were deregulated except the Super Computer, which remained under investigation. At the request of Dr. Czekajewski, the Commerce Department called the Customs Service to advise them of the change in regulations and to ask them to return the laboratory equipment to Columbus Instruments. The Customs Service refused to return the equipment, claiming that a criminal investigation of the company was underway. Shortly thereafter, the office manager of the company was again called by the grand jury, but this time was required to appear.

The case finally reached the Undersecretary of Commerce, whose office also tried to get Customs to release the seized equipment. Customs once again refused, alleging that the equipment was involved in a criminal investigation. Eleven months after the fact, Customs relented and returned six of the seven computers, but retained a $50,000 rat respirator and the clone of the IBM PC-XT, maintaining that the Super Computer could have military use to the Soviets.

Dr. Czekajewski then made a trip to Eastern Europe to conduct his own investigation of the availability of microcomputers in Poland, Finland and Bulgaria. To his surprise he found that IBM PC-XT and AT computers are readily available in Poland, and that one could purchase microcomputers from the local IBM office in Helsinki without any type of special license. (Recall that Helsinki was the original destination of Dr. Czekajewski's shipment.) When he reached Bulgaria, Dr. Czekajewski purchased a Bulgarian clone of the IBM PC-XT that was virtually identical to his Super Computer. After bringing it back to the United States, he wondered if he would need an export license to ship the Bulgarian computer back to Sophia?

Not only has his bout with the Reagan administration cost Dr. Czekajewski several hundred thousand dollars in legal fees, time, energy, and lost sales, but two years later he still did not have all of his equipment back. In addition, he is still the target of a grand jury investigation, even though no charges have ever been filed against him. Dr. Czekajewski had fled Poland in 1967 to escape the repressive shackles of communism. Today he stamps all of his correspondence with the inscription, "Warning! Exporting Can Be Hazardous to Your Mental Health."

Obstacles to U.S.–Soviet Trade

Although the climate for U.S.–Soviet trade has improved since 1982, some formidable obstacles remain, including a number of anti-Soviet regulations such as export, import, and financial controls, and other political and legal constraints. Since the 1970s, the United States has engaged in a series of hostile acts against the Soviet Union including boycotts, embargoes, sanctions, and broken trade contracts. There are also a number of cultural factors that constrain U.S.–Soviet trade as well.

Export Controls

The most onerous of the U.S. government regulations affecting U.S.–Soviet trade are export controls, which were first introduced after the end of World War II as the cold war was beginning to heat up. The philosophy of these restrictions was laid out in the Export Control Act of 1949, which was revised by the Export Administration Act of 1969, and more recently in the Export Administration Act of 1979. Their objective was to restrict the export of technologies to the Soviet Union that might prove detrimental to national security. No technology can be exported to the Soviet Union without a license approved by the U.S. Commerce Department. During the last three years of the Carter administration, export controls were used as punitive sanctions against the Soviets to support the administration's policies, particularly in the area of "human rights." Dresser Industries, Sperry-Rand, and Control Data were denied export licenses by the Carter administration. (Despite objections from the Pentagon, the Reagan administration lifted controls on exports of oil and gas equipment and technology to the Soviet Union in January 1987.)

Another form of export control, the Consultative Group Coordinating Committee (COCOM), was also initiated by the United States in 1949. It provides an institutional basis for Western multilateral trade controls. The membership of COCOM includes all of the members of NATO (except Iceland and Spain) and Japan. The authority of COCOM has consistently been limited by the inability of the member nations to reach a consensus on rules and procedures. In the 1980s, COCOM agreed to tighten export controls on high technology but opposed export controls on energy-related technologies. The Western European members of COCOM have tended to favor a much narrower scope for export controls than the United States, covering only those exports that are directly associated with significant military applications. Recently, COCOM lifted the export restrictions on some low-level, eight-bit digital computer systems and on some peripheral equipment, including CRT displays, floppy disks, and impact printers. This means that Apple II and IBM PC computers will become even more available in the Soviet bloc.

Import Controls

Products imported from the Soviet Union are also subject to numerous controls. The Tariff Act of 1930 covers all imports and provides two separate schedules for duties—most-favored-nation rates and higher rates. Since 1962 Congress has either refused to grant MFN status to the Soviet Union or has conditioned that status on requirements that are unacceptable to the Soviets. As I have previously noted, the Jackson–Vanik Amendment prevents the president from granting the Soviets MFN treatment until they comply with the emigration provisions mandated by that amendment. As a result, Soviet imports are subject to full tariff rates, which puts them at a substantial disadvantage compared to countries selling comparable goods with MFN status. The absence of MFN status affects 25 percent of the goods imported from the Soviet Union.

A number of Soviet products (including furs, crab meat, gold coins, and nickel) have been totally banned. However, the Reagan administration lifted the ban on Soviet nickel in 1987 and has recommended to Congress that the ban be removed on Soviet furs (including ermine, fox, mink, muskrat, and weasel). Antidumping laws prevent Soviet-bloc countries from selling their products in the United States below the market price.

Financial Controls

Although the U.S. Export-Import Bank was established originally to facilitate trade with the Soviet Union, congressional amendments enacted in 1945 and 1974 have severely restricted its activities. A 1945 amendment prevented the Export-Import Bank from financing Soviet trade unless the U.S. president deemed that trade with the Soviets was in the national interest. In 1972, President Richard Nixon was the first president to make such a determination. As a result, the bank granted approximately $500 million in credit to the Soviets to finance purchases of U.S. exports over the next two years. This practice ended abruptly in 1974 when the Jackson–Vanik Amendment prohibited the bank from financing U.S.–Soviet trade so long as the Soviets continued to impose certain restraints on emigration. A second 1974 amendment, known as the Stevenson Amendment, set a $300 million limit on new credit to the Soviet Union over the next four years. Since 1974, no Export-Import Bank credits have been extended to support trade with the Soviet Union.

In addition to the laws restricting the practices of the Export-Import Bank, there are also laws that inhibit the financing of Soviet trade by private banks and financial institutions. The Johnson Debt Default Act of 1934 prohibits the loan of funds to any foreign government that has defaulted on its debts to the United States, except for members of the World Bank and the International Monetary Fund. The Soviets have debts to the United States that predate the 1917 revolution, as well as lend-lease obligations accrued at the end of World War II and the Soviet Union is neither a member of the World Bank nor the IMF. Further the National Bank Act limits U.S. bank credit to a total of $1.5 billion for any one customer. Because the Soviets usually borrow through a single bank, many U.S. banks would soon reach their legal lending limits very quickly if U.S.–Soviet trade were to increase significantly. This situation differs from Japan and Western Europe, where export credits are routinely extended to the Soviet Union and Eastern Europe.

Cultural Barriers

The fact that the Soviet Union has a highly centralized economic system and the United States has a decentralized, market-oriented economy is a source of numerous misunderstandings related to trade. Although most Soviet business and academic leaders are familiar with English, few U.S. business-people make any effort whatsoever to learn Russian. Most Americans demonstrate an appalling ignorance of Soviet history, culture, and economics. The Soviets, on the other hand, seem to possess a great deal of knowledge about life in the United States. Both the U.S. government and U.S. business leaders seem to have an inordinate amount of difficulty viewing East–West trade issues from the Soviet perspective. Negotiations with the Soviets are not made any easier by Americans who approach the Soviet Union with a condescending, know-it-all attitude. Many Americans who attempt to deal with the Soviet Union know the Soviets only through the eyes of writers such as Solzhenitsyn, and don't seem to realize that the Soviet Union has changed a great deal since the 1950s.

Among the other practical problems involved in dealing with the Soviets is their preference for barter arrangements and countertrade. Often it is necessary to work with several Soviet ministries in very large deals. Sometimes the lack of access to the end-user or final consumer of a product is frustrating to more market-oriented U.S. executives. Given the vastness of the Soviet bureaucracy, U.S. business-people often find it difficult to follow up on major proposals submitted to Soviet ministries.

Soviet Export Strategies

Given the Soviet Union's strong appetite for Western imports, and its shortage of hard currency to finance these imports, the Soviets are strongly motivated to increase the quality and quantity of the products that they export to the West. The United States represents the largest market in the world in terms of total purchasing power, so it follows that the Soviets have a particular interest in increasing exports to the United States. To increase their exports to the United States, they are likely to consider a number of different strategies.

Huge economies of scale, an abundance of natural resources, and relatively low labor costs make it possible for the Soviets to be *low-cost producers* in a number of U.S. markets, including automobiles, chemicals, furniture, refrigerators, and fertilizers. In 1985, the Soviets sold 112,600 automobiles to the West, including seventeen thousand each to France and the United Kingdom, and sixteen thousand to Belgium. If granted most-favored-nation status by the United States, the popular Soviet auto Lada, priced at $5,000, could easily penetrate the economy-conscious segment of the U.S. market. The U.S. government's decision to get out of the commercial satellite launching business may have created a new opportunity for the Soviet Union. If granted permission to do so by the U.S. government, the Soviets could launch commercial satellites for U.S. firms. The Soviets' price for launching satellites is the lowest in the world.

Product differentiation may represent another viable strategic option for the Soviets with products such as helicopters, hydrofoils, laser technology, pharmaceuticals, surgical instruments, and furs. The Ka-26 helicopter has achieved a reputation for reliability, performance, and endurance in Japan, Sweden, France, and West Germany. It is best known for its ability to operate under severe weather conditions. Soviet sable, mink, lynx, polar bear, and silver fox are premium-quality furs that would command premium prices in the United States. Furthermore, wines and brandies produced in the Soviet republic of Georgia are among the best in the world. With relatively little effort, they could find a ready market among U.S. yuppies. The same is true of Georgian fabrics and oriental rugs. The uniqueness of these exotic Soviet products would have great snob appeal in the United States. Undoubtedly there are dozens of handicraft products from all over the Soviet Union that would be well received in the United States. Those Americans who have been introduced to Soviet jewelry—particularly jewelry made of amber—really like it. An aggressive marketing effort supporting the sale of some of these products could yield high dividends for the Soviet Union.

The near-desperate condition of U.S. agriculture may represent an interesting *market niche* for the Soviet Union. The Soviets might offer to purchase more grain, if, in return, U.S. farmers would buy more Balarus tractors and other farm equipment from the Soviet Union. To assist the Soviets in finding and developing specific market niches in the United States, Soviet trade officials should seek out small- to medium-size U.S. import-export companies. Many of these smaller U.S. trading companies have much more imaginative, creative approaches to trade than do the large companies with whom the Soviets have traditionally traded. If the Soviets are truly interested in breakaway export strategies for the U.S. market, then they should find some more innovative trading partners in the United States.

Joint ventures represent another strategic option available to the Soviets to increase the quantity and quality of their exports to the West. The Swedish engineering firm Sandvik was the first Western company to start a joint venture in the Soviet Union under the new joint-venture law. The joint venture will be located in the city of Orsha in the republic of Belorussia, and will produce block tool systems that are used in machine manufacturing. Mitsubishi and Nisho have agreed to joint ventures in lumber and food processing, Mitsui in cutting tools, and Maruichi in snack foods. By early 1987, the Soviets had received several dozen proposals from U.S. companies for joint ventures. Again, the Soviets should not rule out the possibility of doing some joint ventures with smaller, more innovative U.S. companies. With over seventy joint ventures with the West, Hungary provides an excellent example for the Soviets to follow.

Joint ventures based on science and technology represent another area in which the Soviets may strengthen their market position in the West. The Soviets are much better at basic research than applied research. The Americans and the Japanese are stronger in converting technology into marketable products. These differences provide a unique opportunity for scientific cooperation and joint ventures—a point that the Japanese and the West Germans have been much quicker to grasp than the Americans. With the high cost of research and development in the West and the Soviets' strength in basic research, joint ventures combining Soviet research with Western product development and marketing skills may become increasingly attractive to U.S. firms. European drug companies such as Ciba-Geigy and the Wellcome Foundation have had successful joint clinical studies with Polish scientists for several years. One advantage of such coventures to the Soviets is that it decentralizes research and development and brings it closer to the market.

To make any of these marketing and joint-venture strategies work will require well-defined strategic plans from the Soviet side. Just as Western businesspeople have only limited experience in doing business with the Soviet Union, Soviet managers are also deficient in their knowledge of Western business practices. I believe there is a definite need for a high-level management consulting group based in Moscow to facilitate trade and investment possibilities between Soviet enterprises and Western companies. Such a consulting firm should have close ties with the Soviet Chamber of Commerce, the Ministry of Foreign Trade, Gosbank, and the Soviet Trade Mission in Washington. The China United Trading Corporation has been extremely effective in increasing bilateral trade between China and the United States. A Soviet equivalent could have a similar impact on Soviet–U.S. trade and joint ventures.

It may be beneficial for some Soviet trade officials and enterprise managers to consider participating in executive education programs conducted by graduate schools of business in Western Europe or the United States. The Soviets may eventually want to develop their own schools of management in collaboration with their CMEA allies in Budapest and Warsaw. What is important is that these programs have strong courses in market-oriented management practices. Like the Chinese, the Soviets are now represented by a public relations firm in the United States.

One of the keys to the success of the Hungarians in trading with the West has been the extent to which they have improved their financial and banking structure. These financial reforms have made it much easier for Western companies to trade with Hungary. If Gorbachev truly wants to integrate the Soviet economy into the international economy, steps must be taken to monetize the Soviet economy and eventually make the ruble a freely convertible currency. Monetary reforms will be initiated in 1988.

Implications for Economic Reform

If the Soviets expect to compete effectively in the Western international marketplace, then they must both improve the quality of what they produce and produce in a more efficient manner. But improved product quality and increased production efficiency are two more reasons why Soviet leaders have turned to radical economic reform. Their Stalinist economic system is simply incapable of producing high-quality products in a cost-effective manner. Thus the international market provides an important incentive for changing the economic mechanism in the Soviet Union.

By increasing its exports to the West, the Soviet Union can afford to increase its Western imports. But there is an indirect benefit of Western imports that may be far more important to the Soviet economy than any of the goods imported from abroad. Increased Western imports will help break the monopolistic stranglehold that some Soviet enterprises possess over certain industries. More foreign imports will lead to more competition in the Soviet domestic market. Through this strategy, combined with decentralized planning, flexible prices and wages, and the increased use of production incentives, Gorbachev

is injecting new vitality and flexibility into moribund Soviet enterprises. Thus the power of the international marketplace is one of
Gorbachev's most important instruments of economic reform.

Already, Soviet trade officials are using the impressive World Trade
Center (WTC) to attract Western business leaders to Moscow. Included in this complex are an ultramodern office building to accommodate foreign companies accredited in the USSR, six hundred first-
class hotel rooms, Russian and continental restaurants (as well as the
only Japanese restaurant in the Soviet Union), cafes, bars, and a first-
rate international nightclub. The WTC also boasts a 625-unit resi-
dential hotel, a meeting hall with a seating capacity of two thousand,
a data processing center, and a health club with a swimming pool
and sauna.

As was the case in Hungary, we may see an even greater interest
in international trade on the part of Soviet managers as the government eases up on the reins of control over the economy. The freedom
to manage their enterprises for profit and the lure of Western customers and financial markets may prove to be an irresistable temptation to Soviet managers. With improvements in quality and
efficiency, Soviet enterprises can receive higher prices for their products in the West, thus leading to higher profits and higher bonuses
for managers and employees alike.

Just as Hungary faced serious productivity problems and shortages of agricultural products and consumer goods in the 1970s, causing them to turn to the international market for solutions, so too is
the case with the Soviet Union today. Given the success of the Hungarians and the Chinese in dealing with trade and economic problems
similar to the ones faced by the Soviets today, it is not surprising that
the Soviets are looking to them for alternative solutions to their
problems.

There is an important feedback relationship between bilateral trade
and economic reforms in the USSR. Increased trade provides a positive incentive for economic reform. But economic reform enables the
Soviets to increase their exports to the West. Increased exports provide the foreign currency to buy more imports. Thus both the Soviet
Union and the rest of the world gain from Gorbachev's foreign-trade
policy as well as his policy of radical economic reform.

6
The Reagan Effect

In May 1985, near the banks of Lake Balaton in Hungary, while having lunch with the president of a Hungarian electronics firm located near the town of Szombathely (near the Austrian border), my Hungarian host asked me, "Which leader has done more to strengthen the Soviet Union economically and militarily than any other leader since the death of Stalin?" Naturally, I assumed he was referring to a Soviet leader, and my first response was, "Khrushchev," then I guessed, "Brezhnev." With a sly smile, the Hungarian shook his head and said, "Ronald Reagan." He then went on to say that "the foreign policy of the Reagan administration has created an atmosphere in the Soviet Union that will make it extremely difficult for Mr. Gorbachev to fail in his attempts to reform the Soviet Union." After the initial shock of his answer, I began reflecting on the underlying premises of President Reagan's foreign policy, which is based on ten maxims:

1. You can't trust the Russians.

2. The Soviet Union is the source of all the evil in the world.

3. The economy of the Soviet Union is on the brink of total collapse.

4. The Soviets can obtain modern technology only by buying it or stealing it from the West.

5. The Soviets have achieved strategic military superiority over the United States.

6. Through technology and increased military spending we can protect ourselves from the Soviets and ensure our immortality.

7. It is possible for the United States to fight and win a nuclear war with the Soviet Union.

8. Arms control negotiations are a waste of time and should not be taken seriously.

9. The views of Eastern Europe and Western Europe on U.S.–Soviet relations are fundamentally irrelevant.

10. In the name of freedom, the United States has the right to impose its values and its way of life on any country in the world.

I will examine each of these foreign policy maxims and its effects on Soviet economic reforms, foreign policy, and defense policy.

Russophobia

That Ronald Reagan made the epithet "You can't trust the Russians" the overriding foreign-policy theme of his administration came as little surprise, when one considers the fact that his entire political career had been based on hard-line opposition to communism. From the first day he came into office, Reagan acted on the belief that insult and intimidation were the only viable means of dealing successfully with the Soviet Union. Tough talk and military strength were viewed as necessary and sufficient conditions for bringing the Soviets to their knees at the bargaining table.

Certainly there is nothing new about the use of anti-Soviet rhetoric to increase the president's popularity with the electorate. Every president since Harry Truman has from time to time engaged in red-baiting—some more than others. Although Richard Nixon used anticommunism in his earlier political campaigns, once he was elected president he took a more flexible and tolerant view towards the Soviets and the Chinese. But the undeniable fact is that there is a very big market for anticommunism in the United States. Not only have politicians like the late Senator Joseph McCarthy in the 1950s and North Carolina's Senator Jesse Helms in the 1980s built their careers on being against the Russians, but many a politician who was about to go down to defeat has bailed out the campaign with a last-ditch anticommunism strategy. Being against the Russians is a very safe position for a U.S. politician to take.

But President Reagan's fear and distrust of the Soviets knows no equal. He seems to be driven to show that literally everything the Soviets do is suspect and that no part of the Soviet arms buildup in the 1970s and 1980s is a response to U.S. arms building or to the Soviets' perception of U.S. motives. According to this logic, the only way to end the arms race is for the United States to press the Soviets to the wall and force them to back down. Diplomatic negotiations have little value with this type of mind-set. Everything that is true and good is on our side, and the Soviets are to blame for everything that goes wrong in the world. Simplistic though it may be, people in the United States seem to be mesmerized by this view of the Soviet Union.

Psychologist Ralph K. White has written an excellent book on U.S.–Soviet relations entitled *Fearful Warriors*. White contends that the United States and the Soviet Union suffer from a number of common maladies—an exaggerated fear of each other, "macho pride," and a complete inability to admit their own shortcomings.

Most Americans have a paranoid fear of Soviet-style communism—particularly the repressive form that it took in the 1930s and 1940s under Stalin. Many of our attitudes towards the Soviets today, as well as our foreign policy, seem to be based on the belief that the Second Coming of Stalin is imminent. What is particularly interesting is our complete lack of trust of the Soviets, who were our allies in World War II, in contrast to our attitude towards the West Germans, who were our enemies. Because most Americans have neither visited the Soviet Union nor ever known any Soviet people, they rely entirely on the U.S. press for information about the Soviets. But with very few exceptions, the editorial policy of most U.S. newspapers is, "You can't trust the Russians."

The Russians' paranoia towards the United States stems from a fear of foreign invasion. They live in the midst of a vast plain with no natural barriers to protect them from hostile forces. For over a thousand years, they have been the object of countless invasions. They have been successfully invaded by the Teutonic knights, in the days of Aleksandr Nevsky; by the Tatars, who arrived in 1237 and cut Russia off from Europe for over two centuries; by the Turks, Poles,

and Swedes; by the French under Napoléon; by the British and French
in the Crimean War; and by the Germans in World Wars I and II—
the latter the most disastrous of all the invasions.[1]

It is virtually impossible for Americans to conceive of the psychological impact that World War II has had on the Soviet Union. Over
and over again the Soviets remind Americans that they suffered 20
million casualties in World War II in contrast to only 300,000 for
the United States. Although the Germans occupied the Soviet Union,
our homeland remained untouched during World War II. To add
insult to injury, few Americans know that between 1918 and 1920
the United States actually sent troops to the Soviet Union to fight
against the revolution. Thus when President Reagan speaks of "containing" Soviet aggression, the Kremlin is contemplating the risks of
"encirclement." We simply do not speak the same language.

Both sides view each other as diabolical enemies. Soviet leaders
portray Americans as "imperialist warmongers," and President Reagan depicts the Soviets as the source of all evil in the world. Though
these epithets may have popular appeal on the home front, they harden
bellicose attitudes on the other side far more than U.S. and Soviet
politicians seem to realize.

Exaggerated fear of an opponent is one of two forms of delusion
often associated with paranoid personalities. Psychiatrists call this
type of behavior the *delusion of persecution*. The other forms of paranoia shared by U.S. and Soviet leaders are *macho pride* and *narcis-
sism*. Macho pride is a form of delusion of grandeur characterized by
Napoléonic empire building that first blinds the leader and then the
followers, thus paving the way for aggression. It often accompanies
an overstated fear of an opponent's strength and hostility. In a psy-
chotic person, delusions of persecution stem from a projection of
one's inner conflicts, which are too painful to acknowledge, onto
other people. On the other hand, delusions of grandeur are also based
on dissatisfaction with oneself. They are derived in part from delusions of persecution ("They must think I am important because they
persecute me") and in part from a cover-up of the individual's basic
sense of weakness and unworthiness. These ideas fit the personalities
of Hitler and Stalin like a glove.[2] As evidence of macho pride in the
United States, Ralph K. White cited polls that show that a majority
of Americans subscribe to the view that the United States should

maintain its position as the world's most powerful nation at all costs, even going to the brink of war if necessary.[3]

The need to be in control underlies much of the macho pride behavior found among U.S. and Soviet leaders today. If we are to ever make any real progress in reducing the arms race, we must abandon—at great cost to egos in Washington and Moscow—the illusion of control.

Both the United States and the Soviet Union have an excessively high moral self-image. We Americans believe we can do no wrong. Although the Vietnam War caused some U.S. leaders to be more hesitant about intervening in foreign conflicts, it has not deterred President Reagan in Grenada, Libya, or Nicaragua. Soviet leaders justify their intervention in Afghanistan as a necessary defensive action to prevent the United States from destabilizing its socialist neighbor.

Examples abound of the Reagan administration's distrust of the Soviets. In spite of substantial evidence to the contrary, President Reagan and Defense Secretary Caspar Weinberger have repeatedly accused the Soviets of violations of the SALT II arms agreement. In walking away from SALT II, Reagan chose to ignore an intelligence report made public by the Joint Chiefs of Staff that completely contradicts his assertion that the Soviets have violated key arms control provisions in the treaty.

One of the most imaginative of the Reagan administration's accusations against the Soviets was the "spy dust" scare. In 1985, the administration charged the Soviets with using a powdery chemical to track employees of the U.S. Embassy in Moscow. It was insinuated that "spy dust" might be carcinogenic. Six months later the administration quietly backed away from these charges. During that same year the administration claimed that the Soviet Embassy in Mexico City was being used to mount espionage operations against the United States. It charged that the embassy had become a conduit for the illegal diversion of advanced technology to the communist world.

One of the more blatant forms of tension-increasing activities is the practice of making national heroes out of defectors from the Soviet Union—particularly celebrities from the arts, well-known sports figures, Soviet dissidents, and former KGB officers. Obviously, Reagan is not the first president to engage in this type of anti-Soviet hype; nor is he likely to be the last. Even completely unknown Soviet immigrants to the United States soon learn that they can find receptive audiences on the Rotary Club circuit if they present one-sided views of how tough life is in the USSR.

The U.S. entertainment industry has been quick to capitalize on the anti-Soviet feelings engendered by the administration's policies. Hollywood has produced *Red Dawn, Rocky IV,* and *Rambo: First Blood Part II,* each of which portrayed the Soviets as cruel and treacherous enemies. The 1986–87 bestsellers by Tom Clancy, *The Hunt for Red October* and *Red Storm Rising,* had similar themes. And while President Reagan and General Secretary Gorbachev were meeting in Geneva, U.S. television advertisers had discovered a new way to appeal to anti-Soviet prejudices—red-bashing. Miller Lite beer, MCI (the long-distance telephone service), and Wendy's (the hamburger chain) all ran anti-Soviet commercials during this period. Not to be outdone by the movie industry, the ABC television network ran a miniseries depicting life in the United States after a Soviet takeover.

Nothing more accurately reflects the current status of U.S.–Soviet relations under the Reagan administration than the 1986 Daniloff–Zakharov affair. Paranoid fear, macho pride, and an inability to admit one's mistakes are all firmly embedded in this episode. It began that March with the Reagan administration calling for a reduction in the size of the Soviet, Ukrainian, and Belorussian missions to the United Nations from 275 to 170 over a two-year period, with the first cut of twenty-five to be implemented by 1 October 1986. President Reagan claimed that at least 40 percent of the Soviet officials living in the United States were known or suspected intelligence officers and that all could be "called upon by the KGB." In a related event, on 23 August, U.S. agents arrested Soviet physicist and United Nations employee Gennadi F. Zakharov and charged him with espionage. One week later, the Soviets detained *U.S. News & World Report* correspondent Nicholas S. Daniloff in Moscow and charged him with espionage also. On 15 September the United States ordered twenty-five members of the Soviet UN mission to leave by 1 October. In the meantime, Daniloff was allowed to leave the Soviet Union and Zakharov left the United States. Shortly after the twenty-five Soviet diplomats left New York, the Soviets retaliated by expelling five diplomats from the U.S. Embassy in Moscow. The United States countered by expelling five Soviet diplomats from the Soviet Embassy and ordering fifty more Washington-based Soviet diplomats to leave so as to bring the size of the U.S. and Soviet diplomatic delegations to parity. The affair was concluded when the Soviets expelled five more U.S. diplomats from Moscow and ordered 260 Soviet nationals to stop working in the U.S. Embassy.

Prior to each Reagan–Gorbachev summit meeting, the administration has precipitated a major spy scandal. In 1985 before the Geneva summit there was "spy dust;" in 1986 before Reykjavík, the Daniloff–Zakharov affair; and then in 1987 before the proposed Washington summit, the bugging of the U.S. Embassy in Moscow, which involved illicit sexual relations between U.S. Marines and attractive female KGB agents.

The White House has justified sending U.S. arms to Iran by citing the potential Soviet military threat to Iran. But a Brookings Institution study claims that the administration has exaggerated the Soviet Union's ability to invade Iran.

And how has all of this affected the Soviets? When I was in Moscow in May 1982, the attitude of Soviet officials and academic leaders concerning Reagan's anti-Soviet campaign was one of shock, disbelief, and a genuine fear that the United States was planning to attack the Soviet Union. My next visit to the Soviet Union was in May 1985, six weeks after Gorbachev came to power. By this time the Soviets were expressing anger and cynicism about Reagan's never-ending arrogance in his public statements about the Soviet Union. But there was a feeling in the air that things would be different under Gorbachev. He not only would stand up to Reagan but would provide the Soviet Union with a new vision of the future. By 1986, renewed self-confidence was emanating from the Soviet Union. "We have solved our geriatrics problem; what about the United States?"

The Evil Empire

In March 1983, President Reagan told a group of Christian fundamentalist broadcasters in Florida that our conflict with the Soviet Union was a "struggle between right and wrong, good and evil." He then went on to call the Soviet Empire an "evil empire" and a totalitarian state that is "the focus of evil in the modern world." He described the Soviets as "immoral, ready to stop at nothing, including lying and cheating, to advance their goal of world domination." Thus began a well-organized series of attacks by President Reagan on the Soviet Union—probably the most vitriolic attacks against a foreign nation ever waged by a U.S. president since the end of World War II. There appeared to be no limitations on the amount of anti-Soviet venom President Reagan was prepared to spread in the name of "freedom." He called for a "global campaign for freedom" that would "leave Marxism-Leninism on the ash heap of history."

When Korean Air Lines Flight 007 was destroyed over Soviet territory on 1 September 1983, President Reagan launched a series of well-aimed attacks on the Soviets, even though there was substantial evidence to suggest that his administration knew considerably more about the underlying causes of this disaster than it shared with the American people. Reagan turned the tragedy into a public relations bonanza for U.S. foreign policy. Just prior to his 1984 landslide reelection, while preparing for one of his weekly Saturday afternoon radio broadcasts, he said, "My fellow Americans, I am pleased to tell you I just signed legislation which outlaws Russia forever. The bombing begins in five minutes." And the American people loved every minute of it.

To support its claim that the Soviet Union is an evil empire, the Reagan administration embarked on a broad-based campaign of often-repeated accusations of Soviet adventurism, Soviet arms treaty violations, Soviet arms race initiatives, Soviet inflexibility in arms negotiations, Soviet nuclear war plans, Soviet use of chemical warfare, Soviet human rights violations, and Soviet support of international terrorism.[4]

There is a serious gap between U.S. perceptions of the Soviet Union and reality. Few Americans realize that even before Gorbachev came to power that the Soviet Union had already changed a great deal since the 1950s. When such changes do occur, the Reagan administration very often turns them into new indictments. Rather than commending the Soviets for permitting nearly 270,000 Jews to emigrate since 1968, the administration persists in its practice of condemning them for not allowing more to leave. In his 1987 State of the Union speech, President Reagan chose to ignore the fact that on that very day Gorbachev had called for secret balloting and a choice of candidates in Soviet party elections. Little or nothing has been said by the administration about the alcohol reforms, the clampdown on corruption, increased openness, and the release of political dissidents.

But the really fundamental problem of Russophobia in the United States is that, unlike most other countries, we have never acknowledged the fact that, whether we like it or not, the Soviet Union is a major power in the world with interests and entitlements in international affairs not unlike our own. We continue to deny the Soviet Union the status of a coequal legitimate power. This strategy of denial has a high price tag in terms of human energy and military expenditures. We continue to pour endless amounts of resources into defense to assure ourselves that we are still the greatest power in the world.

How have the Soviets reacted to the administration's demeaning anti-Soviet rhetoric? Initially, the self-esteem and patriotic pride of Soviet leaders were severely shaken by Reagan's self-righteous moralistic pronouncements that reduced Soviet achievements to criminal acts implemented by international outlaws. They were stunned and humiliated.

It did not take them long to realize that Reagan's real objective was to deny them the legitimacy and status of a global superpower. What particularly enraged the Soviets was their belief that Reagan was attempting to deny them the respect and influence to which they felt they were entitled by virtue of having achieved military parity with the West. Reagan was in essence refusing to acknowledge what the Soviets considered to be their single greatest accomplishment. They deeply believed—and not without some justifiable reason—that there are very powerful forces in the United States that will never accept the Soviet Union as a preeminent power and will never cease to try to undermine its position.

Even before Gorbachev came to power, the effects of President Reagan's "evil empire" slur were already in evidence in Moscow. Once their anger began to subside, a consensus soon emerged among Soviet leaders to strengthen their resolve to prove to the United States and the rest of the world that the Soviet Union is indeed a global superpower. Today the Soviet Union is much stronger economically and militarily than it was when President Reagan was elected. Reagan's policies have helped create a political climate in Moscow that is very supportive of Gorbachev. Reagan has single-handedly made Gorbachev's task of injecting new vitality into the Soviet political and economic systems inordinately easier than might otherwise have been the case. History may very well show that Ronald Reagan inadvertently virtually guaranteed Gorbachev's success as a Soviet leader.

If Gorbachev had written Reagan's script over the past six years, it's hard to imagine that he would have changed one word of it. His task of taking control of the party, the Politburo, the military establishment, and the government was greatly facilitated by the policies of President Reagan.

The "Inevitable" Economic Debacle

Pentagon strategists argue that the United States should use its military buildup as well as economic sanctions to increase the pressure on the Soviet economy, eventually leading to its collapse. Studies suggest that the Soviet Union is vulnerable to economic sanctions by the West. This view assumes that the United States has the power to cause the economic collapse of the Soviet Union by spending the Soviets into the ground and cutting off trade with them. With the Soviet economy in shambles, the military will lose control, thus paving the way for a popular revolt and the collapse of the regime, which in turn will lead to either military surrender or disarmament.

Wishful thinking about the collapse of the Soviet Union is not new to U.S. politics. Although this view is shared by many Americans—particularly émigrés from Eastern Europe and the Soviet Union—it is based on economic poppycock.

Although the Soviet economy has lots of problems, it is not on the brink of collapse. Among our foreign-policy options, none have the power to cause the collapse of the Soviet economy. This was true before Gorbachev came to power and is even more so now that the Soviet economy is improving.

Gorbachev has inherited some big economic problems, not the least of which is finding the resources to satisfy competing demands for increased consumer goods, plant modernization, improved computer technology, and increased military spending. He is going to have to make some tough choices as to how he allocates his scarce resources. The issue is not economic collapse and never has been.

John W. Kiser argues that the arms race may help the Soviets more than it helps the United States. Military spending has both positive and negative effects. Although it does divert scarce resources away from the more productive civilian sector, defense spending generates economic benefits as well. Kiser argues that in the Soviet Union these benefits may be even greater than in the United States.[5]

In the United States, the marketplace is an important source of energy and discipline. The market not only provides incentives for innovation and technological change, but it is also a severe disciplinarian in the case of firms that cannot carry their own weight. With its highly centralized, planned economy, the Soviet Union has no commercial penalties (such as bankruptcy) for economic failure. The only two institutions that are concerned with institutional survival are the Communist party and the military establishment.

Both of these institutions have a paranoid fear of internal revolution as well as of invasion by an outside force. This fear provides the military with a kind of discipline that demands high quality and efficiency, neither of which are widespread in the civilian sector of the Soviet economy. In many ways, the Soviet military emulates some of the important features of the private sector of the U.S. economy. For example, it generates technological spinoffs and improved management techniques.

Thus, contrary to the view of the Reagan administration, we, rather than the Soviets, may be spending ourselves into the ground by eroding our competitive position abroad through the excessive concentration of research and development resources in the defense sector rather than in the private sector. There is little evidence to support the view that the administration's foreign policies have weakened the Soviet Union either economically or militarily. Indeed, the evidence suggests that exactly the opposite is true.

Technology Bandits

According to the Pentagon, the only way the Soviets will ever be able to obtain sophisticated technology is by buying or stealing it from the West. Implicit in this view is the assumption that the Soviets fear U.S. technological prowess as well as the Reagan administration's military buildup.

Although the U.S. weapons buildup may concern the Soviets in the long run, this threat may strengthen the Soviets by pushing them

into the computer age and causing them to develop even more sophisticated defense systems than those of the United States. Administration officials completely underestimate the effects of the threat of
war on technological progress. From the days of the crossbow to the
age of jet engines, nuclear power, and high-speed computers, war has
been a powerful stimulus to technological change. Some historians
have even suggested that at least part of the impetus for the Industrial
Revolution was generated by the demands of British soldiers fighting
on the Continent at that time. Why should the Soviet Union's response to the threat of war be any different?

It is a misperception of the Reagan administration to assume that
the Soviets are completely lacking in computer technology. Nothing
could be further from the truth. The Soviets have demonstrated repeatedly the capacity to implement very sophisticated computer-based
projects, such as guiding missiles accurately and putting probes on
Venus. Their problems lie primarily in the depth of their computer
base and in the integration of computer systems into their economy.
Although the Soviets have the most highly planned economy in the
world, the computer software used to support it is absolutely primitive.

The arms race could be a blessing in disguise for the Soviet Union,
for it may greatly accelerate the pace of development of computer
technology, electronic process controls, and robotics. Thus we have
yet another example of a Reagan administration policy yielding results that are quite contrary to their intended purpose.

Strategic Military Superiority

At his news conference on 31 March 1982, President Reagan became
the first U.S. president in history to tell his people that the United
States no longer held the lead in the arms race with the Soviet Union.
"The truth of the matter is that on balance the Soviet Union does
have a definite margin of superiority—enough so that there is risk
and there is what I have called, as you all know, several times, a
window of vulnerability."

Then in 1985, after spending more than $1 trillion on defense
since he came into office, with plans to spend another $1.7 trillion
by 1990, President Reagan said, "At the moment I have to say the
United States is still well behind the Soviet Union in literally every

kind of offensive weapon, both conventional and in the strategic weapons."

President Reagan has traded heavily on the United States' paranoid fear of the Soviet Union to gain public and congressional support for his staggering military program. He not only convinced Congress that the weapons he wanted were urgently needed to redress what he called an "adverse imbalance" of military power, but that the Soviets held a definite margin of "strategic superiority" over the United States.

In an extremely well documented book, *The Myth of Soviet Military Supremacy,* which contains 219 pages of tables and detailed appendices, Tom Gervasi provides convincing evidence that both of these statements are "lies." Gervasi argues that not only has the Soviet Union never had a margin of strategic superiority over the United States, but it probably never will.[6] Instead, according to Gervasi, it is the United States that holds the lead in strategic power by virtually every significant measure. In most categories of military hardware, the United States and its NATO allies actually hold a numerical lead over the Soviet bloc. In a few categories such as tanks where the Soviets hold the numerical edge, the Soviet lead is more than offset by NATO's advantage in terms of quality.[7]

On the one hand, we are told by the Pentagon that the Soviets are technologically incompetent and lag significantly behind the West. On the other hand, the president tells us that the Soviets have managed to achieve strategic superiority over the United States. Is it really possible for the Reagan administration to have it both ways?

How has the administration been able to deceive such a large percentage of the U.S. public for such a long time? Why has the press been so passive in its treatment of the arms race? Why is there so little criticism of Reagan's defense policies? Again, according to Dr. Gervasi, the administration has pushed state-of-the-art information management to its upper limits. It has demonstrated an almost uncanny ability to not only control the agenda of the national media, but to ensure that the public draws the desired conclusions from the issues defined by the White House. Until the story leaked out about illegal arms shipments to Iran and aid to the contras in Nicaragua, the U.S. public was prepared to believe virtually anything Reagan said about the Soviet menace.

As an example of the type of deceit practiced by Reagan, consider the speech he made in February 1981 in which he said, "Since 1970, the Soviet Union has invested $300 billion more in its military forces than we have." Later that year the CIA updated this estimate to $420 billion. But in a carefully written analysis of the actual situation, Franklyn D. Holzman showed that, in fact, the West outspent the Soviet bloc by $740 billion between 1971 and 1980. In other words, Reagan was off by more than $1 trillion in his assessment of Soviet military spending.[8]

Or consider the case of the T-80 Soviet tank described in detail by Defense Secretary Weinberger in a 1981 publication entitled *Soviet Military Power*. When pressed about the matter, Pentagon officials sheepishly admitted that not only did such a tank not exist, but they had absolutely no intelligence data whatsoever on its design specifications. What had been published in the Pentagon publication was a complete fabrication.[9]

In June 1984, the North Atlantic Treaty Organization quietly revised downward its estimate of the number of Warsaw Pact divisions in Europe from 173 to 115. In so doing it tacitly admitted that it had been exaggerating the numerical superiority of Soviet-bloc armies available for combat in Europe.

On one occasion when President Reagan was claiming that the Soviets had achieved nuclear superiority over the United States, he was challenged by Senator Sam Nunn, a highly respected Democratic specialist on military and arms control. "That's not correct," asserted Nunn. "I think the President needs to sit down with the Joint Chiefs and learn about our submarines, about our aircraft carriers, about our tactical aircraft, about our cruise missiles, about our bombers and other advantages."

But why does the Pentagon continue to prepare for a Soviet threat, if there is more than sufficient military force in place to meet any conceivable Soviet challenge that might arise? Why does the Reagan administration continue to deceive and manipulate the American people into supporting what is essentially a wholly gratuitous effort? The answer is that there is no other way to meet the never-ending demands of what President Dwight D. Eisenhower called the military-industrial complex. In his farewell address to the American people on 17 January 1961, President Eisenhower defined the dilemma we face today:

In the councils of government, we must guard against the acquisition
of unwarranted influence, whether sought or unsought, by the military-industrial complex. The potential for the disastrous rise of mis-
placed power exists and will persist.

　　We must never let the weight of this combination endanger our
liberties or democratic processes. We should take nothing for granted.
Only an alert and knowledgeable citizenry can compel the proper
meshing of the huge industrial and military machinery of defense
with our peaceful methods and goals so that security and liberty
may prosper together.[10]

The military-industrial complex has become the most powerful
and the least democratic institution in the United States today. It is
powerful not only because it appeals to our patriotism and exploits
our need for security, but also because it distributes income and wealth.
The more wealth the military establishment can control, the more
dependent on it do business, labor, and government become. The
more dependent they become on the military, the more actively they
will support its goals and objectives.[11]

　　Even though the Soviet Union is a socialist country, many of the
same institutions exist there, as do very similar political processes.
Soviet leaders, like their U.S. counterparts, play on the fears of the
Soviet people to gain popular support and consolidate their political
power. Soviet ministries concerned with the design and production of
weapons have about as much interest in arms control as senior executives of U.S. defense contractors.

　　Thus we see that tension between the United States and the Soviet
Union is a necessary and sufficient condition for the survival of the
military-industrial complex in both countries. The real battle is not
over ideological differences between the two superpowers but rather
between the military power structure of the United States and the
military establishment of the Soviet Union. In both countries, it is the
military that wields the ultimate power, and the U.S. and Soviet people bear the tremendous economic and social costs of our respective
military programs. Unfortunately, both the American people and the
Soviet people appear to be powerless to do anything about this
situation.

　　The ultimate weapon used by the Reagan administration to support its defense policies is the suggestion that anyone who opposes its policies is by definition "un-American" and "pro-Communist." Any member of Congress who votes against the president's military agenda—the MX missile, the Strategic Defense Initiative, the B-1 bomber, or aid to the contras—is said to be soft on communism and disloyal and becomes the target of a vicious negative advertising campaign the next time reelection comes around. Needless to say, there are relatively few members who can stand up to this kind of intense pressure.

How will Reagan's myth of Soviet strategic military superiority play in Moscow? How will the Soviets respond to the administration's unprecedented military buildup? Let there be no doubt that Gorbachev knows that Reagan's claim of Soviet military superiority is a lie. If Reagan is prepared to go to such extremes to misrepresent the facts to his own people, how could he be trusted in any arms control agreement? Indeed, Reagan's behavior during and after the Reykjavík summit must have raised even more doubts about his credibility in the eyes of the Soviets. When Reagan accuses the Soviets of not being serious about arms control, he may be absolutely correct, but for the wrong reasons. The Soviets not only want an arms control agreement, but given the condition of their economy, they need a major arms control deal.

Under Stalin, Khrushchev, or Brezhnev, forces would have been set loose in the Kremlin for the Soviets to respond in kind. No doubt Soviet military leaders have been pressing for increased defense outlays. But there are also forces in the Politburo calling for improvements in the Soviet economy. There is little evidence to suggest that the Soviets have sufficient resources to increase their military budget significantly while simultaneously increasing the production of agricultural products and consumer goods. In response to these dual economic and military pressures, Gorbachev has carved out a strategy of radical economic reform and international tension reduction.

Strategic Defense Initiative

On 23 March 1983, President Reagan called on U.S. scientists to develop a missile defense shield in space that would render nuclear weapons "impotent and obsolete." Although the official name of this project is the Strategic Defense Initiative (SDI), it has been dubbed "Star Wars" by critics of the program and the U.S. press. In proposing SDI, Reagan attacked the traditional theory of nuclear deterrence by retaliation as immoral and unreliable.

As envisaged by the Pentagon, SDI would consist of a complex network of systems including laser beams; particle beams; electromagnetic "sling shots" that would hurl nonexplosive projectiles (called "smart rocks") through space at great speed; and sensing, tracking, and aiming devices. All of these weapons systems would require the extraordinary coordination of advanced computers and other technologies to detect missiles and compute their trajectories and to direct intercepting weapons over great distances. The administration suggested an initial six-year SDI research program to be funded at the $33-billion level. Scientists estimate that SDI could take between fifteen and twenty years to complete at a cost in excess of $1 trillion.

That Reagan is attracted to SDI should come as no surprise to anyone, given his penchant for large-scale, high-tech enterprises such as the MX missile, the B-1 bomber, the Clinch River breeder reactor, and the space shuttle program. In addition to SDI's alleged military benefits, administration proponents claim that it will spawn valuable nonmilitary technologies that will lead to enormous commercial benefits for U.S. industry.

In his 1986 State of the Union address, President Reagan was almost euphoric over SDI:

> Technology transforming our lives can solve the greatest problem of the twentieth century. A security shield can one day render nuclear weapons obsolete and free mankind from the prison of nuclear terror.
>
> After all we've done so far, let no one say that this nation cannot reach the destiny of our dreams.
>
> America believes. America is ready. America can win the race to the future, and we shall.

But many U.S. scientists do not share President Reagan's optimism over SDI. In February 1986 pollster Peter D. Hart surveyed the members of the American Physical Society and found that 67 percent of the members, all physicists, thought that it was improbable or extremely unlikely that SDI could defend the U.S. population. Only

16 percent of the physicists surveyed thought it was probable or very likely that SDI could protect the population. Sixty-two percent of the physicists said it was very likely that the Soviets would deploy countermeasures that would render SDI ineffective; 25 percent said it was somewhat unlikely. SDI would be dangerously unreliable, 63 percent said, because the system as a whole could never be adequately tested. Finally, 58 percent of the physicists polled thought that proceeding with SDI would escalate the arms race between the United States and the Soviet Union.[12]

The explosion of the space shuttle *Challenger,* the grounding of the Titan and Delta rockets, and the Chernobyl nuclear disaster have all raised serious doubts in the minds of some experts as to whether it is possible to make SDI as invincible as Reagan administration officials have attempted to lead the U.S. public to believe.

Some scientists believe that it would be much easier to design, build, and deploy countermeasures to defeat SDI than it would be to construct the system itself. They argue that any space-based defense system would be useless against bombers, low-flying cruise missiles, short-range submarine-launched weapons, and concealed nuclear devices.

Several seemingly insurmountable problems have already emerged from the early stages of research on SDI.

1. It would be relatively easy for the Soviets to deploy weapons that have the capability to defeat a space-based defense system. So-called fast-burn rockets on Soviet missiles might require an SDI system to shoot down the missiles in less than two minutes, thus imposing a severe time constraint on the system.

2. The complexity of the computer software that would be required to manage the large array of computers necessary to support a weapons system, that would work when confronted with a salvo of nuclear missiles, is virtually beyond belief. The computer program used to support the space shuttle's launch sequence consisted of over ten thousand lines of computer code. By comparison, the software required to support SDI would involve tens of millions of lines of computer code.

3. It would be virtually impossible to test realistically the huge

array of computers that would operate and control a complex system of sensors, antimissile weapons, guidance and aiming devices, and battle management stations.

4. Many of the SDI weapons would have to be placed in extremely low orbits and would travel along predictable paths, thus making them vulnerable to attack by Soviet missiles, space mines, and other countermeasures.

5. The *Challenger* disaster and a series of other major setbacks in the U.S. space program in 1986 have thrown SDI's schedule of complex space-based experiments into confusion and disarray, sending shock waves through the program and demoralizing some of the scientists involved with SDI.

To counteract the effects of the barrage of criticism leveled against SDI by the scientific community, the Pentagon has embarked on a strategy of exaggerated claims, cover-up of scientific failures, hyperbolic tests, and high-priced public-relations razzle-dazzle. The objective is to create the illusion of major technical breakthroughs, no matter how great or small the actual accomplishments may be. The Pentagon trades heavily on the fact that many of the people who are skeptical about SDI are scientists and engineers with security clearances and are therefore legally barred from revealing classified information to the press about the limitations of SDI. Pentagon advocates of SDI also have complete access to all classified information about the project, but they can say whatever they like about SDI and not risk being charged with security violations. Thus the public gets a very one-sided view of SDI.

In addition to all the hype that the Pentagon has used to promote SDI, its most powerful vehicle for attracting support is the lure of fat government research contracts. With over $90 billion targeted for the research phase of SDI, the Defense Department has had little difficulty in stimulating the interest of U.S., Western European, and Japanese military contractors, not to mention U.S. universities that are also anxious to share in the financial bonanza. Cal Tech, Stanford University, Carnegie–Mellon University, and MIT were among the first to jump on board the Star Wars bandwagon and claim their share of the $600 million that the Pentagon expects to spend on SDI-related university-based research between 1986 and 1990. By the end of 1985 TRW and Boeing had already received SDI contracts amounting to $424 million and $217 million, respectively, and the program had just barely gotten off the ground.

We have been told repeatedly by President Reagan that we have Soviet leader Gorbachev on the run and that the only reason he came to Reykjavík was out of fear of SDI. Nothing could be further from the truth. Star Wars has made Gorbachev's task of injecting new vitality into the Soviet political and economic systems much easier than might otherwise have been the case.

Publicly Gorbachev denounces SDI, claiming that it is a destabilizing threat to world peace which will accelerate the arms race. He warns that if the U.S. deploys SDI, the Soviets will take countermeasures which "will be effective though less expensive, and quicker to produce." But what does Gorbachev really think about SDI?

Not unlike some of their U.S. counterparts, many Soviet scientists, including Nobel laureate Andrei Sakharov, have expressed serious doubts about the technical feasibility of President Reagan's vision of SDI.

On 4 October 1957, the Soviets launched the first artificial satellite, *Sputnik*. This shock to U.S. pride generated an enormous commitment on the part of the private and public sectors of the U.S. economy to not only catch up with the Soviets, but to surpass them. Politicians such as John F. Kennedy were quick to pick up on the mood of the U.S. public and exploit it for their own political gain. I believe that Star Wars in the 1980s will be to the Soviet Union what *Sputnik* was to the United States in the 1960s. SDI will enable Gorbachev to play on the national pride of the Soviet people to get their act together and close their economic and technological gap with the West. Indeed, it is hard to imagine a more effective instrument for motivating the Soviet people in the direction Gorbachev would like to lead them. Every time President Reagan opens his mouth about Star Wars, Gorbachev's job is made easier.

The implied military threat of Star Wars to Soviet security has helped Gorbachev consolidate his political power base within the party and the Politburo. Given the Soviets' fear of being attacked by outside forces, they quite naturally gravitate to a strong leader like Gorbachev who promises to protect them from a Reagan. While publicly condemning Star Wars, Gorbachev continues to benefit from its political fallout. Gorbachev's 1987 proposal to de-couple medium-range nuclear missiles in Europe from an overall arms agreement is further evidence that he is not intimidated by SDI.

SDI has also provided Gorbachev with a global issue that he can use to enhance his image as an international peacemaker opposed to the continuation of the arms race. When Gorbachev came to power, the NATO members in Western Europe were still chafing over the Soviets' unsuccessful attempt to intimidate them into not deploying cruise and Pershing missiles. The level of trust between Western Europe and the Soviet Union was not very high.

Many Europeans view Star Wars as an immoral, irresponsible exercise in high-tech adventurism that has significantly increased the risk of a nuclear war. SDI enables Gorbachev to project himself as a man of peace in contrast to President Reagan, who is depicted by Gorbachev as an inflexible warmonger with an unyielding commitment to SDI at any price.

Nuclear Deterrence

Since the Soviet Union joined the nuclear club in the early 1950s, *mutual deterrence* has been the philosophy on which the Soviets and the Americans have based their respective nuclear strategies. The underlying premise of nuclear deterrence is that it is impossible to win a nuclear war. Therefore, neither superpower will be willing to launch a first-strike nuclear attack on the other out of fear of the devastating effects of retaliation on the part of the other superpower. Thus a peaceful equilibrium will prevail in which neither side is willing to risk attacking the other.

For the first time in the history of the nuclear arms race we may be witnessing a breakdown of the strange nuclear logic described by Winston Churchill: "It may well be that we shall, by a process of sublime irony, have reached a stage in this story where safety shall be the sturdy child of terror, and survival the twin brother of annihilation." In 1983 and 1984, when U.S.–Soviet relations were approaching an all-time low, the Reagan administration began talking about preparing to *fight* and *win* a nuclear war with the Soviet Union. In an article in the *New York Times Magazine* in 1984, Leslie H.

Gelb cited a Pentagon planning document approved by Defense Secretary Weinberger and leaked to the news media, which read, "Should deterrence fail and strategic nuclear war with the USSR occur, the United States must prevail and be able to force the Soviet Union to seek earliest termination of hostilities on terms favorable to the United States."[13] According to Gelb, the Pentagon publication emphasized three themes: developing the capability to strike military targets, being able to control and fight a prolonged battle, and having the power to prevail.

Some military policy analysts believe that the overall objective of the Reagan administration is nuclear superiority over the Soviet Union. Several of the new weapons in the Reagan administration's arsenal appear to be first-strike offensive weapons rather than merely defensive weapons. These include the Trident II missile, the sea-launched cruise missile, the Stealth bomber, and the Midgetman.

The Reagan administration's foreign policy contains a number of interesting paradoxes, which are no doubt related to the fact that there is widespread disagreement within the administration as to what its policy should be towards the Soviet Union. While preparing to fight and win a nuclear war with the Soviet Union, the Pentagon is simultaneously claiming that the Soviets have achieved strategic and conventional military superiority over the United States. Politburo members in Moscow must undoubtedly be asking the question, "Will the real Ronald Reagan please stand up?"

The schizophrenic nature of the administration's foreign policy must be a source of confusion and bewilderment to Soviet leaders. Do the Soviets believe that they have military superiority over the United States, as Reagan claims, or do they view Reagan's pronouncements as merely an attempt to justify increases in the Pentagon's budget? Do they take the Pentagon seriously when it claims that it is possible for the United States to win a nuclear war with the Soviet Union? We do not know the answers to these questions, and we doubt that the Reagan administration knows the answers either.

The combined effects of the administration's record military buildup and its movement away from nuclear deterrence must have had a sobering effect on the Kremlin. So long as Reagan remains in the White House, the Soviets undoubtedly feel that it is impossible to let their guard down militarily. Taken in the aggregate, the effect of

Reagan's foreign policies is to cause Gorbachev to maintain military preparedness at least at present levels while combining radical economic, political, and cultural reforms with international tension-reduction activities.

Arms Control

By April 1987, the Reagan administration had spent $1.4 trillion on defense. In his 26 February 1986 speech in support of his $320.3 billion 1987 national defense budget request, of which Congress authorized only $291.9 billion, President Reagan summarized his views on arms control:

> We want to make this a more peaceful world. We want to reduce arms. We want agreements that truly diminish the nuclear danger. We want real agreements, agreements that really work, with no cheating. We want an end to state policies of intimidation, threats and the constant quest for domination. We want real peace.
>
> We've come so far together these last five years; let's not falter now. Let's maintain that crucial level of national strength, unity and purpose that has brought the Soviet Union to the negotiating table and has given us this historic opportunity to achieve real reductions in nuclear weapons and a real chance at lasting peace. That would be the finest legacy we could leave behind—for our children and for their children.

Prior to the exposure of the Iran–contra affair, this was the first U.S. administration since the nuclear arms race began in the 1950s that had not made a serious effort to reduce the danger of nuclear war by limiting nuclear weapons through negotiations. Presidents Eisenhower, Kennedy, Johnson, Nixon, Ford, and Carter were all committed to the use of diplomatic negotiations to reduce the arms race. In spite of the lip service that he gives to arms control, President Reagan's track record hardly suggests that he is a champion of arms control. He opposed the Limited Test Ban Treaty of 1963, the Non-Proliferation Treaty of 1968, SALT I, SALT II, and the Peaceful Nuclear Explosions Treaty of 1976.

In August 1985, the Soviet Union initiated a unilateral nuclear test ban that was repeatedly extended until 1 January 1987. However, the Soviets announced in December 1986 that they would end their halt of nuclear testing as soon as the United States conducted its first test in 1987. By the end of 1986, the United States had conducted over twenty nuclear tests during the course of the Soviet test ban. Not only did the United States continue testing nuclear weapons throughout this period, but Reagan refused to even talk about the possibility of a mutual test ban, claiming that the Soviet initiative was purely a propaganda move. The Soviets resumed nuclear testing in early 1987.

Much to the chagrin of our NATO allies, in 1986 the Reagan administration deliberately breached the SALT II nuclear arms treaty, which had been signed by President Jimmy Carter in 1979 but never ratified by the U.S. Senate. Also in 1986, the administration began backing away from the 1972 Anti-Ballistic Missile Treaty. Reagan's response to most of Gorbachev's 1986 arms control initiatives was not only chilly, but more often than not was downright insulting. Until the October 1986 summit in Reykjavík, literally all of Gorbachev's proposals were summarily dismissed by Reagan as merely communist propaganda and not to be taken seriously.

On 11–12 October 1986, President Reagan met General Secretary Gorbachev in Reykjavík in a hastily prepared summit initiated by Gorbachev. The two leaders apparently reached a tentative understanding on a number of far-reaching proposals, including a ban on medium-range missiles in Europe, a nuclear test ban, drastic reductions in strategic offensive nuclear weapons, as well as a number of nonarms issues. Negotiations broke down between the two superpower leaders when it was not possible to reach a compromise on President Reagan's SDI. But for the first time, Gorbachev had been taken seriously by the Reagan administration.

Under pressure from U.S. conservatives and the leaders of our NATO allies in Europe, within a matter of a few days, President Reagan began to back away from some of the Reykjavík proposals to which he had apparently previously agreed. For the next few weeks, there was considerable debate in the international press as to what had been said or not said by Reagan and Gorbachev at Reykjavík.

Fundamentally, the Reagan administration has never treated arms control as an important part of national security. Positions have been put forth in negotiations, not so much to find common ground, but rather to create the appearance of flexibility while continuing the arms buildup. The administration has shown little flexibility in negotiating with the Soviets. At times the administration's proposals have been so one-sided that they have made Moscow more truculent and more persuaded of Washington's ulterior motives.

At least part of the problem lies in the fact that the Reagan administration is so divided in its attitude towards the nuclear arms race. Some officials in the Pentagon obviously regard the arms race as a good thing for the United States. In their view, either the Soviets will keep pace with the United States militarily (which will destroy their economy) or they will fall behind (which will leave the United States with a decisive military advantage). Because this group favors a policy of U.S. nuclear superiority rather than mutual deterrence, it consistently opposes all arms control proposals.

State Department officials would probably favor some type of agreement with the Soviets that limits the arms race. President Reagan claims that he too favors arms control. But he lets the Pentagon define the terms of an acceptable agreement. An acceptable agreement to the Pentagon is an agreement that would primarily limit intercontinental ballistic missiles. Because the Soviets have invested 75 percent of their retaliatory power in ICBMs and the United States only 25 percent, the Soviets do not respond very positively to such proposals. Rather consistently, the Pentagon makes little or no effort to view the arms race from the perspective of the Soviet Union. Given the arrogance with which the Pentagon approaches arms control, it is not surprising that the Reagan administration has not signed an arms control agreement with the Soviets.

Although some believe that Reagan genuinely does want an arms control agreement with the Soviets, he does not seem to know how to deal with the Soviets—or, more importantly, with his own advisers in the Pentagon. At times it appears as though his foreign-policy and national-security advisers are more concerned about war with each other rather than with the Soviet Union. These bureaucratic disputes have made it impossible to reach a consensus on where we are going, what we want to accomplish, and how we are going to get there. After six years in office, President Reagan's advisers can't even agree on how SDI fits into future security plans, let alone whether it should be used as a bargaining instrument in negotiations with the Soviets.

Gorbachev has installed a top-notch team of national-security advisers who have kept the United States totally off balance with their foreign-policy initiatives. There is a sense among diplomats that Gorbachev and his new team of young, dynamic, and relatively pragmatic advisers have managed to capture the high road in diplomatic maneuvering. He has made what many analysts feel is a sincere and concerted effort to negotiate an arms control agreement with the Reagan administration. Until the Iran–contra affair surfaced in late 1986, Reagan showed only superficial interest in arms control.

Europe

President Reagan has severely strained the NATO alliance with his frequent unilateral actions affecting our Western European allies—the 1982 attempt to block the Soviet trans-Siberian gas pipeline; the intimidation tactics used to pressure our allies into accepting more U.S. missiles and participating in SDI; the bombing of Libya; the breach of SALT II; and the entire Iran–contra affair. All of these events have had a very unsettling effect on the people and governments of Western Europe. After each such event, Secretary of State George P. Shultz makes a quick trip to Europe and attempts to soothe the ruffled feathers.

When NATO was founded in 1949, it was essentially a unilateral U.S. nuclear guarantee disguised as an alliance. Forty years later the situation remains largely unchanged, only the United States has 360,000 troops stationed in Europe and spends 56 percent of its entire defense budget on military forces in Europe or forces in the United States available to reinforce Europe in a conflict. NATO's founders never envisaged what has become a continuing occupation of Western Europe by U.S. troops. And how did all of this come about? Starting with President Truman and continuing through President Reagan, every U.S. administration has succeeded in convincing Western Europe that it needs our protection from the Soviet Union and that the only adequate protection is an extension of the U.S. nuclear umbrella.[14] To make certain that our European allies remain convinced, we offer to pay for most of this protection.

When President Reagan first unveiled his Star Wars proposal in 1983, the initial response in Western Europe was that SDI would not protect Europe from a Soviet missile attack, could possibly precipitate a conventional arms race, might result in a breakup of the NATO alliance, and increase the risk of war. Some Europeans believe that no more nuclear weapons need be based in Western Europe for Europe's deterrence. They believe that any additional nuclear weapons that might be deployed in Europe serve no European purpose. Consequently, some Europeans want no part of SDI or any other nuclear weapons. They feel that the United States has simply used them as a hostage to serve its own strategic interests.

The Reagan administration has cleverly used the attraction of lucrative contracts and the fear that Western Europe might be falling behind the United States and Japan in high technology to win important industrial support for SDI in the United Kingdom, France, the FRG, and Italy. Denmark and Norway, also members of NATO, have categorically rejected space weapons cooperation.

Some Europeans have become impatient with their role as pawns in the superpower conflict between the United States and the Soviet Union. President Reagan's foreign policies in Europe have exacerbated these feelings—particularly on the part of young European peace activists. According to Hungarian political dissident George Konrad, some Europeans are no longer willing to remain silent while the two superpowers turn Europe into "a heap of ashes."[15] Konrad and other European intellectuals have called for a more independent Europe—independent of the United States and the Soviet Union.[16] Thus far the Reagan administration seems oblivious to the fact that a new European identity is emerging in the East and the West that is independent of either of the two superpowers.

Recognizing the political opportunities created by President Reagan's alienating policies in Europe, Gorbachev has embraced the concept of "Europe for Europeans." In July 1986, while hosting President François Mitterrand in Moscow, Gorbachev called for greater Western European self-reliance:

> Everybody sees that Europeans are tired of nerve-wracking confrontation and tension. They need the air of détente. Europe's economic and political potential is large enough for it to speak more definitely and confidently on its own behalf, to press for progress at all the ongoing talks.
>
> It is necessary to get rid of the political thinking that views

Europe as a "theater of operations." Europe must set an example of coexistence among sovereign, different but peaceful countries, countries aware of their interdependence and building their relations on trust.[17]

Gorbachev managed to attract the attention of both Eastern and Western Europe in his 18 April 1986 speech to the East German Socialist Unity Party Congress in Berlin when he called for "the simultaneous disbandment of the Warsaw Treaty and NATO, or at least the military organizations of both alliances to begin with." Gorbachev gained Warsaw Pact approval for this proposal in Budapest in June 1986. He then went on to propose that NATO and the Warsaw Pact begin by demobilizing up to 150,000 troops in Europe within a year or two.

Regardless of the outcome of Gorbachev's 1987 arms control initiatives, he will continue to play his European card and concentrate on strengthening the Soviet economy through economic reform and international trade.

Freedom Fighters

By 1986, the Reagan administration was participating or assisting in nine wars—in Afghanistan, Angola, Cambodia, Chad, El Salvador, Ethiopia, Lebanon, Morocco, and Nicaragua. In each case, U.S. participation was justified by the claim that we are fighting for freedom and democracy. In the case of the war in Nicaragua, anyone who is opposed to the United States sending military aid to the contras is accused of being "un-American" and "pro-Communist."

U.S. intervention in the Third World is based on the "Reagan Doctrine," which claims that the United States has the right to intervene in any country where there is an opportunity to fight either the Soviet Union or communism. Under the assumptions of the Reagan Doctrine the U.S. invasion of Grenada, military aid to the contras in Nicaragua, and the bombing of Libya are fully justified. In all cases, the Reagan Doctrine stands above the United Nations and international law. The corollary of the Reagan Doctrine is that the Soviet Union has no legitimate interests whatsoever in the Third World, and it must reconcile itself to giving up its recently acquired positions in the Third World.

What is so interesting about the Reagan Doctrine is its similarity to the Brezhnev Doctrine of 1968—a doctrine that President Reagan has vehemently denounced over the years. Under the Brezhnev Doctrine, the Soviet Union and the community of socialist nations have the right to intervene if, in their judgment, one of their number is pursuing policies that threaten the essential common interests of the others. The Brezhnev Doctrine was first used by the Soviets to justify overthrowing the Czechoslovakian government in 1968. But the Brezhnev Doctrine is much more limited in scope than the Reagan Doctrine. The former applied only to socialist countries whereas the latter is much more global in nature.

One of the principal attributes of the Reagan Doctrine is its flexibility. It enabled President Reagan, without any apparent sense of irony, to proclaim his duty to wage war on terrorism in Libya at the very moment he was seeking $100 million in military aid from Congress to export terrorism, via contra clients, into Nicaragua. In this perspective, Nicaragua is the sine qua non test of the Reagan Doctrine.

Thus, at a time when Gorbachev appears to be pulling the Soviet Union back from its Third World adventures, the Reagan Doctrine seems to provide limitless opportunities for the United States to impose its form of government on literally any country in the world. Thus far, the Soviet response to the Reagan Doctrine has been amazingly subdued.

The Soviet Response

During Reagan's first four years in office, his foreign policy was based on a combination of hard-line, anti-Soviet rhetoric and the greatest military buildup in the history of the United States. Although there were periods of temporary restraint in his anti-Soviet rhetoric, for the most part Reagan's foreign policy has remained unchanged since Gorbachev came to power in 1985. What is truly amazing is Gorbachev's disciplined, restrained response to Reagan. More often than not, Gorbachev has simply ignored him.

Consider, for example, the Iran—contra affair, which in the past would have been an ideal target for anti-U.S. Soviet propaganda. Gorbachev has said virtually nothing about this matter and certainly cannot be accused of using it for his own propaganda advantage.

The ultimate effect of Reagan's foreign policy on the Soviets has been to encourage the Soviets in three directions—international tension reduction, foreign trade, and economic reform. Gorbachev realizes that it is extremely unlikely that Reagan will ever change his way of thinking about the Soviet Union. But Gorbachev can have a positive influence on U.S. public opinion as well as the public opinion of Western Europe, Japan, Israel, and the rest of the world. The way to influence global public opinion is through international trade and tension-reduction activities rather than through international saber rattling.

Under the leadership of former Ambassador to the United States Anatoly F. Dobrynin, and Foreign Minister Eduard A. Shevardnadze, Gorbachev has put together a first-rate foreign-policy team that in a very short period of time has demonstrated that it is flexible, pragmatic, and nonideological. Not only have the Soviets pursued a policy of improved relations with the United States, but they have made strong diplomatic overtures towards Western Europe, China, Japan, and more recently even Israel. Gorbachev has been particularly forthcoming toward China. Soviet and Israeli officials met in Helsinki in 1986—the first move towards improved relations since the Soviet Union broke diplomatic ties with Israel during the 1967 Arab–Israeli War.

Although a comprehensive arms control deal with the United States is unlikely before 1990, Gorbachev has already responded positively to the unexpected window of opportunity created by the weakened Reagan presidency as a result of the Iran–contra fiasco. In less than two years, the United States and the Soviet Union have completely reversed foreign-policy roles. No longer is it the Soviet Union that is locked into a rigid, moribund foreign policy, but rather the United States.

In the meantime, Gorbachev will continue to pursue a flexible, pragmatic foreign policy and will make every effort to turn the rigidities of Reagan's foreign policy into Soviet advantages—particularly in Western Europe and in the Pacific. In 1990, Gorbachev will go for a sweeping arms control agreement with the next U.S. president.

When Ronald Reagan ran for the presidency in 1980, he ran on a platform calling for a dramatic reduction in government regulations, claiming that more often than not government regulations end up causing more harm than good. Yet he has spent his entire term in office trying to regulate, manipulate, and control the Soviet Union. The irony of all ironies is that when Reagan leaves office, the Soviet Union will be stronger economically, militarily, and politically than at any time in its history. And Ronald Reagan will have played a fundamental role in creating precisely the kind of psychological environment in the Soviet Union to make all of this possible. To President Reagan, Mikhail S. Gorbachev owes a very big *spasibo*.

Part III
Opening the Closed Society

———

7
Changing the Culture of a Risk-Free Society

Changing the Corporate Culture

If the new CEO of a major U.S. company such as IBM or General Motors wants to introduce fundamental policy changes, then the CEO must come to grips with the company's culture—the attitudes, values, and customs of the company's managers and employees. The failure to address strongly ingrained cultural factors has led to the demise of many a new CEO in the United States.

But this is precisely the situation in which Soviet leader Gorbachev finds himself as he attempts to de-Stalinize the Soviet Union and open the closed society. He has embarked on a systematic strategy to change the centrally planned economy, the Communist party, the vast government bureaucracy, the military establishment, and the KGB. Since the 1950s, various Soviet leaders (including Khrushchev, Kosygin, and Brezhnev) have unsuccessfully attempted to "change the economic mechanism" in the Soviet Union, that is, introduce decentralized, market-oriented planning. In each case, these efforts got bogged down in a sea of bureaucratic resistance and inertia. Each of these Soviet leaders learned the hard way that it is impossible to change the economic system of a country like the Soviet Union without first coming to grips with the uniqueness of its culture.

Many of the important characteristics of the Soviet culture can be traced back to the eighteenth and nineteenth centuries when Russia was still ruled by the czars. Some of these cultural mores include a penchant for military authority and secrecy; an aversion to risk; a lack of commitment to democratic principles; a distrust of markets and capitalism; corruption; an underdeveloped consumer sector; and underinvestment in human resource development.

If Gorbachev is to succeed, he must confront the culture of the largest risk-free society in the world—a society characterized by full employment, inexpensive housing, free education and medical care, low-cost transportation, the absence of bankruptcy, and cradle-to-grave socialism. But that is exactly what he is doing, and he is doing it very effectively. The alcohol reforms, the clampdown on corruption, increased openness, the release of political dissidents, and the recent call for secret balloting and a choice of candidates in party elections are all examples of significant changes taking place in the Soviet culture under Gorbachev.

Gorbachev's Management Style

Even before he officially came to power, Mikhail S. Gorbachev was giving off signals that his style of management represented a marked departure from that of his recent predecessors. In December 1984, Prime Minister Margaret Thatcher had this to say about Gorbachev's first visit to London: "I like Mr. Gorbachev. I can do business with him." *Time* magazine described Gorbachev as "younger, smoother, and probably formidable" in its 25 March 1985 cover story.

Almost immediately, reports out of Moscow began depicting Gorbachev's management style as more open, relaxed, and streamlined. He was said to work long hours, to expect the same from his subordinates, and to reject the traditional effusive personal tributes so cherished by his predecessors. He declared war on vodka, cracked down on corruption, and began implementing programs to improve industrial safety and discipline. The press and the arts were given increased license to criticize Soviet society.

Even in the politically sensitive area of human rights, Gorbachev has made some significant moves. Soviet dissident Anatoly B. Shcharansky was permitted to immigrate to Israel, and Yelena G. Bonner, the wife of Andrei D. Sakharov, was allowed to travel to the United States for surgery. Then in December 1986, to the surprise of the entire Western world, Professor Sakharov himself was allowed to leave Gorky, where he had been confined since 1980.

The new Soviet style of management has been particularly noticeable in the field of foreign affairs. First in Paris, and then in his meetings with President Reagan in Geneva and Iceland, Gorbachev demonstrated repeatedly that he is a cool, competent leader. Foreign

Minister Eduard A. Shevardnadze handled the Daniloff–Zakharov affair from the Soviet side with self-confidence, diplomacy, and professionalism. Not only did Shevardnadze obtain the release of accused spy Gennadi Zakharov, but he sent a clear signal to the White House that the United States should think twice before it arrests another Soviet spy suspect. Gorbachev was also able to take credit for arranging the superpower meeting in Reykjavík and salvaging the East–West dialogue on arms control.

On more than one occasion, Gorbachev has managed to put the White House squarely on the defensive with his dramatic change of management style and adroit diplomatic initiatives. This aggressive, more open style of management, whether applied to foreign affairs or domestic policy, bodes well for the future of Gorbachev's economic, political, and social reforms.

Not so many years ago, a clash of Soviet and Chinese troops along the Chinese border would have given rise to a tirade from Moscow. In the summer of 1986, the Soviet Foreign Ministry merely brushed off such a skirmish with a few calm words. The muted response to this clash not only demonstrated a change in management style in the Kremlin, but reflected the priority that Gorbachev assigns to improved Sino–Soviet relations. Today Soviet diplomats no longer talk about the inevitability of conflicts between socialist and capitalist nations, but rather they speak of the importance of "global interdependence." Gorbachev's response to the Iran–contra affair has been professional and low-key. He has resisted the temptation to reap short-term political gains from this venture in favor of a longer-term view of U.S.–Soviet relations.

That there are noticeable similarities between Gorbachev and President John F. Kennedy has not escaped the attention of the Soviets. They are quick to point out that just as Kennedy tried to change the culture of the United States in the 1960s, so too is Gorbachev attempting to reshape the Soviet culture in the 1980s. For the first time since Lenin, the Soviet people have a leader whom they respect and admire.

Glasnost

Gorbachev has repeatedly called for more *glasnost,* or openness, in the media coverage of domestic and international affairs. Soviet citizens are able to enjoy increasingly open television and press coverage of a broad range of events including the economic reforms, the campaign against corruption, the Geneva and Reykjavík summits, the party congress, the Chernobyl nuclear accident, the sinking of the *Admiral Nakhimov* in the Black Sea, and the nuclear submarine accident in the Atlantic Ocean.

In the past, Soviet television almost never reported civil disturbances or political unrest in the Soviet Union. Yet in December 1986, Moscow television reported student riots in Alma-Ata, the capital of the Central Asian republic of Kazakhstan. The Kremlin recently stopped jamming the Russian-language broadcasts of the Voice of America and the British Broadcasting Corporation.

Gorbachev frequently makes televised jaunts around the Soviet Union in which he speaks candidly about the nation's economic and social problems. He has encouraged a degree of openness and self-criticism that is unprecedented in the history of the Soviet Union. In September 1986, in Krasnodar in the deep south of the Russian republic, Gorbachev said, "We've got problems, urgent problems—housing, foodstuffs, health care, education, and, finally, democracy. Our people should feel in command." The Soviets have even acknowledged that drug addiction, prostitution, and AIDS are among their social problems.

Not only do Soviet leaders now hold frequent press conferences, but the spokesperson for the Soviet Foreign Ministry makes press statements on an almost daily basis. Soviet news commentator Vladimir Posner makes regular appearances before U.S. television audiences with his perfect English and smooth style. Most of Gorbachev's speeches are published in English in the *Soviet Weekly,* which is distributed via air mail in the United States. Some have appeared in full-page ads in the *New York Times,* paid for by the Soviet government. Others have been published in full-length books in the United States. Upon writing to the Soviet Embassy in Washington for a copy of Gorbachev's party congress speech, I received a bound copy with a color photograph of Gorbachev on the cover.

The Soviets have entered into agreements with U.S. public television stations and the Turner Broadcasting System for an exchange of programs. They plan to air the anti-Soviet television miniseries, *Amerika,* on Soviet television. It is now possible to purchase some

Western newspapers, such as the *International Herald Tribune*, in Moscow.

The Soviet cultural newspaper, *Sovetskaya Kultura*, has begun publishing articles by noted Soviet authorities that challenge some of the fundamental underpinnings of Marxist-Leninist ideology. In one article, economist Tatyana Zaslavskaya challenged the Soviet government's official position that the Soviet Union had become a classless society as prescribed by Marxist theory. She noted that "opportunities for the timely development of one's abilities are still dependent to a large extent on one's geographical location and on the social and economic standing of one's parents." In another article published by *Sovetskaya Kultura*, Vladimir G. Kostakov, a leading government economist, reported that Gorbachev's economic reforms may throw millions of Soviet people temporarily out of work. He also indicated that the government would pay unemployment compensation to those who lost their jobs as a result of the reforms. This was the first time the Soviet government has acknowledged the existence of unemployment since it was defined to be out of existence in the 1930s.[1]

Recently Soviet newspapers such as *Pravda* and *Sovetskaya Rossiya* have taken to publishing letters from readers that are highly critical of the party, the government, labor unions, economic agencies, and even the Komsomol (communist youth organization). These letters have been particularly critical of those special privileges that are available only to members of the Communist party. Letters have been published that advocate giving voters a choice of candidates in elections.

Increased freedom of expression in art, literature, drama, and music is not only being tolerated by Gorbachev but is actually being encouraged. In 1986, Gorbachev replaced the aging, conservative minister of culture with a younger, more flexible person who is fully supportive of more open cultural activities. Soviet poet, dissident, and now filmmaker Yevgeny Yevtushenko has been openly critical of government censorship, which prevents Soviet writers, artists, film directors, scientists, and workers from saying what is on their minds. One of the most popular plays in Moscow is called *The Silver Anniversary*, and deals with corruption, morality, and renewal of the Soviet ruling class. The Soviet record company Melodia has recently released

300,000 copies each of two albums of the Beatles that were previously banned by the government. Funds were raised for victims of the Chernobyl nuclear accident at a rock concert in Moscow. U.S. films are now widely available in the Soviet Union on video cassettes.

Two movies that have attracted a great deal of attention in the Soviet Union are *Repentance,* a film dealing quite openly with Stalin's purges, and *Is It Easy to Be Young?,* a film about alienated young people and disturbed Afghanistan veterans. The novels of Vladimir Nabokov and the poetry of Nikolai Gumilev, who was shot in the 1920s for anti-Soviet behavior, began appearing in 1986. The long-suppressed novel, *Doctor Zhivago,* by Boris Pasternak, and Anatoly Rybakov's book on Stalin's reign of terror, *Children of Arbat,* were published in 1987. The Bolshoi Ballet has invited émigrés Mikhail Baryshnikov and Natalia Makarova to perform in Moscow.

In the past, Soviet authorities would not permit émigrés to return to the Soviet Union. However, fifty émigrés who had found it difficult to adjust to life in the United States were allowed to return to Moscow in 1986 and received a warm reception from Soviet officials.

After years of withholding data on infant mortality rates, grain harvests, and other socioeconomic statistics, the Soviets began publishing these figures again in 1986. The new figures showed that infant mortality rates have remained more than twice what they are in the West.

In 1986 Gorbachev had to deal with three major tragedies—the Chernobyl nuclear accident, the sinking of the *Admiral Nakhimov,* and the fire on a Soviet nuclear submarine in the Atlantic.

Although the Soviets were initially subjected to widespread criticism for their two-day delay in reporting the 26 April 1986 nuclear tragedy at Chernobyl, they later displayed a high degree of openness in their explanation of the event to the Soviet people and to the rest of the world. This was in sharp contrast to their blustery response to the international outcry following the invasion of Afghanistan in 1979 and the shooting down of Korean Air Lines Flight 007 in 1983. Not only did they admit to error in judgment and to responding too slowly to the crisis, but they openly sought the advice of Western physicians and nuclear engineers to help them deal with the human and technical problems caused by the accident. Both the director and chief engineer of the Chernobyl nuclear power station were fired for mishandling the disaster. Within a month of the accident the Soviets began releasing an enormous amount of very detailed information about the cause of the accident as well as of its adverse effects. A Soviet diplomat appeared before a congressional committee in Washington and testified about the accident only a few days after it happened.

Four months later, when the Soviet passenger ship, the *Admiral Nakhimov*, was hit broadside by the freighter, the *Pyotr Vasev*, and sank in the Black Sea, the Soviet press was very forthcoming with timely details about the accident. Nearly four hundred people were killed. Not so many years ago, Soviet officials might not have even reported such an accident. In the past, commercial airline crashes were rarely reported by the press in the Soviet Union. This too has changed.

In October 1986, when a Soviet nuclear submarine caught fire and sank about a thousand miles east of New York, Gorbachev notified President Reagan of the accident within two hours after it happened. The accident received substantial television and newspaper coverage back in the Soviet Union.

A new high-water mark in openness was reached in early 1987 when *Pravda* reported that two KGB officials had been disciplined for the illegal arrest of a reporter who had exposed corruption in the Ukraine. This event was followed within a few days by the arrest of former Soviet leader Brezhnev's son-in-law, Yuri M. Churbanov, on charges of corruption.

Finally, for the very first time, the Soviets have agreed to on-site inspections to verify compliance with arms control agreements. The Soviets permitted a team of Western scientists to set up an array of sensitive instruments to monitor their main underground nuclear test site in 1986. For years the United States has unsuccessfully sought this type of verification of nuclear tests in conjunction with various arms control proposals. In the past, the Soviets have systematically refused to consider on-site verification.

Sense of Meaning

A common malaise found in developed countries is a lack of meaning in the lives of individual citizens, which can give rise to feelings of alienation towards one's government, employer, and family, as well as one's self. In the United States hardly a month goes by in which there is not at least one article in the business press about some well-known corporate executive who has opted out of corporate life to pursue a quieter, more reflective existence far removed from the management of a major corporation. Often referred to as a midlife identity crisis, this phenomenon appears to be caused by the absence of a sense of purpose or meaning in the lives of many executives. In many U.S. firms, managers are forced to subscribe to the values of the company in order to advance up the corporate ladder. The values they must embrace often place too much emphasis on greed, the acquisition of power, and the desire to dominate and manipulate others. For such executives, motivation comes not from internal personal goals but from recognition and approval by others. Eventually, this type of behavior results in anxiety, depression, feelings of emptiness, and burnout. Some executives turn to drugs and alcohol to combat their loneliness and emptiness.

There is little evidence to suggest that Marxist-Leninist ideology has provided an effective shield against similar feelings of alienation and meaninglessness in the Soviet Union. Problems of meaninglessness are further confounded by the fact that the Soviet people live in a risk-free society. The absence of risk and the heretofore limited possibilities for significant improvements in the quality of their lives have taken their toll on the Soviet people.

How do the Soviets cope with problems of alienation and meaninglessness? Among the more destructive ways in which they deal with such problems are alcohol and drug abuse; the excessive consumption of cigarettes; divorce; and suicide. The severity of these problems cannot be overemphasized. It was not by chance alone that one of Gorbachev's first actions after coming to power was a very tough alcohol reform program. Recently, as a part of their new openness, the Soviets have acknowledged that some of their young people have turned to drugs as a means of escaping from their feelings of meaninglessness.

In a more positive vein, the government fights alienation by promoting sports activities and cultural events as well as the restoration of historical buildings, palaces, churches, and even Turkish baths. Sporting events of all types, but particularly soccer, are strongly encouraged by the government at the local, regional, and national levels.

Success in sports is synonymous with patriotism. At enormous expense, the government is restoring palaces used by the czars to their prerevolutionary splendor. There appears to be a particularly strong need to restore anything that is old. For example, every effort is being made by a Finnish construction company that is restoring the Metropol Hotel in Moscow to preserve the historical and architectural features of the hotel. In no other nation in the world are their more statues of artists in cities, parks, and streets than there are in the Soviet Union. Public buildings are frequently named after writers, composers, dancers, painters, and actors. It is as though the state hopes that the Soviet past will be able to provide its citizens with something that Marxist-Leninist ideology has been unable to provide—meaning.

Although atheism appears to be much less important to the Soviets today than it was in the 1930s, it is still the official religion of the eighteen million members of the Communist party. One of the most fascinating ways in which the Soviets are attempting to cope with the problem of meaninglessness is by emulating Judeo-Christian religious symbolism. Recent New Year's greeting cards that I have received from friends in the Soviet Union are almost identical to U.S. Christmas cards in terms of colors, style, and design. Since the death of Brezhnev, Soviet New Year's cards have become decidedly more upbeat. A much more dramatic use of religious symbolism can be found in certain state-run wedding chapels.

When I was in the city of Tbilisi in the republic of Georgia, I visited the magnificent Palace of Marriages. Located on a hillside overlooking the Kura River, the Palace of Marriages looks like a modern U.S. church or synagogue and features stained-glass windows and a pipe organ imported from West Germany. On the altar was a book that looked like a Bible but was not. It was the official government marriage register for Tbilisi. The altar was identical to altars in Christian churches with one exception. At precisely the place where one might expect to see a cross displayed on a Christian altar, instead there was the hammer and sickle. There was a special hall for silver anniversaries and another for golden anniversaries. But my favorite room of all was the "naming hall," where parents would bring their children to be officially named by the state.

Being somewhat taken back by all of this, I turned to our Georgian guide and asked the following question. "You have told us that it is possible to get married here, to name your baby, and to celebrate your wedding anniversary. Is it also possible to have a funeral here?" Obviously annoyed by my question, she turned to me and said, "No, funerals are handled by another bureau." She then went on to explain that if you were an ordinary citizen of Tbilisi, you would probably have your funeral in your office. If you were a particularly prominent person you might be able to have your funeral in the opera house.

The notion that the Soviet Union is the home of godless communism has undoubtedly contributed to the feelings of distrust that Americans have towards the Soviets. The view which many Americans share about the importance of atheism in the Soviet Union is captured in the following vitriolic statement by Aleksandr Solzhenitsyn:

> But the world had never before known a godlessness as organized, militarized, and tenaciously malevolent as that preached by Marxism. Within the philosophical system of Marx and Lenin and at the heart of their psychology, hatred of God is the principal driving force, more fundamental than all their political and economic pretensions. Militant atheism is not merely incidental or marginal to communist policy; it is not a side effect, but the central pivot. To achieve its diabolical ends, communism needs to control a population devoid of religious and national feeling, and this entails a destruction of faith and nationhood. Communists proclaim both of these objectives openly, and just as openly put them into practice.[2]

This is a very strong anti-Soviet statement, but is it representative of the actual situation in the Soviet Union today? Certainly it is well known that churches did not fare very well in the Soviet Union in the 1930s under Stalin or during the period 1959–64 under Khrushchev. However, in 1943 Stalin signed a compact with acting patriarch Sergei that provided the basis for a stable church–state relationship that was resumed after Brezhnev came to power in 1964.

Today there are 7,500 active Russian Orthodox churches in the Soviet Union, with approximately 50 million members. In addition, there are 500,000 Jewish believers (out of a population of 1.8 million Jews); 5 million Protestants; and 3.5 million Roman Catholics. Although it is hard to imagine, there are actually a half million Baptists in the USSR. Between 1980 and 1984, 76 new Baptist churches were registered and 118 prayer houses were either built or acquired. If one includes Moslems and Buddhists as well as others, it is estimated that at least 100 million people in the Soviet Union profess a belief in God. This means that there are five times as many believers as there are members of the Communist party. Party members, of course, are not permitted to belong to a church or synagogue.

During a trip to Moscow in May 1982, U.S. evangelist Billy Graham got himself in hot water with liberals and conservatives in this country when he said, "I think there is a lot more freedom here than has been given the impression in the United States." On a return visit to the Soviet Union in 1984, Graham reconfirmed his optimistic view of Soviet religious life. When I visited the Soviet Union in May 1985, I attended services in a dozen or so Orthodox churches in Leningrad and Tbilisi as well as the Moscow Baptist church. In a country where Christianity has been proscribed by Marxist-Leninist ideology, the Orthodox churches with their icons and fantastic onion-shaped domes are in an excellent state of preservation. Not only were most of these churches full during the services I attended, but in some cases they were literally packed with people of all ages—young, old, and middle-aged.

Recently the Patriarchate of Moscow outlined proposed revisions in legislation on religion and church life in the Soviet Union. Under the new regulations, congregations will be recognized as legal bodies and may also own property. Congregations have not been able to own property since 1918. In addition, congregations may invite non-local clergy to conduct open services, and allow children under ten to participate in services.

When he was interviewed by *Time* magazine in 1985, Gorbachev said, "Surely, God on high has not refused to give us enough wisdom to find ways to bring us an improvement in our relations." To be sure, none of this is meant to suggest that the Soviet Union is on the brink of some sort of religious revolution. Indeed, nothing could be further from the truth. However, there is considerable evidence to suggest that atheism is much more important to certain fundamentalist religious leaders in the United States than it is to party leaders in the Soviet Union. Religion is simply not a big deal to most officials in the party. Although they may be professed atheists, they spend little time talking about atheism.

As for the increased level of religious activity in the Soviet Union, is it possible that under Gorbachev that the Kremlin is deliberately looking the other way because it realizes that religion may be meeting some of the spiritual needs of the Soviet people that can never be satisfied by the state alone? Maybe the Soviet leaders have come to view religion as a less-threatening alternative for dealing with problems of meaninglessness than is alcohol.

The Nomenklatura

U.S. critics of Gorbachev's economic reforms argue that the 250,000 or so self-perpetuating elites, known as the *nomenklatura* (who are said to control the party, the KGB, and the Soviet military) have no incentive to change and will systematically block any serious attempts to change the economic mechanism in the Soviet Union. These Soviet elites enjoy a number of privileges including high salaries, larger flats, dachas, private cars, trips abroad, and access to foreign goods and special state-run food stores. The thousands of middle-level bureaucrats, mainly in the branch ministries (who act as intermediaries between the central-planning bodies and the enterprises) constitute another source of opposition to economic reform.

But this view of economic reform overlooks two important points. A forty-year-old Soviet manager does not remember World War II and was only a small child when Joseph Stalin died. This means that the manager has not experienced firsthand the oppressive political and economic conditions of the 1930s and 1940s, and has been spared some of the paranoid fears characteristic of Soviet leaders who were adults during World War II. The new breed of Soviet managers is pragmatic, nonideological, and ambitious. They want a better lifestyle than they have enjoyed before. Those who have sampled Western-style consumerism—including aerobics, video cassettes, Adidas running shoes, blue eye shadow, designer clothes, and fancy automobiles—seem to like it. Indeed, their value systems often appear to be dangerously close to those of U.S. yuppies. But these are precisely the kinds of values that are necessary to drive the incentives that are built into the Gorbachev economic reforms.

These younger Soviet managers also understand that in order to achieve personal success under the Gorbachev reforms they must be successful in motivating the employees who work for them to increase their productivity and efficiency. Most important of all, they are open to the possibility of using markets to achieve these goals.

When Raisa Gorbachev visited the Paris fashion houses of Pierre Cardin and Yves Saint Laurent in 1985, Americans were told that this was communist propaganda aimed at the United States. It was propaganda, but the target audience was the Soviet Union, not the United States. Six months later Pierre Cardin announced a new line of clothing for the Soviets, to be manufactured in Soviet plants and sold in posh Moscow boutiques.

To increase productivity, Gorbachev has offered financial incentives to motivate managers and employees alike. Previously such incentives met with only limited success, because there were no high-quality consumer goods available on which the Soviets could spend their extra rubles. French designer clothes and other consumer goods imported from the West help energize the reforms.

One thing is certain—no matter what form the new economic mechanism finally takes under Gorbachev, it will be based more firmly on the principles of pragmatism than ever before. Indeed, pragmatism may be the only viable option that is open to him.

Specific Reforms

At the party congress, Gorbachev had a lot to say about the reconstruction of Soviet society. This need stems from a demographic and social revolution that is taking place in the Soviet Union, and includes rapid urbanization, high divorce rates, the break-up of the family, a reduction in the birth rate, alcoholism, juvenile delinquency and crime, and drug abuse.

In an unprecedented action in October 1986, the Soviet government announced a legislation plan to codify Gorbachev's five-year plan to reconstruct Soviet society. This plan contained a list of thirty-eight laws and decrees that covered most of the areas in which Gorbachev has called for changes in his campaign to modernize and revitalize Soviet society. The list included laws on voting and referendums, economic incentives, pricing, the media, government structure, and the activities of the KGB. These legal measures are necessitated by the fact that many of the social and economic reforms proposed by Gorbachev contravene existing legislation.[3]

Many of these reforms are already being implemented even though they have not yet been expressed as formal decrees. I will summarize some of the social reforms that Gorbachev has already implemented.

Although population growth is exploding among the Moslems in the Central Asian republics, the birthrate in the Slavic and Baltic republics has either been stagnant or is declining. For a variety of reasons, Soviet families in the north typically have only one child. Among the reasons cited most often for the relatively small family size are insufficient income, small apartments, professional ambitions, high divorce rates, and rapid urbanization. A major concern of the government over the declining birthrate in the north is that it exacerbates an already tight labor market. To motivate people in the northern republics to have more children, the government has offered a number of incentives including rubles for each baby, longer maternity leaves, and free food and uniforms.

By far the most widely publicized of Gorbachev's social reforms has been his radical alcohol reform program. Until Gorbachev clamped down on the consumption of alcohol in June 1985, the Soviets were literally well on their way to drinking themselves to death. With his dramatic campaign against drunkenness, Gorbachev closed most of the country's hard liquor stores, raised vodka prices, slashed production, and prohibited the sale of alcoholic beverages in restaurants before 2:00 P.M. each day. Furthermore, workers found drunk at the workplace can be fined 50 rubles (or $76), which is equivalent to one-fourth of the average monthly wage of a Soviet worker.

The results of the alcohol reform campaign have been dramatic. Sales of alcoholic beverages were down by 40 percent in 1986. Many liquor factories have closed, and others have been converted to the production of other products. The loss of revenue received by the state has been made up by a 25-percent drop in the crime rate, a 20-percent reduction in automobile accidents, and a 33-percent decline in absenteeism from work. Sales of soft drinks and juices have risen correspondingly. Coca-Cola has joined Pepsi-Cola in the vast Soviet soft drink market.

The alcohol reform program is changing the social habits of the country. Diplomatic social functions are not what they used to be. Long queues form outside liquor stores before they open at 2:00 P.M. and before they close at 7:00 P.M.

In addition to his campaign against the excessive use of alcohol, Gorbachev has come down hard against corruption, bribery, illegal incomes, and some black-market activities. On the other hand, he has legalized some private-sector service businesses such as automobile repairs, home repairs, and taxis, which were previously illegal. Moscow now has a few private restaurants as well.

Gorbachev has also proposed a sweeping program to make the nation's system of higher education more responsive to the needs of a modern high-tech industrial economy. The objective of the program is to replace the existing higher education system (with its focus on narrow vocational and professional specialization) with a broader-based approach to education that would better prepare graduates to adapt themselves more readily to new technology and a rapidly changing environment. The program includes new teaching methods, a more rigorous evaluation of professors, new curricula, alternative funding structures, administrative reorganization, increased power and authority for local colleges, and an increase in student rights to better equip them to function in a more decentralized market-oriented society.

As an integral part of his education reform program, Gorbachev has also inaugurated a program to raise the level of computer expertise of high school and university graduates. Some U.S. cynics have expressed skepticism about how much Gorbachev will be able to accomplish with his computer education program in a "closed society." I believe that computers will set loose forces in the Soviet Union that will make Soviet society more open rather than less. When young Soviet computer jockeys begin communicating among themselves, Soviet society may never be the same. In Moscow, a city that has no telephone directory, computers could revolutionize communications. For example, there would be nothing to prevent computer technicians from creating a large database of Moscow telephone numbers and making it available across a wide network of users. The notion that the Soviets cannot benefit from the microcomputer revolution is not based on reality.

Since the Geneva summit in November 1985, Gorbachev has actively supported a broad range of exchange programs with the United States in a variety of different fields including art, music, literature, sports, education, science, and religion, to mention only a few. Particularly noteworthy was Gorbachev's 1986 exchange of New Year's greetings with President Reagan, which was carried on live television in the Soviet Union and the United States. Unfortunately, this event was not repeated in 1987.

Human Rights

Presidents Jimmy Carter and Ronald Reagan have devoted considerable attention to what they call Soviet human rights violations—the treatment of political dissidents and Soviet Jews who want to emigrate to the West. In the past, this issue has always enraged Soviet leaders, who argued that the United States was meddling in Soviet affairs and should spend more time trying to solve its own human rights problems—unemployment, poverty, racism, violent crime, and drug abuse.

Moscow and Tel Aviv have not had diplomatic relations since the Soviets severed diplomatic ties after the 1967 Arab–Israeli war. Since that time, Soviet Jewish emigration policies have become one of the most divisive issues separating the East and the West. Between 1968 and 1985, 265,657 Jews emigrated from the Soviet Union, but the Israeli government claims that another 400,000 want to leave. As I noted in Chapter 5, after allowing 51,320 Jewish emigrants in 1979, the Soviets cut back sharply on Jewish emigration and allowed only a thousand or so Jews to leave each year between 1983 and 1986. The Soviets say that most Jews who wanted to leave have already done so, and that those who have applied for exit visas have received them, with the exception of those who possess classified government information and have been turned down for national security reasons.

In September 1986, Soviet Foreign Minister Eduard A. Shevardnadze and Israeli Prime Minister Shimon Peres met in New York at the United Nations and agreed to consider normalizing relations between the two countries. Although the total number of Jews and political dissidents allowed to leave the Soviet Union in 1985 and 1986 did not increase significantly, Gorbachev did permit some very well known dissidents to leave in 1986. They included Anatoly B. Shcharansky, as well as his mother and brother, who emigrated to Israel; Yelena G. Bonner, the wife of Nobel laureate Andrei D. Sakharov, who was permitted to visit the United States for surgery; and Yuri F. Orlov, who was granted permission to emigrate to the United

States as part of the deal the Reagan administration made with the Soviets to free U.S. journalist Nicholas Daniloff and Soviet physicist Gennadi Zakharov.

Just prior to the summit in Reykjavík, Irina Ratushinskaya, a poet who had been critical of the Soviet Union, was unconditionally released from a twelve-year sentence in a Soviet labor camp. U.S. industrialist Armand Hammer arranged for Jewish geneticist David Goldfarb and his wife to immigrate to the United States. But in December 1986, the most famous political dissident in the Soviet Union, Dr. Sakharov, was permitted to leave Gorky where he had been in exile since 1980. Not only was he allowed to return to his home in Moscow and resume his work as a physicist at the Soviet Academy of Sciences, but he was also permitted to speak his mind quite openly to the Western press.

Then in February 1987, nearly two hundred political prisoners were freed and Soviet authorities announced plans to release even more political dissidents. The number of Soviet Jews permitted to emigrate increased dramatically during the first half of 1987, and Israel and the Soviet Union appeared to be inching gradually towards a resumption of diplomatic relations. These actions suggest increased flexibility on the part of the Soviets in an area where they were completely unapproachable in the early 1980s.

Implications

What is so astounding about Gorbachev's assault on the Soviet culture is that it is not merely an attack on the postrevolution culture of Lenin, Stalin, Khrushchev, and Brezhnev, but rather a culture that dates back at least six centuries and includes a whole chain of authoritarian rulers—Ivan the Great, Ivan the Terrible, Peter the Great, and Nicholas I. It represents by far the most radical set of reforms ever attempted by any Soviet leader since Vladimir Ilyich Lenin introduced his New Economic Policy (NEP) in the 1920s, which combined elements of capitalism and socialism.

The implications of these cultural reforms are far more profound than any of the specific economic, political, or foreign-policy reforms that have already been implemented. They were completely unanticipated by U.S. politicians, economists, and Sovietologists. Indeed, a great deal of the cynicism expressed by U.S. economists about the likelihood of Gorbachev's success in achieving the goals of FYP12 is directly linked to the failure of these economists to fully grasp the practical significance of these cultural reforms.

The cultural reforms not only pave the way for economic, political, and foreign-policy reforms, but they also serve to reinforce them as well. For example, the alcohol reforms and the educational reforms both make it much more likely that decentralized, market-oriented planning will succeed. There is a two-way feedback effect between the cultural reforms and the other reforms in which each reinforces the other.

Many historians believe that what led to the demise of Khrushchev in 1964 was the fact that he did not adequately prepare the party for his attempts to decentralize government ministries along regional lines. He tried to change the structure of the bureaucracy and the economic mechanism without changing the Soviet culture, and he failed.

The types of economic reforms being introduced by Gorbachev would be impossible to implement in the traditional risk-free Soviet culture. But some of the cultural changes, such as the introduction of French designer clothes, serve to energize the economic reforms in particular.

The conclusion of Gorbachev's speech to the Central Committee of the Communist Party on 27 January 1987 contains a concise description of his cultural model for the Soviet Union:

> We wish to turn our country into a model of a highly developed state, into a society with the most advanced economy, the broadest democracy, the most humane and lofty ethics, where the working man would feel that he is master, would enjoy all benefits of material and spiritual culture, where the future of his children would be secure, where he would have everything that is necessary for a full and interesting life.[4]

Although the speeches by Gorbachev and Prime Minister Ryzhkov still contain numerous examples of anticapitalistic, Marxist-Leninist rhetoric, they are, nevertheless, much more subdued than similar speeches in the past given by Stalin, Khrushchev, and Brezhnev. Gone are the forecasts of the imminent demise of capitalism and the blustery predictions of communism overtaking capitalism. Instead, there are frequent articles in the Soviet press explaining how Lenin's New Economic Policy was used in the 1920s to overcome some of the disastrous results of War Communism between 1918 and 1921.

Most of what is happening today in the Soviet Union has little to do with Marxist-Leninist ideology. It has much more to do with pragmatism rather than politics. It is neither socialism nor capitalism yet it combines elements of both.

8
Opening the Closed Society

S oviet leader Gorbachev is being driven towards radical economic, political, and foreign-policy reforms by a combination of internal problems as well as a number of international forces. The domestic problems, many of which predate the 1917 revolution, include a stagnant economy; inefficient agriculture; an inadequate supply of consumer goods and services; a substantial technological gap with the West; a rigid political and governmental structure; a police-state mentality; a high death rate; and an increasingly alienated population. On the international side, Hungary, China, Soviet bilateral trade needs, and the Reagan administration's foreign policy are not only pushing Gorbachev towards radical reform, but they also enhance the possibility that he will be successful in implementing those reforms.

But unlike previous leaders who have tried and failed to change the rigid Soviet socioeconomic, political system, Gorbachev has attacked the root cause of the Soviets' problems, namely, their culture. It is the Soviet culture that has always been the binding constraint on Soviet leaders who have attempted to respond to the plethora of Soviet domestic problems as well as an ever-changing external environment. Just as the culture has blocked every Soviet leader since Stalin, it also holds the key for Gorbachev's success. To open the closed society Gorbachev has concentrated his attention on the Soviet culture, which is precisely where his attention must be focused.

I will now summarize some of the more important economic, political, and foreign-policy reforms initiated by Gorbachev during his first two years in power. In addition, I will speculate on the future direction of these reforms and examine their implications for the Soviet Union, the United States, and the rest of the world.

Changing the Economic Mechanism

Even though the Soviet economy has remained virtually unchanged since the 1930s, Soviet economists have been talking about "changing the economic mechanism" (which is code for decentralized, market-oriented planning) since the 1950s. Ironically, the very first Soviet economic reformer in the 1920s was none other than Lenin. Lenin's so-called New Economic Policy (NEP), which combined features of free enterprise and socialism, was a replacement for the disastrous War Communism that was implemented in the Soviet Union immediately after the 1917 revolution. Although NEP was relatively short-lived (1921–28), it nevertheless provides the economic, political, and ideological basis for the Hungarian, Chinese, and Soviet economic reforms. Indeed, some of Gorbachev's descriptions of the Soviet economic reforms in the 1980s are taken almost verbatim from Lenin's NEP.

In the 1930s, Stalin replaced NEP with the highly centralized, command economy that is still in place in the Soviet Union. Economic reform was anathema to Stalin, with his forced collectivization of agriculture and the nationalization of all industry. During the repressive Stalin years, those who openly expressed their desires for economic reform often paid a very high price; namely, they were either imprisoned or, in some cases, they actually lost their lives. Economics was virtually snuffed out as a legitimate academic discipline and did not reemerge until after Stalin's death in 1953. Stalin's view was that economists were unnecessary in a centrally planned economy. Soviet economists had little or no influence on the party or the government until Yuri V. Andropov came to power in November 1982.

Nikita S. Khrushchev and Aleksey Kosygin were each associated with unsuccessful attempts to change the economic mechanism in the Soviet Union in the 1950s and 1960s. In each case their economic experiments were blocked by a combination of bureaucratic resistance and Marxist-Leninist ideology. In fact, Khrushchev's overthrow in 1964 may have been related to his relatively liberal views on economic reform. Thus, it is not surprising that until recently, Soviet economists and politicians who were interested in serious economic reform took a relatively guarded approach.

On 26 July 1983, Soviet leader Yuri V. Andropov announced a

package of "economic experiments," the objective of which was to introduce decentralized, flexible planning in all of the enterprises belonging to five industrial ministries in the Soviet Union. The five ministries selected to implement the new ideas included two national ministries (heavy electrical equipment and transportation machinery) and three regional ministries (the food industry in the Ukraine, light industry of Belorussia, and local industry in Lithuania). Under the decree from the Central Committee of the Communist Party, which established these experiments, plant managers were given wider authority over their budgets, with greater discretion in matters of investment, wages, bonuses, and retained earnings, all of which had been tightly controlled by the supervisory ministries and Gosplan in the past.

The Andropov experiments began on schedule on 1 January 1984. One month later Andropov died, and Konstantin U. Chernenko presided over their implementation until his death in March 1985. Although the Soviet press had a great deal to say about these experiments throughout 1984, the U.S. press virtually ignored them until the latter part of 1985, after Gorbachev had taken control of the Soviet government. Most U.S. experts on the Soviet economy scoffed at them as merely cosmetic changes rather than much-needed structural changes.

Although Chernenko had little to say about these experiments during his year in power, he did nothing to impede their progress. However, he did introduce an important reform in foreign-trade practices that helped pave the way for the more sweeping foreign-trade reforms announced by Gorbachev in 1986. For the first time, Soviet managers were permitted to trade directly with their counterparts in enterprises in other CMEA countries without having to go through the Foreign Trade Ministry. This was an important step towards the decentralization of foreign trade.

In May 1985, six weeks after Gorbachev came to power, I met with enterprise managers and government officials involved with the economic reforms in Moscow, Leningrad, and Tbilisi. By that time the number of ministries participating in the economic experiments initiated by Andropov had been increased from five to twenty-one—one-third of all of the Soviet ministries. When asked why the experiments had been extended to include all of the enterprises in sixteen additional ministries, the Soviet officials indicated that the experiments had been extremely successful. Enterprise managers who participated in the experiments reported increased output and efficiency, reduced production lead times, lower costs, higher profits, increased benefits and wages, and significantly improved employee morale. Not bad for the first year by almost any standards.

How was this accomplished? Enterprise managers were given the freedom to determine prices, output, product mix, new product development strategies, domestic marketing strategies, and even international marketing strategies with CMEA countries. The ministries to whom the enterprises reported still retained control of technology and funding. More recently, some Soviet enterprises have developed their own technology, now trade directly with Western companies, and have become self-financing.

Gorbachev understands the futility of attempting to manage the production and distribution of twenty-four million different types of goods through Gosplan and a handful of highly centralized government ministries. Today the emphasis on enterprise plans is focused on qualitative indicators reflecting efficiency in the use of resources, rates of plant modernization, and the growth of labor productivity through the achievements of science and technology. Government ministries now set efficiency targets and cost-reduction rates. The rigid centrally planned targets and controls of the past are being replaced by more flexible, bottom-up enterprise planning. The role of Gosplan is being redefined along the lines of the Hungarian state planning office as one of providing guidelines and long-term forecasts. All of this is rationalized by Soviet ideologists as "the extension of the rights of economic enterprises and broadening the participation of employees in the management of these enterprises."

I will now examine some of the specific economic reforms introduced by Gorbachev in such areas as agriculture, industry, consumption, foreign trade, and defense. I will also analyze some of the preliminary results of these reforms as well as some of the obstacles that may impede their further expansion.

Agriculture

In his previous position as the party official responsible for agriculture, Gorbachev expressed harsh criticism of the failings of Soviet agriculture and was very supportive of the Hungarian agricultural reforms. It was not surprising that he devoted so much attention in his 1986 party congress speech to "solving the food problem." That Gorbachev is well acquainted with the Responsibility System of Chinese agricultural reforms was clear from his address. Much of what he has proposed has been strongly influenced by the Chinese and Hungarian agricultural reforms.

Problems with Soviet agricultural production can be traced back to the czars in the eighteenth century; the problems have persisted during every important period in recent Soviet history—World War I, the 1917 revolution, War Communism, the New Economic Policy, Stalin, World War II, Khrushchev, and Brezhnev. Soviet agriculture has never fully recovered from the forced collectivization schemes of Stalin in the 1930s.

Gorbachev moved quickly to reform large Soviet agricultural co-operatives. He has encouraged collective farms to assign acreage to groups of farmers called "brigades," which operate under contracts that permit them to keep most of the profits associated with increased production. Sometimes the members of a single family make up a brigade. Profit is no longer a dirty word with the brigades, for the more they produce, the more they eat. Because farmers working on collectivized farms have traditionally received the lowest wages in the Soviet Union, they have responded quite positively to the incentives associated with the brigades. Whether they are state-owned farms or cooperatives, once Soviet farms have met their production targets at fixed prices, they are then free to sell the remainder of their crop anywhere they can at the market price. If all of this sounds familiar, it is virtually identical to Lenin's "proportional agricultural tax" that was implemented in the 1920s under NEP. It is also very similar to some of the early Hungarian and Chinese agricultural reforms.

Another Gorbachev move was to abolish six government agencies responsible for the production of processing of agricultural products and to create a new agency called the State Committee for the Agro-Industrial Complex that would have central authority over all Soviet agriculture. Among the six agencies abolished were the State Committee for Production and Servicing of Agriculture; the Ministry of Rural Construction; the Ministry of the Meat and Dairy Industry; and the Ministry of the Food Industry. The aim of the new agricultural superagency is to improve coordination between the central planners, the farmers, the processors, and the distributors.

Since 1984, Imperial Chemical Industries (ICI) of London has been conducting farm management experiments with four large Soviet farms in widely different locations. The ICI consultants visit the four Soviet farms monthly and advise the farm managers on the proper input mix of seed, fertilizer, and insecticides, and other farming issues. Within two years the output of these experimental farms had already doubled. Output has risen five to ten times on several experimental farms in Hungary and Bulgaria where ICI has played a similar role since the mid-1970s. The techniques used by the ICI consultants are identical to those used by China and India to transform their grain deficits into grain surpluses. There is every reason to believe that the technology used on these experimental farms will be embraced by Gorbachev and employed on all Soviet farms.

Although small plots tilled privately by individual farmers only constitute 3 percent of the tillable land in the Soviet Union, they far outproduce the large collective farms in terms of yield per acre. In 1984, private farms accounted for 30 percent of the milk, eggs, and meat produced in the Soviet Union as well as 24 percent of the wool, 61 percent of the honey, 58 percent of the potatoes, 30 percent of the vegetables, and 59 percent of the fruit and berries. In a country where food is often in short supply, it is not surprising that Gorbachev is encouraging the development of privately cultivated plots.

As evidence that the Soviet agricultural reforms are beginning to have some impact, the CIA estimates that the 1986 Soviet grain harvest rose to 210 million tons, up from 192 million tons in 1985, and the highest level of production since 1979. Soviet imports of grain from the United States dropped precipitously in 1986. In spite of significant improvements in grain production, 1986 grain targets were not fully realized. However, meat, milk, and egg production were well above the FYP12 targets.

Industry

On 1 January 1987, the Andropov–Gorbachev economic reforms were extended to all forty-six thousand state-owned industrial enterprises in the Soviet Union. No longer are the reforms merely experiments, but rather they are now the law of the land. Soviet enterprise managers have been given a great deal more decision-making freedom than was the case in the past. They not only are able to make their own product mix and production volume decisions in response to market demand, but they may purchase raw materials from alternative suppliers and have the right to hire and fire employees based on market needs and performance. They may even make their own pricing and wage decisions within guidelines provided by Gosplan. Differential wage rates across industries will be permitted, with higher wages being paid to managers and workers in high-priority industries such as computers, machine tools, and robotics. A portion of the profits of an enterprise may either be reinvested in the business or shared with the managers and employees as a form of incentive compensation. The state, of course, will also claim a share of the profits.

The driving force underlying the Andropov–Gorbachev economic reforms is the improved management and use of human resources, including reduced job security, greater wage differentiation among workers with different skills, increased freedom for managers to hire and fire workers, and improved managerial incentives to encourage increased labor productivity.

In 1986, 13 percent of the factories in the Soviet Union operated at a loss and were only able to avoid bankruptcy through substantial government subsidies. State-owned enterprises are increasingly expected to be self-financing. The state bank, Gosbank, has indicated that it will no longer extend credit to enterprises that produce poor-quality products, have large unsold inventories, and are unprofitable.

In 1986, two major firms experimented with self-financing—the Vaz automobile factory in Tolyatti and the Amalgamated Engineering Plant in Sumy. On 1 January 1987, the enterprises of seven ministries were converted to the principle of self-financing. These include the ministries of machine-building for the chemical industry, the petrochemical industry, light industry, the instrument-making industry, the automobile industry, and the merchant marine and trading industries. All of the firms in these seven ministries are expected to be able to cover their production and marketing expenses through revenues generated from the sale of their products. The government has prohibited these ministries from subsidizing the losses of unprofitable businesses from the profits of more efficient enterprises. The government has also indicated that it will pay unemployment compensation to workers who lose their jobs as a result of reorganization or bankruptcy. Undoubtedly, the Soviets will soon implement a bankruptcy law similar to the ones found in Hungary and Poland. Fifteen state-owned enterprises went bankrupt in Poland in 1986 and another five were preparing for closure under the new law on bankruptcy.

The state bank will offer liberal credit terms including low-interest rates to firms that modernize their equipment and invest in new technology and research and development. One major obstacle to economic reform is the fact that research and development in the Soviet Union is still highly centralized, either in large national research institutes or national ministries. Research and development must also be decentralized and in some cases brought down to the level of individual enterprises. This is the only way to make research and development more responsive to the needs of Soviet enterprises and consumers. (China has recently taken such a step.) Five of Moscow's thirteen research and design institutes have been closed because their research was of an inferior technological level, the volume of the research that they produced was too small, and their impact on Soviet socioeconomic development was only minimal.

In June 1986, the Supreme Soviet voted to invest 80 percent more in engineering over the period 1986–90 than in the previous five years. Spending on retooling in the major enterprises will be doubled. Nearly 60 percent of fixed assets in engineering will be modernized by 1990—the biggest retooling plan in Soviet history. Much of it will be done by special facilities being built to produce technology exclusively for this industry.

Frustrated by the Reagan administration's attempts to block it from acquiring U.S. technology, the Soviet Union hopes to become independent of Western technology by 1990. The objective is to produce world-class products based on state-of-the-art technology by the early 1990s.

More resources are being pumped into the computer and electronic industries, and the Academy of Sciences has set up a department in charge of information and computer technology to run a chain of research and design centers. All of this work is being done on a mammoth scale. It involves 430 major production companies and 150 research and manufacturing associations, employing 700,000 scientists, designers, and engineers.

Small, private, high-tech enterprises in Poland and Hungary are an important new source of computer hardware and software for the Soviet Union. Some of these Polish and Hungarian firms are providing the Soviet Union with state-of-the-art microprocessors, process control computers, as well as sophisticated software.

As was the case in Hungary, cooperatives are also expected to take on increased importance in the Soviet Union. In his party congress address, Gorbachev suggested that cooperatives should play a greater role in "the production and processing of goods; in housing, orchard, and garden construction; and in the provision of consumer services and trade." In an attempt to reduce energy and raw material costs, the Politburo has called for the establishment of manufacturing cooperatives to produce consumer goods, household wares, and various services.

The Soviet industrial reforms are virtually a mirror image of the Hungarian and Chinese reforms. The only difference is that Gorbachev appears to be determined to move ahead at a much faster pace.

One of the Soviet enterprises that began participating in the original Andropov economic experiments on 1 January 1984, was Sibelekroterm, a manufacturer of high-temperature metallurgical furnaces outside Novosibirsk. According to *Business Week*, the management of Sibelekroterm was given considerable latitude to set prices and wages, make investment decisions on new technology and equipment, and grant bonuses to employees. At the end of the first year of operations under the economic reforms, industrial productivity at the company had increased by 11 percent by comparison to 7 percent in the previous year. Furthermore, industrial output increased an additional 8.5 percent during the first half of 1985 compared with an average gain in industrial productivity in the Soviet Union of 7.8 percent in 1984.[1]

When the Amalgamated Engineering Plant in Sumy became autonomous in 1985, both labor productivity and profits increased twice as fast as those for the machine building industry as a whole; the average wages of workers grew almost 50 percent faster.[2]

Another major Soviet enterprise which has been involved in the economic experiments since 1984 is the Belorussia Railroad. Time-and-motion studies and automatic signal controls were used to reduce employment at the railroad by twelve thousand workers—10 percent of the work force. Of these, four thousand retired, five hundred were transferred to railroad construction, and the remaining seventy-five hundred given new jobs in other branches of the Belorussia economy. Labor productivity rose by 11.2 percent in 1985 and 27 percent during the first quarter of 1986. Wages increased by 25 rubles per month. Not surprisingly, the Soviets have decided to extend the Belorussia experiment to all railroads in the USSR by 1990.[3]

Consumption

Consumer goods and services, long neglected by previous Soviet leaders, have been singled out by Soviet officials as a sector of the economy that merits special attention. The objective is to improve the quality and the range of choice of consumer goods and services available to Soviet citizens. By the Soviets' own admission, only one-sixth of the goods produced in the Soviet Union meet world standards for quality.

Government planners hope to streamline the management of the production and distribution of consumer goods, to improve planning, and to introduce incentives in light industries that manufacture consumer goods. The same reforms described previously are beginning to be applied to the consumer sector, only more intensively. Financial incentives are provided to improve the manufacturing technology of the industry. Improved distribution channels are also being developed. Those enterprises that produce goods for export abroad are permitted to retain a portion of their hard-currency earnings to be used at the discretion of their management. Fashionable clothes designed by French designers Pierre Cardin and Yves Saint Laurent have been introduced in the domestic market.

If the incentives of the Gorbachev economic reforms are to be expected to work, Soviet managers and workers must be able to purchase more and better-quality consumer goods with their extra incomes generated from improved productivity and efficiency. Otherwise economic reform will fall flat on its face. Implicit in the entire reform movement is the assumption that employees will respond positively to economic incentives in order to improve their lifestyles. The whole program will collapse if high-quality consumer goods and services are not available. Soviet yuppies are not any different from yuppies in any other part of the world.

Beginning in 1987, it became legal for a Soviet citizen to open a private business to produce consumer goods such as cosmetics, apparel, and furniture, and to provide services such as automobile and home repairs. At least for the time being, hiring other employees is still strictly prohibited. As a result of this change in Soviet law, private taxi drivers can now operate legally. The first private restaurants since the 1920s are beginning to appear in Moscow.

Ital New Food Trading of Italy is opening thirty-six fast-food pizza restaurants in the Soviet Union and Pepsico has announced plans to open one hundred Pizza Huts. Following on the heels of its entry into the fast-food markets in Budapest and Bucharest, McDonald's is currently negotiating with the Soviets.

Defense

In the 1960s, President Lyndon B. Johnson learned the hard way that it is very difficult to support a major military buildup (such as the Vietnam War) and also maintain a healthy economy. Likewise, in the late 1970s and early 1980s, the Soviets found it equally difficult to support a policy of "guns and butter." As the competition for resources between the military and civilian sectors of the Soviet economy intensified in the 1980s, the Soviet economy was slowly grinding to a halt. This tension between the military and civilian sectors of the Soviet Union is a major internal factor pushing Gorbachev towards radical reform. The old ways of doing things simply are not adequate to meet the needs of the Soviet people as well as the Soviet military-industrial complex. Something has to give, and that something may turn out to be Marxist-Leninist ideology. It is obviously impossible for Gorbachev to achieve his ambitious economic and military objectives while maintaining the status quo. The economy possesses neither the resources nor the flexibility to satisfy the economic and military needs of the nation simultaneously.

Previous Soviet leaders have always been willing to sacrifice consumer goods to provide the necessary resources to meet the nation's military and industrial needs. Gorbachev is the first Soviet leader to appreciate the importance of consumer goods to the overall health of the Soviet economy. As I have noted before, high-quality consumer goods help energize the economic reforms that are necessary to strengthen the Soviet economy and the Soviet defense capability. It is, therefore, not surprising that the production of consumer goods increased by 4.0 percent in 1986.

Two reasons are often cited for Gorbachev's increased interest in an arms control agreement with the United States. First, reductions in military spending would free up much-needed resources for investment in the civilian economy. Second, better relations with the United States might improve the Soviets' access to U.S. technology and financial credits. Others claim that Soviet arms control proposals would have only limited effects on the Soviet economy in the short run, because they are aimed primarily at retiring older weapons systems rather than canceling new ones.

U.S. cynics often cite the Soviet military establishment as a group that might be expected to resist radical economic reform. This view overlooks the fact that economic reform may free up more resources for use by the military than might otherwise have been the case.

Strategic Implications

By the end of 1986, there were strong indications that the Soviet economy was responding favorably to the Gorbachev reforms—decentralized planning, self-financing, financial incentives, improved worker discipline, reduced alcohol consumption, and sweeping personnel changes. According to the CIA, the Soviet GNP increased by 4.2 percent over 1985, industrial output was up by 3.6 percent, and agricultural output increased by 7.3 percent. The CIA also estimates that 1986 fixed capital investment increased by 7.5 percent. Soviet statistics indicate that the production of consumer goods increased by 4.0 percent in 1986 and that labor productivity increased by 3.8 percent, average wages by 2.7 percent, and real per capita income by 2.3 percent. There were also significant increases in the production of all types of energy—electricity by 4.0 percent, oil by 3.0 percent, natural gas by 7.0 percent, and coal by 3.0 percent. Although the physical volume of two-way foreign trade increased in 1986, the monetary value of foreign trade decreased by 8.0 percent as a result of the decline in the price of oil and some agricultural products.[4]

Not only has the Soviet economy responded positively to the economic reforms, but there have also been improvements in Soviet social statistics. The birthrate increased in 1986 and the death rate declined. The decline in the death rate has been attributed to the success of the alcohol abuse campaign and a decrease in accidental deaths. Of course, cynics claim that Soviet officials manipulate economic and social statistics to suit their own political purposes.

Even when confronted with substantial evidence to the contrary, most U.S. experts on the Soviet economy still deny the possibility that Gorbachev may actually be successful in implementing radical economic reforms before 1990. They argue that he will be blocked from doing so by a combination of Marxist-Leninist ideology; the bureaucracy of the party, the government, and the military establishment; and the Soviet people, who have become all too complacent with life in a risk-free society.

The real obstacle to Gorbachev's reforms is not political ideology, but rather the lack of experience of Soviet managers in market-oriented planning and management practices including marketing strategies, international finance, and organizational development.

I believe that the importance of Marxist-Leninist ideology in the Soviet Union today is seriously overstated by most Americans. It is an ideology that is going through a major transformation in all parts of the world including China, Eastern Europe, the Soviet Union, and the Third World. It often seems the only country that has not changed its view of communist ideology is the United States. At least in the foreseeable future, most large industrial enterprises in the Soviet Union will be owned by the state and there will remain a concern over the equitable distribution of income—much more so than in the United States. However, even these large state-owned enterprises will be patterned after their Chinese and Hungarian counterparts. They will be highly decentralized and market oriented. When the Soviet economy reaches a steady state, I believe that it will resemble some combination of Austria, the most socialistic of the Western European countries, and Hungary, the most capitalistic of the Eastern European countries. Thus far neither China, Hungary, nor the Soviet Union have publicly admitted that they have moved a long way from Marxist-Leninist ideology. But the facts speak for themselves.

As for the Soviet bureaucracy and Soviet society, Gorbachev is using a dual strategy to encourage their participation in the reform movement. First, he has embarked on a systematic effort to change the culture of the Soviet Union by introducing such radical ideas as alcohol reform, bankruptcy, flexible hiring and firing policies, increased freedom of the arts and the press, and greater religious freedom. Second, he is using the power of the international marketplace to motivate Soviet managers and workers to work harder and more efficiently and to produce higher-quality goods. By producing more and improving the quality of what is produced, Soviet managers and employees will receive higher pay, thus enabling them to purchase higher-quality consumer goods, some of which will be imported from the West. By improving the quality of Soviet exports, the Soviets can earn more hard currency to purchase Western consumer goods and technology. As I have indicated, there are already positive signs that the process of internationalizing the Soviet economy is starting to work.

Since the days of Lenin, the Soviets have maintained a strong interest in U.S. trade. Political ideology has never been a problem for Soviet officials in their trade relations with the United States. Today Marxist-Leninist ideology seems to be much more important to some U.S. politicians than it is to Soviet trade officials. The United States is paying a high price for its inability to compete internationally. Ironically, the Soviets have a similar problem. Hasn't the time come to put aside our ideological differences and begin relating to each other on the basis of economic self-interest rather than political rhetoric? We both stand to gain from the experience.

U.S. businesspeople have two options as to how they may respond to the revolutionary new Soviet trade initiatives. They may either sit cynically on the sidelines and wait until the new Soviet trade and joint-venture laws have been cast in concrete, or they may opt to work with the Soviets to help create a set of joint-venture laws and practices that are mutually advantageous. If U.S. businesspeople do choose to lay out during the opening round, they may find themselves squeezed out of future rounds not only by the FRG and Japan, but also by China, Israel, India, Brazil, Argentina, and Mexico, to mention only a few. For example, it was not by chance that Gorbachev plans to visit Mexico, Brazil, and Argentina in 1987. The name of the game is trade and technology and it is being played on a global field.

Isn't it time for U.S. businesspeople and politicians to push aside some of their ideological stereotypes about the Soviet Union, and begin responding to the Soviet trade overtures in a more pragmatic, open-minded fashion? If we mean what we say about wanting to encourage the Soviet Union to become a more open, market-oriented society, then why don't we offer them more positive encouragement rather than continuing to impose endless government restrictions on U.S.–Soviet trade and denying them membership in GATT, the World Bank, and the IMF? If we truly believe in the power of the free market, why don't we give it a chance to work in the Soviet Union?

There may be some unique opportunities for U.S. business leaders to contribute to global peace by assuming a stronger leadership role in East–West trade and joint ventures. Rather than resisting global interdependence, we should embrace it. As *Megatrends* author John Naisbitt says, "If we get sufficiently interlaced economically, we will probably not bomb each other off the face of the planet."

Political Reform

In his most poignant speech to date, on 27 January 1987, General Secretary Gorbachev charged the Communist party with stagnation, corruption, and systematic incompetence. He then went on to say that "we need democracy like air. If we fail to realize that, or if we realize it but make no real serious steps to broaden it, to advance it and to draw the country's working people extensively into the reorganization process, our policy will get choked, and the reorganization will peter out, comrades."[5]

Without mentioning them by name, the speech was a broadside attack on the stultifying legacy of Stalin and Brezhnev. It provided the most solid evidence yet that Gorbachev intends to pursue political reforms as well as economic and cultural reforms.

Many Sovietologists express the view that Gorbachev will be severely constrained by the power of the enormous Soviet bureaucracy in his attempts to reform the party and the government. But this view significantly underestimates the political power possessed by Soviet leaders throughout history. If anything, the accelerated pace of the Soviet reforms under Gorbachev indicates that he, in fact, has far more power than anyone could possibly have imagined.

We are constantly told by the U.S. news media that Gorbachev has substantial political opposition in his policies of radical reform and that he is proceeding with great caution. Each time he makes a significant step towards further reform, our press hints that this could very well be his last move in that direction and that political disaster lies just around the corner. But where is the evidence to support this pessimistic view? It seems to be based on a combination of wishful thinking and a psychological need to deny that the Soviet Union could ever be anything other than what we have always said it was, namely, a completely closed society.

Democratization

Just as Deng Xiaoping often falls back on Chairman Mao to justify his sweeping economic reforms of China, Gorbachev frequently leans on Lenin's NEP to legitimize his program of radical economic reform and *democratic centralism*. On 22 April 1983, the 113th anniversary of the birth of Lenin, Gorbachev said, "Lenin persistently defended centralism as the point of departure in the organization of the economy of socialism, which represents a uniform entity. At the same time he called for a free rein to be given to creativity and initiative at the base: 'Our main task is to provide an impetus everywhere in the country, to mobilize a maximum of initiative and to display a maximum of independence.' "[6] Thus Gorbachev was paving the way for structural changes in the Soviet political and economic systems rather than settling for a strategy based entirely on discipline.

An entire section of Gorbachev's 1986 party congress speech was devoted to the promotion of "democracy" and "socialist self-government."

> Comrades, Lenin regarded democracy, the creative initiative of working people, as the principal force behind the development of the new system. Unmatched in his faith in the people, he showed concern for raising the level of the political activity and culture of the masses, stressing that illiterate people were outside politics.
>
> Democracy is the wholesome and pure air without which a socialistic public organism cannot live a full-blooded life. Hence, when we say that socialism's great potential is not being used to the full in our country, we also mean that the acceleration of society's development is inconceivable and impossible without a further development of all the aspects and manifestations of socialist democracy.[7]

But what does Gorbachev have in mind when he speaks of promoting democratic centralism and socialist self-government? Prior to his January 1987 speech to the central committee, Gorbachev's pronouncements on economic reform were much clearer than his statements calling for "democratization of society" and the promotion of self-government. By the end of his first two years in power, the major elements of economic and foreign-trade reforms were clearly visible. Not only had he laid out the strategic direction of economic reforms, but there was tangible evidence of their implementation and results. Indeed, there has been a high degree of correlation between Gorbachev's rhetoric on economic and trade reforms and what is actually taking place in the Soviet Union.

Although there is visible evidence of increased political freedom under Gorbachev, the overall sense of direction of political reform is less clear than is the case with economic reform. How far is Gorbachev prepared to go with the liberalization of the Soviet political system? Will he permit political parties to emerge that are opposed to the Communist party? Will opposition parties be permitted to field candidates in local, regional, or national elections? Will independent trade unions be allowed? Will employees of an enterprise be able to select their own general managers or will these decisions continue to be controlled by the party through the respective ministries? Will members of the Communist party continue to enjoy special privileges not available to other citizens? Will the Communist party expand its membership? These are very tough questions, but they are the kinds of questions which Gorbachev began to answer in his January 1987 report to the central committee, in which he called for a choice of political candidates in party elections as well as secret balloting. He also elaborated on what he means by "re-organization."

> Re-organization is reliance on the creative endeavor of the masses, all-round extension of democracy and socialist self-government, encouragement of initiative and self-organized activities, better discipline and order, greater openness, criticism and self-criticism in all fields of public life, and high respect for the value and dignity of the individual.[8]

And there is indeed evidence of increased freedom and openness in the press, literature, theater, art, and even religion in the Soviet Union. There is considerably less secrecy in reporting national disasters and politically sensitive statistics such as agricultural production, alcoholism, and infant mortality rates. Soviet officials now openly acknowledge that drugs, prostitution, and AIDS are very real problems in the Soviet Union.

Some aspects of life in the United States are being portrayed more positively these days. Until recently U.S. fast-food restaurants were always depicted by Soviet television as examples of capitalistic exploitation of teenage workers. In November 1986, Soviet television reporter Vladimir Dunyev did a piece on a McDonald's restaurant on Fifth Avenue in New York that praised the quality of food and service of the highly successful U.S. chain. Phil Donahue's television talk show was broadcast from Moscow in February 1987 for an entire week and was aired simultaneously in the United States and the Soviet Union.

The level of tolerance of political dissent appears to be rising gradually. In July 1986, an underground document calling for increased democracy and political opposition to communism was released to Western journalists. It advocated freedom of the press, an end to the persecution of political dissidents, and alternative political organizations that would compete with the Communist party for the most effective means of "building socialism." The Soviets have begun releasing political prisoners and have indicated that more will be released in the near future. The 1961 criminal code is being revised to bring it in line with the economic reforms and the new openness in the Soviet Union. The laws against "anti-Soviet agitation and propaganda" and "slandering the Soviet state" are expected to either be repealed or significantly softened in the near future.

Thus far, the overall conceptual framework for political reform has yet to be unveiled. However, the specific political changes already implemented by Gorbachev are certainly consistent with the objective of broadening the base of participation of the Soviet people in the political process. Again Hungary and China are likely to be the models followed by Gorbachev as he gradually liberalizes the Soviet political system. In both of these countries economic reforms have eventually been followed by political reforms. Based on the experiences of Hungary and China, I anticipate that Gorbachev is likely to consider the following political reforms before 1990—legalization of opposition political parties and candidates; inauguration of employee councils with the power to elect enterprise managers; further decentralization of some of the powers of the government and the party to the Soviet republics; and possibly the legalization of some independent trade unions on an experimental basis.

Through all of this, Gorbachev must play a delicate balancing game. To increase the output and productivity of the Soviet economy, he must offer the Soviet people more economic and political freedom. But increased freedom generates the desire and expectation of even more freedom. If expectations get too far ahead of the government's ability to deliver additional freedom, or if the government begins to feel threatened by its loss of power, then we have the kind of situation that led to the demise of Solidarity in Poland and the declaration of martial law. Given Gorbachev's close relationship with General Jaruzelski, he will be strongly motivated to avoid replicating the 1981 Polish crisis in the Soviet Union.

To be sure, I am not suggesting that every move that the Soviets make will be consistent with the objective of increased political freedom. For example, in February 1987, U.S. television audiences witnessed the police harassment of Jewish dissidents in Moscow. As distasteful as that incident was, the Soviets did permit it do be filmed by all three of the major U.S. television networks. Not so long ago, that would have been totally out of the question.

The Communist Party

Although the Soviet Union will continue to be dominated by the Communist party in the foreseeable future, it may be a somewhat different party than it has been in the past. In Gorbachev's words,

> [t]he Party is the guiding force and the principal guarantor of the development of socialist self-government. Playing the leading role in society, the Party is itself the highest form of a self-governing sociopolitical organization. By promoting inner-Party democracy and intensifying the activity of Communists at all levels of the political system, the CPSU sets the right direction for the process of furthering the people's socialist self-government and broadening the participation of the masses and of each person in the affairs of the country.[9]

Gorbachev's political reforms are likely to lead to a number of changes in the Communist party. Already there are signs that both the party and the government are becoming less centralized geographically under Gorbachev. This is not surprising when one considers the backgrounds of the party leaders appointed by Gorbachev, most of whom did not come from Moscow. For example, chief party ideologist Yegor K. Ligachev and economic advisor Abel Aganbegyan both came from Siberia. Prime Minister Nikolai I. Ryzhkov and Moscow party chief Boris N. Yeltsin were former Party leaders in Sverdlovsk. Foreign Minister Eduard A. Shevardnadze was previously the party leader in Tbilisi, which is in the republic of Georgia. For this reason, regional decentralization may be expected to replace bureaucratic centralism in the management of party affairs.

The new party leaders are nonideological technocrats rather than hard-line Marxist-Leninist ideologues. Their views on economic and political reforms are much more pragmatic than those of their predecessors. By virtue of their age, they do not have the emotional need to defend the old system. They have little reason or desire to justify or preserve the status quo. They judge the Soviet economic and political systems only on the basis of results.

Although Gorbachev has replaced thousands of incompetent party leaders all over the Soviet Union with younger, better-educated officials, he has not resorted to the type of massive retirement program used by Deng Xiaoping to rid China of millions of unproductive civil servants and military officials. In many parts of the Soviet Union, acute labor shortages make such a strategy impractical.

Given the amount of attention that Gorbachev has devoted in his speeches to making the party and the government more democratic, it seems likely that he will open the doors to party membership a bit wider, and perhaps permit the creation of opposition parties as well. However, it seems reasonable to assume that the USSR will in all likelihood remain essentially a single-party state until the end of the twentieth century.

What remains to be seen is whether or not Gorbachev can transform the party into a dynamic source of creative and innovative ideas to lead the Soviet Union out of its current social and economic crises. Most Americans dismiss this possibility out of hand. However, if Gorbachev were to succeed in energizing the Communist party and using it as a catalyst to ignite the rest of the nation, this would surely be his greatest accomplishment.

The Political Structure

The two biggest challenges facing Gorbachev are the decentralization of the Stalinist economic system and the dismantling of the Leninist bureaucratic central structure. Although he has already made significant progress in decentralizing industrial production and foreign-trade decisions to the enterprise level, restructuring the government bureaucracy is quite another matter.

Many Sovietologists believe that Gorbachev will meet his match when he confronts the millions of civilian and military bureaucrats who run the layers of government ministries in the Soviet Union. This is where he will encounter the most entrenched resistance to his radical economic and political reforms. Just as was the case in Hungary and in China, Gorbachev will probably not press vigorously for major reforms in the political structure of the Soviet Union until the economic reforms begin to show visible results. During FYP12, he will probably be content with some reorganization of ministries such as agribusiness, foreign trade, and energy. If he achieves his FYP12 economic targets for 1990, then he will have the self-confidence to devote his energies to political reform. To some extent he will let his strategy of globalizing the Soviet economy help drive the much needed political reforms. Only time will tell whether increased economic freedom in the USSR will set loose forces for greater political change as well.

In the meantime, Gorbachev will continue to replace aging government bureaucrats with his own people. He may also begin appointing some well-qualified nonparty members to key governmental positions.

As long as Ronald Reagan remains in office, Gorbachev will find it relatively easy to consolidate his own political base in Moscow around the issues of economic reform and increased technological development. As I have previously indicated, Reagan has made Gorbachev's mission of radical reform much easier than it would have been otherwise.

With increasing political self-confidence at home and abroad, Gorbachev may be willing to cut back on the degree of military control maintained over the Soviet people at home and reduce the activities of the KGB abroad. In the case of Hungary and Poland, increased political freedom and decreased military control have been closely associated with the increased self-confidence of the leaders of these two countries. As long as the Soviets retain their paranoid fears of the United States, secrecy, political repression, the military police, and the KGB will remain a way of life. Likewise, international travel and emigration restrictions are not likely to be lifted until the Soviets' self-esteem has been raised a notch or so.

Political Dissent

The openness with which Gorbachev handled the release of Andrei Sakharov from exile in Gorky could protend further improvements in human rights in the Soviet Union. Continuing to hold political prisoners and preventing Soviet Jews from leaving the country make little or no sense in light of Gorbachev's economic and foreign-policy objectives. Leaving humanitarian considerations aside, such practices are totally inconsistent with the spirit of *glasnost*.

I believe that in the not-too-distant future it is quite likely that Gorbachev will say to political dissidents and would-be emigrants, "If you don't like it in the Soviet Union, feel free to leave. The door is wide open." Such a move would represent an act of incredible self-confidence on the part of Gorbachev. Imagine the effect it would have on the visa desks of the U.S. State Department and the Israeli Foreign Ministry. Overnight the rules of cold war politics would be turned on their ear. The leaders of the other Eastern-bloc nations might very well emulate the Soviet policy and open their own doors as well.

U.S. politicians who have devoted their entire political careers to unabashed anticommunism might suddenly be rendered impotent. Defense contractors would be shaking in their boots fearing the worst—a reduction in the arms race. Star Wars would be permanently shelved and military spending might actually start to decline. The U.S. budget deficit could be reduced and more funds might become available to improve the competitiveness of U.S. industry and aid the poor and homeless. An impossible dream? Maybe. Maybe not.

The New Soviet Foreign Policy

Gorbachev's principal foreign-policy objective is to strengthen the Soviet economy and reduce international political tensions through a strategy of increased global interdependence based on bilateral trade with the rest of the world. To achieve this objective he has opted for the road less traveled by either United States or the Soviet Union, namely, international diplomacy. By choosing the high ground he has created an image for himself as a statesman and an international peacemaker.

In no sense am I suggesting that Gorbachev is motivated entirely by altruism, nor am I suggesting that he is not. The relatively poor condition of the Soviet economy alone may be sufficient to motivate Gorbachev to pursue global trade and tension reduction strategies.

I believe that Gorbachev is much more interested in exporting Soviet-made goods rather than exporting international communism. The main thrust of his foreign-policy initiatives is to create new opportunities for foreign trade. He is fully aware of the potential economic, technological, and political benefits of this strategy. What is truly amazing is the speed at which he is implementing this strategy.

Europe

If Gorbachev were to be successful in breaking the hammerlock control that the United States maintains over Western Europe through its NATO forces, then he could simultaneously increase trade with Western Europe and significantly scale down the size of his army in Eastern Europe, both of which would represent enormous economic gains for the Soviet Union.

In many ways, Europe represents one of Gorbachev's most important opportunities for making significant breakthroughs in achieving some of his economic, technological, and political objectives. For example, the Soviet Union has 610,000 troops stationed in Eastern Europe; the United States has 360,000 troops in Western Europe. Total Warsaw Pact uniformed military personnel in Eastern Europe amount to 4,788,000 compared to 6,030,889 NATO troops in Western Europe.[10] Gorbachev has proposed joint NATO–Warsaw Pact troop reductions of 150,000 each over the next two years.

If Gorbachev were to announce the unilateral withdrawal of say half of the Soviet troops stationed in Eastern Europe along with reductions in the military forces of the other Warsaw Pact nations in Eastern Europe, this would create tremendous international political pressures on the United States and Western Europe for reciprocal troop reductions. Not only would such a move dramatically reduce the level of tension between the Soviet Union and Western Europe, but it would also significantly lower the cost of the Soviet Union's defense budget. Furthermore, West Germany, France, Holland, and Belgium would be much more likely to break with the United States over the question of the export of technology to the Soviet Union.

Thus it is within Gorbachev's power to reap substantial windfall political and economic gains in Europe by playing the European card and reducing the level of Warsaw Pact troops in Eastern Europe. Such a move would require no negotiations or arms control agreement with the United States.

Obviously, the reduction of Soviet troops in Eastern Europe implies greater political freedom for the Soviets' Warsaw Pact allies—a step that Gorbachev may not yet be ready to take. But with increased self-confidence in his domestic economic programs as well as foreign policy, Gorbachev may feel this is an affordable risk. It would reduce Eastern Europe's economic dependence on the USSR and free up more resources to be used in achieving the civilian targets of FYP12. More importantly, Soviet troop reductions would go a long way towards reducing anti-Soviet feelings in Eastern Europe as well as Western Europe. Younger Europeans in the East and the West who are both anti-American and anti-Soviet would obviously be attracted to such an initiative on the part of the Soviets. Finally, Soviet troop reductions in Europe could turn out to be both a necessary and sufficient condition for significant arms control agreements with the United States in the 1990s.

Asia and the Pacific

In July 1986, in a speech made in Vladivostok, on the Pacific coast of the Soviet Union, Gorbachev made it clear that Japan, China, and the Pacific Basin were major targets of Soviet foreign policy. There is increasing evidence to suggest that the Japanese model for economic development has not only captured Gorbachev's attention but is strongly influencing his foreign-trade policy. The Soviets are particularly anxious to tap into Japanese technology as a means of neutralizing the effects of the U.S. embargo on the export of U.S. technology to the Soviet Union. Although the Japanese do sell some technology to the Soviets, they are members of COCOM as a result of U.S. coercion. The COCOM restrictions limit the extent to which they can sell technology to the Soviets.

Undoubtedly the Soviets have also noticed that Japan has become a global economic superpower, though it spends only 1 percent of its GNP each year on defense, in contrast to 6 percent for the United States and 14–15 percent for the Soviet Union.

A sore point in Soviet–Japanese relations is the occupation by the Soviet Union (since the end of World War II) of the Kuril Islands off the northern coast of Japan. To Japan these islands are ancestral lands that must be repatriated. To the Soviet Navy they are critical military outposts for protecting Soviet submarines in the Sea of Okhotsk. The real question is whether or not the Soviets would be prepared to turn over the Kuril Islands to the Japanese in return for improved access to Japanese technology. One way or another, the Soviets must find a strategy to break the Pentagon's technological embargo against them.

Gorbachev appears to be particularly anxious to normalize relations with China. In his Vladivostok speech he acceded to China's view of where the Sino–Soviet border should run in the Amur River region. Six Soviet divisions have been withdrawn from Afghanistan and a six-month cease-fire was announced in early 1987. The Soviets began removing some of their troops from Mongolia in April 1987. The remaining sticking point in Sino–Soviet relations is Moscow's support for Vietnam's occupation of Cambodia, an issue that is not likely to be easily resolved.

In general, Gorbachev has signaled his strong interest in expanding the Soviet Union's economic, political, and military influence in the Pacific Basin. Thus far, Thailand, the Philippines, Malaysia, Singapore, and Indonesia are among the Pacific Rim countries that have been singled out for special attention. In November 1986, Gorbachev visited Prime Minister Rajiv Gandhi in New Delhi in pursuit of stronger ties with India. In each case, Gorbachev's primary reason for courting these Asian countries was trade and economic development.

Middle East

As further evidence of Gorbachev's break with the Soviet Union's xenophobic past, consider the case of the Middle East, where the United States has managed to deny the Soviets a position of influence in the peace process. The Soviets have made no secret about their interest in possibly restoring diplomatic relations with Israel. Through Isreal the Soviets hope to gain a position of influence in the Middle East peace process and purchase sophisticated technology. Even before the Reagan administration acknowledged that it was shipping arms to Iran, Washington's influence over the moderate Arab states was on the wane as a result of the bombing of Libya.

The biggest hurdle to overcome in Israeli–Soviet relations is the Soviet Union's policy on Jewish emigration. I fully expect the Soviet Jewish emigration issue to be resolved in the near future and that Israeli–Soviet diplomatic relations will be reestablished shortly thereafter.

In addition to working on its relations with Israel, the Soviet Union appears to be on the brink of establishing diplomatic relations with Qatar and Bahrain and reestablishing diplomatic links with Saudi Arabia, which were curtailed in 1939 because of World War II. The Soviets are also cooperating these days with OPEC. In August 1986, at the request of Iran, the Soviets reduced their oil exports to the West by 6 percent in support of OPEC's efforts to stabilize the world price of oil. Kuwait leased three oil tankers from the Soviet Union in April 1987.

Africa and Latin America

By virtue of their Marxist governments, three African countries have close ties to the Soviet Union—Angola, Ethiopia, and Mozambique. In addition to their Soviet connections, these countries share three other attributes—extreme poverty, weak government, and a need for substantial foreign economic assistance. With the possible exception of Angola, these countries are of little strategic importance to Gorbachev because they do little to enhance his objective of strengthening the Soviet economy through increased trade. Rather, they represent a net financial drain on the Soviet economy. Only Angola is likely to receive much attention from Gorbachev because of its potential importance for the control of southern Africa, given the current level of political instability in South Africa.

As for Latin America, the Soviet Union's presence is limited to Cuba and Nicaragua, both of which contribute substantially to Gorbachev's economic woes. For the most part, Cuba and Nicaragua represent a form of token opposition to the fact that the Soviet Union is surrounded by NATO missile bases (including Turkey, which lies on the Soviet Union's southern border). Although the Soviet presence in Latin America is minimal, some U.S. politicians insist that it represents a major threat to the national security of the United States.

For the remainder of the 1980s and the beginning of the 1990s, Gorbachev will devote less and less attention to the Soviet Union's existing clients in Africa and Latin America. Instead, he will concentrate his diplomatic initiatives on the more affluent countries, such as Mexico, Brazil, and Argentina. His proposed visit to these countries indicates their importance to Soviet foreign-policy and international trade objectives. Brazil and Argentina represent sources of foodstuffs for the Soviets as well as potential markets for goods manufactured in the Soviet Union. By virtue of its large shipments of meat and grain to the Soviet Union, Argentina has a $1.6 billion trade surplus with the Soviets. The Soviets are encouraging the Argentineans to import more from them. Brazil and Mexico are potential sources of Western technology. Brazil has been quite successful in developing its own technology for microcomputers and process control devices. The Soviet Union represents a huge market for such products.

As for Mexico, the Reagan administration has already registered its displeasure with Soviet diplomatic moves aimed at Mexico City. Washington has not so subtly accused the Soviets of using Mexico to widen their intelligence-gathering capabilities in the southern United States. Of course, the Reagan administration has had no qualms whatsoever about expanding the United States' presence in China— the Soviet Union's most important neighbor. According to the assumptions underlying U.S. foreign policy, the Soviets should not respond even when they feel threatened by U.S. diplomatic and military moves. If the Soviets do counter the U.S. moves with new diplomatic initiatives of their own, then they are accused by Washington of engaging in aggressive expansionist behavior.

United States

As Gorbachev begins his third year as leader of the Soviet Union, he must view U.S. foreign policy with utter bewilderment. Thus far, the radical changes that have taken place in Moscow over the past two years seem to have eluded the White House, the Congress, and most U.S. Sovietologists. As a result, the United States is extremely well positioned to enter the foreign-policy arena of the 1950s—forty years too late. In spite of the truly amazing changes that have occurred in the Soviet Union, U.S. foreign policy towards the Soviets remains as rigid and inflexible as it has been since the early 1950s.

In response to Gorbachev's diplomatic and arms control initiatives, the American people have been repeatedly told by the Reagan administration that Gorbachev's overtures are insincere propaganda moves that should not be taken seriously. We are further told that the United States has Gorbachev on the run, and that the Soviets have returned to the bargaining table primarily out of fear of President Reagan's SDI. President Reagan is lauded for having stood up to Gorbachev at Reykjavík and for having rejected his sweeping arms control proposals. But does the United States really have the Soviet Union on the run? Is it possible that exactly the opposite is the case?

Consider the case of the Reykjavík summit meeting between President Reagan and General Secretary Gorbachev, which took place in October 1986, two months after it was first proposed by Gorbachev. The Soviets arrived at Reykjavík with a number of very specific, well-defined arms control proposals including (1) 50-percent reductions in strategic arms; (2) a ban on Soviet and U.S. medium-range missiles in Europe; (3) negotiations on an accord on missiles in Asia; (4) a freeze on short-range nuclear arms; (5) discussion of a total nuclear test ban; (6) tougher verification procedures; (7) strengthening of the ABM treaty; and (8) limitations on space weapons research. The Americans came to Reykjavík ill-prepared and empty-handed. During the days immediately following the summit and preceding the 4 November congressional elections in the United States, the Reagan administration presented the American people with a wide variety of interpretations of what had actually taken place at Reykjavík—all clearly aimed at the U.S. electorate. The only thing one could be sure of was that Reagan had rejected all of Gorbachev's arms control proposals because Gorbachev insisted on limiting research on space weapons to the laboratory. Reagan's position was that the ongoing research program for the U.S. SDI, which includes real-time tests as well as laboratory tests, was absolutely nonnegotiable.

Again, the American people were assured by President Reagan that the only reason Gorbachev came to Reykjavík was out of fear of SDI. Nothing could be further from the truth.

Gorbachev understands fully that Reagan's claims for SDI as a defensive shield against nuclear attack are grossly exaggerated and and technologically impossible to implement at virtually any price. He is not afraid of SDI per se, but rather is concerned about its potential as a U.S. cover-up for future research on offensive space-based weapons.

Gorbachev not only wants a major arms control agreement with the United States, but his task of revitalizing the Soviet economy would be much easier if he could reduce the level of Soviet military spending. But the Reagan administration made a fundamental strategic error in agreeing to the hurried-up Reykjavík summit. Reagan's advisors assumed that Gorbachev was under so much pressure at home because of the Soviets' economic problems that he would agree to major concessions at Reykjavík, including SDI, in order to get an arms control agreement. But that is precisely what Gorbachev wanted Reagan to believe. In reality, the Reagan administration was a victim of its own ignorance and arrogance in U.S.–Soviet relations.

Gorbachev came to Reykjavík extremely well prepared and he knew exactly what he wanted. Reagan was caught completely off guard, and appeared to be in a state of confusion and disarray. Gorbachev was prepared to agree to all of the sweeping arms control proposals that he put on the table at Reykjavík, provided Reagan would walk away from SDI. However, he knew there was little chance that Reagan would negotiate away SDI, because Reagan had so often told the American people that SDI was absolutely nonnegotiable. Not only did Gorbachev anticipate Reagan's response, but he got exactly what he expected.

Reykjavík provided Gorbachev with much-needed international credibility for his sweeping arms control proposals. Upon his departure from Iceland, President Reagan referred to the proposals discussed at Reykjavík as "the most far-reaching arms-control proposals in history." Thus for the first time, Gorbachev's proposals had been taken seriously by the Reagan administration and the whole world was a witness to the event. Reykjavík was thus a major international public relations coup for Gorbachev. He had beaten President Reagan at his own game.

Gorbachev still wants a comprehensive arms control deal with the United States, but he is prepared to settle for a more limited agreement until 1990. In the meantime he will continue to use the Reagan administration's ill-conceived foreign policy as a means of motivating the Soviet people to make the necessary sacrifices to rebuild the Soviet economy and close their technological gap with the West. To the rest of the world Gorbachev will present himself as an emissary of peace blocked only by President Reagan's obstinance and SDI.

The United States has missed countless opportunities to play a constructive role in shaping Gorbachev's radical economic, political, cultural, and foreign-policy reforms. Our failure to appreciate the international significance of the sweeping changes introduced by Gorbachev has stymied our ability to respond in a creative and imaginative fashion. Gorbachev's foreign-policy initiatives deserve a more positive response from Washington. It is not business-as-usual in Moscow, and it is no longer in the self-interest of the United States to continue pretending otherwise.

Postscript

S ix weeks after I finished writing this book I returned to Moscow and Warsaw to have another look at the rapidly changing scene in that part of the world. To some extent I wanted to find out whether or not I had written the right book: For the past six months both the U.S. press and most Sovietologists have been extremely critical of Gorbachev—claiming that he was facing monumental resistance to his reforms and implying that he was doomed to failure.

During my most recent trip, I visited all of the major economics institutes in Moscow, several government ministries, a number of state-owned and private enterprises, a Russian Orthodox church, and a Jewish synagogue. I even had lunch in one of Moscow's three new private restaurants—a particularly pleasant experience.

What I observed in Moscow bore almost no resemblance to what I had been reading in the U.S. press. Everywhere I went optimism was in the air. Bureaucrats, scientists, and enterprise managers were open and completely self-confident. Heads of economics institutes were jockeying for position among themselves. Each wanted to take personal credit for the reforms that had already been implemented and to make certain that his institute would be a major influence in the next round of reforms.

The biggest single obstacle to Gorbachev's sweeping reforms is obviously not political ideology, but the complete lack of experience of Soviet managers in decentralized, market-oriented planning and management.

To help him de-Stalinize the Soviet Union and open the closed society, Gorbachev has turned to a sophisticated team of five high-level economic strategists, headed by Academician Abel G. Aganbegyan. Their strategy calls for nothing less than the dismantling of the centrally planned economy and a frontal assault on the Communist Party, the government bureaucracy, the military, and the KGB. As one member of the team said to me, "the only way to save socialism is to abolish GOSPLAN."

Gorbachev's strategy team works closely with the new rector of the Academy for the National Economy, Yevgeniy K. Smirnitskiy, to reorient senior level Soviet bureaucrats to the new way of thinking. Ministers, deputy ministers, and heads of the largest enterprises are brought to the Academy for an intense executive development program of seminars, small group experiences, role playing, computer gaming, and private consultation with the architects of the economic reforms. The methods being used to retrain Soviet managers are identical to those being taught in the very best graduate schools of business in the United States.

According to Professor Smirnitskiy, many of these training sessions are open to the press and often result in "stormy, heated debate." Participants are encouraged to speak openly about their reservations and negative feelings concerning the top-down changes being imposed on them. Discussion topics include decentralized planning, participatory management, property rights, international trade, economic theory, computer technology, and scientific management.

To gain a different perspective on the practical problems associated with implementing the reforms, managers are temporarily reassigned to a ministry other than their own. They also spend two weeks abroad observing how other socialist countries, such as Hungary, have dealt with the reforms. The Academy also works with the minister of education to coordinate the work of sixty management training institutes located throughout the entire Soviet Union that are responsible for introducing middle- and lower-level bureaucrats to the reforms.

No one in Moscow claims that this aggressive management development program is a panacea which will eliminate all opposition to Gorbachev's reforms. Indeed, nothing could be further from the truth. But it does represent a creative attempt to confront the Soviet culture.

Soviet managers now have access to a network of private management consultants, including members of Gorbachev's strategy team, who are being encouraged to gain practical experience by consulting with state-owned enterprises. In May a private U.S. management consulting firm began operations in Moscow amidst considerable fanfare in the local press. Soviet economists can now be paid as private consultants to state enterprises and government ministries. From the initial response of economists to these new developments, private management consulting may soon become a high-growth industry in Moscow.

According to Professor Valeriy L. Makarov, a key member of the strategy team, additional reforms even more radical than those already in place will soon be approved by the Central Committee. A new law on intellectual property rights will permit Soviet scientists to earn patent royalties on their inventions. Inventors will be allowed to start their own private businesses or go to work for higher paying Western joint-venture companies which license their inventions. Can it be that Soviet high-tech entrepreneurs may be just around the corner?

Leonid I. Abalkin, the new director of the Institute of Economics, has indicated that financial and banking reforms similar to those in Hungary and China will gradually be introduced in the Soviet Union over a three-year period beginning in January 1988. They will include creation of new financial institutions, introduction of capital markets, application for membership in the World Bank and IMF, and eventually introduction of flexible exchange rates.

In the near future, Soviet elites will pay higher rents for larger apartments and will be charged fees for special health care services such as cosmetic surgery and the use of luxurious health spas on the Black Sea. Additional reforms designed by Gorbachev's strategy team will soon be approved by the Central Committee dealing with such diverse topics as participatory management, the decontrol of consumer prices, the pricing of mineral resources, environmental pollution, and social welfare.

Gorbachev's prompt and decisive response to the small civilian plane that recently landed in Red Square hardly suggests that he is lacking in political clout. Within two days Defense Minister Sergei L. Sokolov and the commander of Soviet air defense forces, Marshal Aleksander I. Koldunov, had been relieved of their responsibilities.

Given the mounting evidence that Gorbachev's economic, political, and cultural reforms are starting to take hold, how is it that most U.S. Sovietologists—particularly economists—continue to deny that there are indeed significant changes taking place in the Soviet Union? Many of the economists who advise the State Department, the CIA, the Congress, and the White House about the Soviet economy have never been in a factory in the Soviet Union—some have never even been in a U.S. factory. They know absolutely nothing about practical management problems either in the United States or the Soviet Union. Their principal sources of information about the Soviet economy are Soviet economists, technical statistical data, and public decrees that appear in the Soviet press. They approach the Soviet economy from a narrow legalistic and technocratic perspective. As a result of their extremely myopic view of Soviet economics, they not only understate the importance of the cultural changes taking place in the Soviet Union, they completely ignore them.

Until very recently, Soviet economists have had almost no influence on Soviet economic policies. Most Soviet economists, not unlike many of their American counterparts, are applied mathematicians with little or no hands-on experience with the operations of the Soviet economy. Even today, one can find relatively few Soviet economists who have first-hand practical experience with Gorbachev's reforms at the factory level. To find out what is really going on inside the Soviet economy today, one has to talk with factory managers and workers, store managers, and union leaders—not just academic economists and bureaucrats. As for public decrees about economic reforms, they often lag behind what is actually happening in the Soviet economy by twelve to eighteen months. Only now are we beginning to read public decrees supporting reforms which were initiated a couple of years ago.

It is well known that the track record of American economists in forecasting the behavior of the U.S. economy is singularly unimpressive. Why should they be expected to do any better with the Soviet economy, about which they know even less?

As for Poland, the situation as usual is very complex. Even though Poland has an imaginative new joint-venture law and an increasing number of new private high-tech businesses, the economic reforms seem to be dragging. The Reagan administration's decision to lift the trade sanctions against Poland has led to an increase in Polish exports to the United States.

Most Poles remain extremely cynical about the likely impact of the Soviet reforms on the Polish economy. They cite countless examples of promises of economic reform made by the Polish government in the past—promises that were never realized. Whereas the air in Moscow is full of optimism, Warsaw remains under a dark cloud of pessimism.

The economic reforms in Poland seem to lack direction, discipline, and energy. In the Soviet Union, Gorbachev provides the sense of direction and the energy. The Party provides the discipline. The biggest obstacle to the Polish reforms is a complete lack of discipline. So much energy is dissipated in the endless conflicts between the Church, the Party, and Solidarity that little energy is left to drive the reforms. Even though Poland has at least a fifteen-year head start over the Soviet Union in terms of experience with economic reforms, the Soviet Union may very well achieve lasting economic, political, and cultural reform much sooner than Poland.

As I reflect on the attitude of many Americans about the radical changes taking place in the Soviet Union, I am reminded of my own experiences growing up in Jackson, Mississippi, during the 1950s. Nearly one hundred years after the Civil War, most white Southerners continued to deny that the North had won the war and that blacks were human beings and should not be treated as though they were slaves. It was not until the late 1960s and early 1970s that white Southerners finally began to abandon some of their stereotyped views of blacks.

Is it any wonder that many Americans find it equally difficult to believe that fundamental changes are actually taking place in the Soviet Union? For at least forty years we have been told over and over again, "You can't trust the Russians." We are so conditioned to always assume the very worst about anything the Soviets do or say that it is extremely difficult to view them in any other way.

It may not be business as usual in Moscow, but at the rate we are going, it will take us another five or ten years to find that out. In the meantime, the military, economic, social, and psychological costs of the arms race will continue to mount.

As for the question, "Did I write the right book?" Only time will tell.

Notes

Chapter 1. The USSR: The Closed Society

1. Central Intelligence Agency and Defense Intelligence Agency (CIA and DIA), *The Soviet Economy under a New Leader*. A report presented to the Subcommittee on Economic Resources, Competitiveness, and Security Economics of the Joint Economic Committee of the U.S. Congress, Washington, D.C., 19 March 1986, p. 12.
2. CIA and DIA, p. 39.
3. Serge Schmemann, "Queues in Soviet Persist," *New York Times*, 6 February 1985, p. 6.
4. Seweryn Bialer, "Politics and Priorities," in *The Soviet Economy: Toward the Year 2000*, edited by Abram Bergson and Herbert S. Levine. London: George Allen & Unwin, 1983, p. 394.
5. CIA and DIA, p. 3.
6. Hedrick Smith, *The Russians*. New York: Ballantine Books, 1977, p. 332.
7. Smith, p. 334.

Chapter 2. Gorbachev's Strategy: Radical Reform

1. Mikhail S. Gorbachev, *Speech to the Twenty-seventh Congress of the Communist Party of the Soviet Union*, Moscow, 25 February 1986.
2. Gorbachev, 25 February 1986.
3. The Soviets do not calculate a value for GNP. They use a Marxist definition of national income that excludes depreciation, as well as most wages in services. To convert the Soviets' national income target into a GNP target, the CIA adds an estimate for growth of most service sectors.
4. Gorbachev, 25 February 1986.
5. Mikhail S. Gorbachev, *Closing Speech to the Twenty-seventh Congress of the Communist Party of the Soviet Union*, 6 March 1986.
6. Gorbachev, 25 February 1986.
7. *Resolution of the Twenty-seventh Congress of the Communist Party of the Soviet Union on the Political Report of the CPSU Central Committee*, Moscow, 6 March 1986.

8. *Resolution of the Twenty-seventh Congress.*
9. Central Intelligence Agency and Defense Intelligence Agency (CIA and DIA), *The Soviet Economy under a New Leader.* A report presented to the Subcommittee on Economic Resources, Competitiveness, and Security Economics of the Joint Economic Committee of the U.S. Congress, 19 March 1986, p. 11.
10. Ed A. Hewett, "Gorbachev's Economic Strategy: A Preliminary Assessment," *Soviet Economy* 1 (October–December 1985), p. 301.
11. CIA and DIA, p. 18.
12. *Resolution of the Twenty-seventh Congress*
13. Nikolai Ryzhkov, *Speech to the Twenty-seventh Congress of the Communist Party of the Soviet Union,* Moscow, 3 March 1986.
14. *Resolution of the Twenty-seventh Congress.*
15. Gorbachev, 25 February 1986.
16. Mikhail S. Gorbachev, *Speech at the G.I. Petrovsky Plant,* Dneipropetrovsk, 26 June 1985.
17. Mikhail S. Gorbachev, *Meeting with U.S. Secretary of Commerce Malcolm Baldrige,* 20 May 1985.
18. Gorbachev, 20 May 1985.
19. Gorbachev, 6 March 1986.
20. Mikhail S. Gorbachev, *Speech at the Extraordinary Plenary Meeting of the CPSU Central Committee,* Moscow, 11 March 1985.
21. Gorbachev, 11 March 1985.
22. Gorbachev, 11 March 1985.
23. *The Programme of the Communist Party of the Soviet Union, Pravda,* 26 October 1985.
24. Francis Fukuyama, "Gorbachev and the Third World," *Foreign Affairs* (Spring 1986), p. 716.
25. Fukuyama, pp. 718–722.
26. Gorbachev, 25 February 1986.
27. *Resolution of the Twenty-seventh Congress.*
28. Gorbachev, 11 March 1985.
29. Gorbachev, 25 February 1986.
30. Mikhail S. Gorbachev, *Speech Commemorating the 113th Anniversary of the Birth of Lenin,* Moscow, 22 April 1983.
31. "The New Edition of the CPSU's Third Programme," *Soviet Weekly* (15 March 1986), p. 5.
32. "Congress Shows the Way Towards Victory over Nuclear War," *Soviet Weekly* (15 March 1986), p. 7.
33. Townsend Hoopes, "The New Soviet Posture on Nuclear Armaments," *East/West Outlook,* American Committee on East–West Accord, May 1986, p. 9.

Chapter 3. The Hungarian Connection

1. John J. Putman, "Hungary: A Different Communism," *National Geographic* (February 1983), p. 242.

2. Putnam, p. 245.
3. Béla Csikós-Nagy, "Development Problems of the Hungarian Economy," *The New Hungarian Quarterly* 23 (Winter 1982), pp. 74–76.
4. National Planning Office, "Guidelines of the Further Development of the Hungarian Economic Management System," Budapest, 1985, p. 3.
5. Mikhail S. Gorbachev, *Speech to the Twenty-seventh Congress of the Communist Party of the Soviet Union,* Moscow, 25 February 1986.
6. Ivan Gara, "The Bank System and Joint Ventures in Hungary," Budapest, 1985, pp. 3–4.
7. Tamás Sugár, ed., "Joint Ventures in Hungary," Hungarian Chamber of Commerce, Budapest, 1986, p. 9.
8. Gara, pp. 1–3.
9. Thomas H. Naylor, *The Corporate Strategy Matrix,* New York: Basic Books, 1986.
10. Michael T. Kaufman, "A Pole Woos, and Wins, Gorbachev," *New York Times* (10 March 1986), p. 6.
11. Flora Lewis, "A Pole in Moscow," *New York Times* (9 March 1986), section E, p. 21.

Chapter 4. The New Chinese Socialism

1. Alasdair Clayre, *The Heart of the Dragon.* Boston: Houghton Mifflin, 1985, p. 141.
2. Rosalie L. Tung, *Chinese Industrial Society after Mao.* Lexington, Mass.: Lexington Books, 1982, pp. 158–59.
3. John F. Burns, "Chinese Let Their Businesses Bloom," *New York Times* (3 October 1985), p. 10.
4. Leonard Silk, "The Open Door Policy in China," *New York Times* (27 September 1985), p. 32.
5. Tung, pp. 237–62.
6. Peter Gumbel, "Peiking Drops Plans to Purchase Nuclear Plants, Siemens Unit Says," *Wall Street Journal* (4 March 1986), p. 35.
7. John F. Burns, "China Alters Course with Sale of Stock," *New York Times* (11 February 1985), p. 26.
8. Tung, p. 91.
9. Tung, p. 218.

Chapter 5. The Globalization
of the Soviet Economy

1. Members of the Council for Mutual Economic Assistance, otherwise known as CMEA or COMECON, include Bulgaria, Cuba, Czechoslovakia, the German Democratic Republic, Hungary, Mongolia, Poland, Romania, the USSR, and Vietnam. CMEA observer countries are Afghanistan, Angola, Ethiopia, Laos,

Mexico, Mozambique, Nicaragua, and the People's Democratic Republic of Yemen.

2. Mikhail S. Gorbachev, *Statement at a Dinner to Honor the Participants in the Ninth Annual Meeting of the U.S.–USSR Trade and Economic Council,* Moscow, 10 December 1985.

3. Based on a case study prepared by Robert R. Gardner and Richard A. Bettis entitled "Dresser Industries and the Pipeline," Edwin L. Cox School of Business, Southern Methodist University, 1984.

4. Based on an article by Jack Robertson entitled "Government Closeup," *Electronic News,* 2 June 1986, and personal correspondence from Dr. Jan Czekajewski, president, Columbus Instruments, Columbus, Ohio.

Chapter 6. The Reagan Effect

1. Ralph K. White, *Fearful Warriors.* New York: The Free Press, 1984, p. 12.

2. White, p. 123.

3. White, p. 119.

4. Tom Gervasi, *The Myth of Soviet Military Supremacy.* New York: Harper & Row, 1986, p. 67.

5. John W. Kiser, "How the Arms Race Really Helps Moscow," *Foreign Policy* (Fall 1985), pp. 40–51.

6. Gervasi, p. 24.

7. Gervasi, pp. 63–64.

8. Franklyn D. Holzman, "What Defense Spending Gap?" *New York Times* (4 March 1986), p. 31.

9. Andrew Cochburn, "The Russians Are Coming? In a Nonexistent Tank," *New York Times* (22 November 1982).

10. Dwight D. Eisenhower, *Farewell Radio and Television Address to the American People,* 17 January 1961.

11. Gervasi, p. 38.

12. Peter D. Hart Research Associates, *Survey of the American Physical Society Conducted for the Union of Concerned Scientists,* Washington, D.C., 20–28 February 1986.

13. Leslie H. Gelb, "Is the Nuclear Threat Manageable?" *New York Times Magazine* (4 March 1984), p. 29.

14. Gervasi, p. 49.

15. George Konrad, *Antipolitics.* New York: Harcourt Brace Jovanovich, 1984, p. 31.

16. Konrad, p. 33.

17. Mikhail S. Gorbachev, *Speech at the Dinner Honoring François Mitterrand,* Moscow, 7 July 1986.

Chapter 7. Changing the Culture
of a Risk-Free Society

1. Philip Taubman, "Classless Soviet Is Far Off," *New York Times* (27 January 1986), p. 1.

2. Alexksandr Solzhenitsyn, *Speech upon Receipt of the Templeton Prize,* Buckingham Palace, London, 10 May 1983.
3. Serge Schmemann, "Soviet to Codify Gorbachev's Social Changes," *New York Times* (7 October 1986), p. 4.
4. Mikhail S. Gorbachev, *Report to the Central Committee of the Communist Party of the Soviet Union,* Moscow, 27 January 1987.

Chapter 8. Opening the Closed Society

1. John Pearson, "Now a Soviet Manager Can Start Thinking for Himself," *Business Week* (11 November 1985), p. 93.
2. *East European Markets,* published by *Financial Times,* 19 September 1986, p. 3.
3. *East European Markets,* 19 September 1986, p. 2.
4. *East European Markets,* 6 February 1986, p. 15.
5. Mikhail S. Gorbachev, *Report to the Central Committee of the Communist Party of the Soviet Union,* Moscow, 27 January 1987.
6. Mikhail S. Gorbachev, *Speech Commemorating the 113th Anniversary of the Birth of Lenin,* Moscow, 22 April 1983.
7. Mikhail S. Gorbachev, *Speech to the Twenty-seventh Congress of the Communist Party of the Soviet Union,* Moscow, 25 February 1986.
8. Gorbachev, 27 January 1987.
9. Gorbachev, 25 February 1986.
10. Tom Gervasi, *The Myth of Soviet Military Supremacy,* Harper & Row, New York, 1986, p. 193.

Index

About the Author

Thomas H. Naylor is Professor of Economics and Business Administration and Director of the Center for Corporate Economics and Strategy at Duke University. He is also Managing Director of The Naylor Group, an international management consulting firm specializing in strategic planning. Some of his clients have included IBM, Shell Oil, *The New York Times*, Burroughs Wellcome, the Federal Reserve Bank, and numerous firms in Hungary, Poland, and the Soviet Union.

He is the author of 22 books of which the most recent is *The Corporate Strategy Matrix*, which has also been published in Hungarian. His articles have appeared in *Business Week, The New York Times, Los Angeles Times,* and *The Journal of Commerce,* as well as many professional journals.

DATE DUE